WITTGENSTEIN AND RELIGION

Wittgenstein and Religion

D. Z. Phillips

Professor of Philosophy
University College of Swansea
and Danforth Professor of the
Philosophy of Religion
Claremont Graduate School
California

St. Martin's Press

© D. Z. Phillips 1993

First published in Great Britain 1993 by
THE MACMILLAN PRESS LTD
Houndmills, Basingstoke, Hampshire RG21 2XS
and London
Companies and representatives
throughout the world

This book is published in Macmillan's *Swansea Studies in Philosophy* series
General Editor: D. Z. Phillips

A catalogue record for this book is available
from the British Library.

ISBN 0–333–52378–4 hardcover
ISBN 0–333–58620–4 paperback

Printed in Hong Kong

First published in the United States of America 1993 by
Scholarly and Reference Division,
ST. MARTIN'S PRESS, INC.,
175 Fifth Avenue,
New York, N.Y. 10010

ISBN 0–312–09639–9

Library of Congress Cataloging-in-Publication Data
Phillips, D. Z. (Dewi Zephaniah)
Wittgenstein and religion / D. Z. Phillips.
p. cm.
Includes bibliographical references and index.
ISBN 0–312–09639–9
1. Wittgenstein, Ludwig, 1889–1951. 2. Religion–
–Philosophy. 3. Theology—Methodology. 4. Religious thought—20th
century. I. Title.
B3376.W564P465 1993
210'.92—dc20
92–47226
CIP

To

The Reverend E. Cadfan Phillips

my brother

Contents

Acknowledgements

The essays included in this collection, apart from minor changes and cross-references, appeared originally in the contexts listed. I decided to collect them because of the obvious bearings they have on each other, and because of the relative inaccessibility of some of the essays.

'Philosophy, Theology and the Reality of God', *The Philosophical Quarterly*, vol. 13, 1963.

'Sublime Existence' *Archivio Di Filosofia*, vol. LVIII, 1990. This paper was read at the 1990 Enrico Castelli Conference in Rome on The Ontological Argument.

'Searle on Language-Games and Religion', *Tijdschrift Voor Filosofie*, no. 2, 1989.

'On Really Believing', in *Is God Real?* ed. J. Runzo (Macmillan, 1992). This paper was read at Claremont Graduate School, California, in a conference on Realism and Non-Realism in Contemporary Philosophy of Religion in 1988.

'Religious Beliefs and Language-Games', *Ratio*, XII/1, 1970.

'Wittgenstein's Full Stop', in *Perspectives on the Philosophy of Wittgenstein*, ed. Irving Block (Oxford: Basil Blackwell, 1981). This paper was read at a Wittgenstein Colloquium held in London, Ontario, in 1976, to mark the twenty-fifth anniversary of Wittgenstein's death on 29 April 1951.

'Primitive Reactions and the Reactions of Primitives', *Religious Studies*, vol. 22. The paper was the 1983 Marett Lecture at Exeter College, Oxford, and was first published by Exeter College.

'Belief and Loss of Belief', *Sophia*, 1970. This discussion with J. R. Jones originated as a Radio Wales BBC discussion.

'From Coffee to Carmelites', *Philosophy*, vol. 65, 1990.

'On Not Understanding God', *Archivio Di Filosofia*, vol. LVI. This paper was read at the 1988 Enrico Castelli Conference in Rome on Theodicy Today.

'Waiting for the Vanishing Shed', *Philosophy and Theology*, vol. V, no. 4, 1991, a special issue on Wittgenstein.

'On Wanting to Compare Wittgenstein and Zen', *Philosophy*, vol. 52, 1977.

'Authorship and Authenticity: Kierkegaard and Wittgenstein', *Midwest Studies in Philosophy*, 1992, a special issue on Wittgenstein.

'Advice to Philosophers who are Christians', *New Blackfriars*, Oct. 1988. This paper was given as one of the 1988 Cardinal Mercier Lectures at the University of Leuven.

'Religion in Wittgenstein's Mirror', in *Wittgenstein Centenary Lectures*, ed. by A. Phillips Griffiths (CUP, 1991). The paper was read in the Royal Institute of Philosophy, 1989–90 lecture series on Wittgenstein.

The author and publisher are grateful to the editors and publishers for permission to reprint the essays in this collection, and to my colleagues Ieuan Lloyd and Timothy Tessin for helping me with the proof-reading.

D. Z. PHILLIPS

Introduction

Wittgenstein's philosophical insights have a major bearing on methodology in the philosophy of religion. These methodological issues are central in this collection of essays. Even when the essays are specifically about Wittgenstein, exposition is never their main aim. The collection is not called *Wittgenstein On Religion*. Rather their aim is to pay the kind of attention to the particular so characteristic of his work. Even when we succeed in expounding his work, we may fail, in practice, to give this kind of attention to the questions which engage us. In my experience, this is nowhere more evident than when we turn from discussions in logic, epistemology or the philosophy of mind, to discussions of religious belief.

In the first essay, 'Philosophy, Theology and the Reality of God', for example, I point out how easy it is to miss the fact that in philosophical discussion of the reality of God, we are discussing a *kind* of reality. In asking whether God is real, we cannot simply assume that we know what 'real' means in this context. Whether we believe in God or not, a task of conceptual elucidation awaits us.

In the second essay, 'Sublime Existence', I explore the suggestion that Anselm was concerned with such conceptual elucidation. He wanted to understand what he already believed. For example, he wanted to emphasise that whatever is meant by the reality of God, it is not akin to the reality of anything which comes to be and passes away. Believers have spoken of the *necessity* of God's existence. Some philosophers have said that talk of necessary existence makes no sense. Other philosophers have responded by saying that no such definite conclusion can be reached since, being human, we have no understanding of ultimate reality or of the necessities which characterise it. These are two examples, among others, of what Wittgenstein called, the tendency to sublime the logic of our language. On the first view, alien criteria of meaning are imposed on religious belief. On the second view, leave is given to say that religious beliefs may have meaning, because the justification for what we want to say lies out of reach in some metaphysical realm. Both views fail to appreciate that what we need to be clear about lies open to view, namely, how we speak of God's necessary existence in the context of religious belief. The clarity to be arrived at is as essential for an understanding of atheism as it is for an understanding of religious belief.

The third essay, 'Searle on Language-Games and Religion', re-emphasises the lessons of the first two essays by reference to Wittgenstein's use of the term 'language games'. The distinction between the real and the unreal is not given prior to the use of various language games. There is no Archimedian point outside all language games by which we assess the adequacy of language in relation to reality. Such a relation is a chimera. It is so easy to forget this when we discuss religion. For example, we find ourselves saying that we would not engage in religious language games unless we *first* believed in the existence of God. But this 'belief' cannot be the external justification of the language games, since it is only in the context of these language games that belief in God has any meaning.

In the fourth essay, 'On Really Believing', I show how these issues take us to the heart of disputes concerning realism and non-realism in contemporary philosophy of religion. In saying that no-one would worship unless he first believed that God exists, the realist assumes that we are *all* realists with respect to religion, believers and atheists alike. This assumption hides the fact that, so far, *no* conceptual elucidation has been provided of what this *prior* belief in the existence of God amounts to. No intelligible account could be given of it. The realist will not allow any appeal to religious worship in elucidating the belief, since to do so, he claims, is to confuse religious belief with its fruits. The religious life, he argues, is the fruit of the belief in God's existence which is its foundation. And so we have a search for a minimal, basic belief in the existence of God, one which involves no affective response. Such a search ends up with a marginal phenomenon far away from the realities of religion.

The realist wants to insist, quite rightly, that God's existence, like the existence of tables and chairs, does not depend on what we say and think. But we must also realise that what saying this amounts to depends on what talk of existence means in these respective contexts. Wittgenstein's attack on realism applies as much to the belief that there is a chair in the next room, as it does to belief in God. Wittgenstein, however, is not advocating non-realist accounts of religious belief in face of the onslaughts of positivism. His philosophical insights cut through the dispute between realism and non-realism.

Wittgenstein's emphasis on distinctive language games has led to considerable discussion, much of it misplaced. This is nowhere more evident than in the ill-conceived notion of Wittgensteinian Fideism.

To talk of distinctive language games in relation to religion, it is thought, is to claim that only religious believers understand religious belief, that religious belief or believers cannot be criticised, that anything called religion determines what is meaningful, and that religious belief cannot be overthrown by any personal or cultural event. I do not give very much attention to these empty charges in this collection. Having heard them for almost twenty years, I undertook, reluctantly, a textually based demonstration of their irrelevance. (See *Belief, Change and Forms of Life* (London: Macmillan, 1986).) Since then, critics have backpedalled, some behaving as though these charges have never been made! Such are the ways of philosophical fashions.

The most unfortunate aspect of discussions surrounding Wittgensteinian Fideism was that they diverted attention from much deeper philosophical issues. I discuss some of these in the fifth essay, 'Religious Beliefs and Language-Games'. One of Wittgenstein's aims, in introducing the term 'language games', is to emphasise that language does not have the unity of a formal system. To get us away from *that* assumption, Wittgenstein asks us to think of the different games we play. We would not dream of suggesting that all these games are part of one big super-game. Why should we think, then, that different uses of language are all variations of one paradigmatic use? Religious uses of language are often distinctive and will be misunderstood if this distinctive character is not recognised. The claim for the distinctiveness of religious language games grows out of what actual usage shows. It can never be any kind of dogma or methodological axiom imposed on language. For example, if attention to use reveals confusions and distortions, they cannot be excused because they are religious. Religion makes its own distinctive contribution to the hold of superstition on us.

Having said all this, it is important to recognise the limitations of the analogy between games and language. The different games we play are not part of one big game, whereas we participate in different language games in the *same* language. The sameness of the language does not consist of anything like the formality of a system. But speaking a language, saying something, cannot be accounted for simply in terms of following the rules of a game. Although Wittgenstein emphasises the distinctiveness of language games, he also speaks of the relations between them. He had in mind the bearings the various things we say have on each other. These bearings do not amount to the same thing for every individual. Think of the ways in which conversations develop. Without such bearings, there could be nothing like a growth in understanding, or an understanding of one's life.

Wittgenstein said that to imagine a language is to imagine a form of life. To imagine a religion, too, is to imagine it in a form of life. Religious beliefs and rituals would not have the importance they do if they were cut off from the life that surrounds them. This does not make what is in them any less distinctive, or mean, when this is so, that they stand in need of external justification.

The difficulty in philosophising about religion, as in philosophising elsewhere, is to know where to stop. Every issue must be taken to its deepest level, but, when that is reached, it is important to stop. Looking for external justifications for religious belief is one way of not knowing where to stop. In the sixth essay, 'Wittgenstein's Full Stop', I discuss the view that emphasising the distinctiveness of religious language games is an example of stopping too soon in philosophy. It seems to make religion immune to criticism. For Wittgenstein, 'confused language game' is a meaningless term, since by a language game he meant a conceptually distinct use of language. If practices are clusters of language games it seems to follow that no practice can be confused. Surely, this is an unwelcome conclusion.

Two unsatisfactory ways of avoiding this conclusion have been suggested. First, by taking a normative view of language games, any practice could be assessed in terms of it. Second, by arguing that language games are concepts which run through many practices without being identifiable with any of them, it can be argued that practices may distort language games. Both would-be solutions ignore how fundamental a notion *practice* is for Wittgenstein. We cannot separate concepts from practice, from what we do, because it is only in practice, in what we do, that concepts have their life and meaning. As we saw in the previous essay, however, there are diverse relations between language games. In this traffic, distinctive language games may lose their character; they may become distorted or confused. These possibilities do not affect philosophy's descriptive task in conceptual elucidations of religious practices. In the case of religion, this task faces special difficulties, since, unlike examples of physical objects, colours and sensations, we cannot assume that everyone is acquainted with religious practices outside the context of philosophical reflection on them. As a result, philosophers may give an intellectualised account of religion.

In my seventh essay, 'Primitive Reactions and the Reactions of Primitives', I refer to Wittgenstein's discussion of such an intellectualised account in Frazer's analysis of ritual. Frazer saw rituals as primitive hypotheses, would-be causal supplements to purposive activities. He neglected their celebratory character which Wittgenstein brings to our attention. Wittgenstein does not simply correct Frazer. His main aim is to attack assumptions concerning what language *must* mean.

Animism is the view that primitive man explained the natural world he did not understand by postulating the existence of spirits greater than himself. It may well be that animism is dead in anthropological theories, but it is alive and well in contemporary philosophy of religion. Early anthropologists, such as R. R. Marett, also thought that animism intellectualised primitive religion. Instead, Marett emphasised the importance of primitive reactions in primitive religion. His emphasis is not without its difficulties, but, at his best, Marett did not want to distinguish between concepts and active responses, emphasising that it is in these responses that concepts are formed. Wittgenstein, too, called to our attention the importance of agreement in reactions in acquiring language. We do not reason our way to our agreed reactions concerning colours, sounds, pains. Our reasonings are later refinements. This is true in the realm of religion too. It is only by looking at religious reactions that we can appreciate concept-formation in this context.

There can be no a priori speculation about religion. Forms of words, in abstraction, will not tell us whether they have sense or not. We must look at what we do with them. This is why giving perspicuous representations in philosophy is so important. As we have already seen, however, even when examples are provided, they may not be appreciated by everyone. This will not be a case of misunderstanding the logic of the language they use, since the language in question does not get off the ground for them. There is an important difference between misunderstanding a use of language, and a use of language which passes beyond one's understanding. In the latter context, one does not misunderstand, one fails to understand.

As I show in the eighth essay, 'Belief and Loss of Belief', it follows from this conclusion that there are times when a non-believer is not contradicting a believer, or advancing rival hypotheses. The firmness of a religious belief may be the firmness of a whole way of regarding the world. This does not mean that it cannot be eroded by the appeal of secular rival attitudes in a person's life, or by more pervasive cultural changes. To appreciate these facts is to see that religious responses to the world are not at our disposal to reform at will, as some theologians have thought. A religious way of looking at the world may be irreplaceable. There may be no other way of saying what it says. If it dies, it cannot be replaced by a substitute. Some have argued, that when such religious responses die, the God they speak of dies with them. This is a puzzling conclusion, since the responses may have something to say about such eventualities. What is said is not that God has died, but that people have turned their backs on God.

The distinction between misunderstanding something and something which passes beyond one's understanding, can be badly misunderstood. I explore such a misunderstanding in the ninth essay, 'From Coffee to Carmelites'. The distinction is important in emphasising that all differences between human beings cannot be cashed in terms of a common rationality by which they are to be assessed. Every lack of understanding is not a matter of a failure within a mode of understanding already possessed. It may be due to the fact that we are confronted by something which passes beyond our present understanding. But from this important fact, a misleading conclusion may be drawn. It may be said that when something passes beyond our understanding, there is nothing we can do, even in principle, to rectify the situation. This ignores the fact that if every lack of understanding is not a mistake within our present mode of understanding, every *acquiring* of understanding is not a matter of correction within that mode of understanding. It is trite to argue that if we come to understand something, it could never, at any time, have passed beyond our understanding. This simply ignores the fact that our present modes of understanding may be extended or transformed.

Yet, it may be argued, there is surely something which passes beyond human understanding as such, namely, God himself. But what does saying this amount to? Is it that the ways of God can be understood, have a rationale, but we, while on earth, cannot understand them? This misunderstands the place of mystery in religion. Another possibility needs to be explored, namely, that in relation to the ways of God, the religious response is not one of understanding.

In my tenth essay, 'On Not Understanding God', I try to show that these different understandings of the sense in which God passes beyond human understanding are nowhere more evident than in discussions of the problem of evil. It can be argued that the great divide in philosophy is not between religious and secular explanations of the evils and contingencies of human life. The greater divide is between those who think that all the evils and contingencies of human life can be explained and those who deny this. Some philosophers seek explanations of God as though he were a human agent. In the Book of Job this possibility is denied. Job said that God is not a man whom he might reason with and subject to judgement. As a result of this denial it has been argued that theodicists are faced with an unresolvable dilemma. Either God is judged by human standards of decency in face of evil, in which case he must be found guilty; or God is said to be someone to whom those standards do not apply, in which case he occupies a position reserved for monsters. I see no answer to these criticisms. Yet, having made them, a critic may recognise that they leave the contingencies of human life, birth, death, the transitoriness of fate, the fickleness of human beings, unexplained. If we are to speak of a god in such circumstances, it may be said, the *only* god which sense allows is a god of caprice against whom the human spirit strives perpetually. While the possibility of belief in such a god cannot be denied, another possibility must also be recognised. From the very same contingencies which may lead to a belief in a god of caprice, may come belief in a God of grace. Reliance on grace shows, no matter what intellectuals say, that the response to life's contingencies is not always one of the understanding.

It is all too easy, however, to misunderstand the sense in which religious responses go beyond understanding. In the eleventh essay, 'Waiting for the Vanishing Shed', I explore a particularly pervasive form such misunderstanding takes. There is a certain religious mentality which insists that there is a great deal to be understood, but which cannot be understood by mere mortals. This insistence has already been explored, to some extent, in the previous two essays. In the present essay I explore the view that this 'more that we cannot understand', is a supernatural realm beyond the natural one. It is said that we know little of this realm but that we have hints of it, now and again, through strange, bizarre or occult events. Such events, marginal from the point of view of ordinary experience, are religiously important. They signify that there is more to reality than we can ever comprehend.

One such strange event might be something simply vanishing. Many people would say that this is impossible: things just do not simply vanish. Against this response some want to argue in the following way: the impossibility of things simply vanishing is only a relative impossibility; it is ruled out relative to our scientific procedures. But this does not mean that the possibility of things simply vanishing can be ruled out absolutely; it has not been shown to be absolutely meaningless. But what is this appeal to absolute meaningfulness or meaninglessness? Wittgenstein teaches us not to indulge in such abstract speculation. The question is: how do the words 'it has simply vanished' enter our lives? What do we want to do with them? Issues concerning the sense of the words cannot be answered in advance of the answers to these questions.

In my essay, these issues are explored in relation to discussions which have surrounded Peter Winch's British Academy lecture, *Ceasing to Exist*. Winch points out that, in our causal enquiries, the exclamation 'It has vanished!' operates neither as a report nor an explanation of an event. It is simply a cry of exasperation in the face of the inexplicable. No one denies that we may be faced by something inexplicable. These inexplicable events are not abstract possibilities. Faced by them, we need not take an interest in explaining them causally. To think we *must* have such an interest in them is a confusion. Given that is not our interest in them, we cannot, at the same time, claim that they show or hint at 'higher' causal activities we do not understand: since that *is* to retain an interest which is essentially causal in character. ('We do not understand how water can be turned into wine, but God does. After all, he must have done it *somehow*.') Without doubt, inexplicable events in the Bible were sometimes regarded as miracles. The inexplicable was perceived religiously. But in the arguments I am combating, there has been a radical cultural shift: it is not religion which gives significance to the inexplicable, but the inexplicable is invoked as possible hints of religious significance. The trouble is that *we* discuss the inexplicable in a culture dominated, not by religion, but by science. We are thus tempted to treat the inexplicable as something which *must* have an explanation, but one which is unavailable to us. Religion becomes a 'super-science' whose answers and explanations will be known after death. Religious mysteries are temporary mysteries. The hubris present in theodicies, with their available answers, now invades the heavens by insisting that we shall have answers there.

The aim of all the essays in the collection, I hope, is conceptual clarification. Many philosophers are not content with this conclusion. They claim that philosophical reflection *must* result in either the acceptance or rejection of belief in God. Some even want to equate conceptual clarification with a form of religious insight. It is this latter tendency that I explore in my twelfth essay, 'On Wanting to Compare Wittgenstein and Zen'.

Philosophical clarification *may* help to clear the path to an understanding of certain perspectives and possibilities previously thought to be meaningless. For example, if we are in the grip of a philosophical picture which sees thoughts as mental events which are the necessary prerequisites of language and action, we may find it difficult to see any sense in the Buddhist ideal of action as 'just doing' with a mind free of thoughts, concepts and ideas. The ideal may seem unintelligible and not even worthy of attention. Freedom from the confused philosophical picture may change one's attitude. A way is opened up for an understanding of the Buddhist ideal.

Some philosophers, however, have made a far more extravagant claim. Not content with saying that Wittgenstein's philosophical methods may help one understand the Buddhist ideal, they have claimed that such methods are a manifestation of that ideal. Emptying oneself of philosophical confusions would thus be an instance of the Buddhist emptying oneself of thoughts. This claim cannot be defended. The generality of the Cartesian tendencies Wittgenstein is combating does not accord with the specific aims of Buddhist teaching. For example, 'cursing' appears in Wittgenstein's list of language games. He would attack the view that a verbal curse is a translation of a mental one which necessarily precedes it. Cursing is an example of 'just doing' in Wittgenstein. This is not so in Buddhist teaching. Where anger is involved in the curse, a person is said to be full of something of which he must empty himself. Anger is called a confusion of soul in Buddhism. Clearly, that confusion must be distinguished from philosophical confusion in this example.

On the other hand, it would be a mistake to draw a sharp distinction always between character in a philosopher's work and the character of the philosopher. The reasons why this should be so are explored in the thirteenth essay, 'Authorship and Authenticity: Kierkegaard and Wittgenstein'.

Kierkegaard and Wittgenstein attacked philosophy's foundationalist pretensions. Philosophy does not provide its own yardstick by which our practices are to be assessed. Instead, it endeavours to give perspicuous representations of these practices when we are tempted to become confused about them. It teaches us differences. Yet, given this characterisation of philosophy, some have become worried about the kind of activity it has become. If philosophy clarifies different perspectives, has it no perspective of its own? Has it become no more than a playful aestheticism which enjoys displaying perspectives without embracing any of them? The struggle for clarity in philosophy can be distinguished from such aestheticism. Neither does it follow that in teaching us differences, philosophy is committed to saying that all perspectives are equal or even that they are alternatives for us, and that no criticism can be made of one perspective from the point of view of another. These denials do not mean that the only alternative is to regard values as the product of the kind of choice or leap of faith expressed by various forms of existentialism.

There are important differences, however, between Kierkegaard's and Wittgenstein's methods. In Kierkegaard, the search for clarity has a religious purpose, whereas in Wittgenstein it does not. Kierkegaard wanted to challenge the wayward by clarifying what it means to become a Christian. Wittgenstein engaged with those issues in philosophy which have always puzzled human beings. Yet, it is too easy to conclude that Kierkegaard fully appreciated philosophy's clarificatory tasks, and simply turned aside from them to pursue his religious purposes. I believe Kierkegaard missed an important dimension of philosophical authorship which we find in Wittgenstein. Kierkegaard saw through philosophy's foundationalist pretensions, but gave insufficient attention to the character of philosophical enquiry. For Kierkegaard, enquiry is taken up into one's life, first, by a revelation of what it cannot achieve: and, second, by then becoming subservient to a personal embracing of a specific perspective, something which philosophy cannot prescribe for. For Wittgenstein, on the other hand, philosophy is taken up into one's life by the kind of attention it asks of one. It is the quality of this attention which shows, or fails to show character. Style was of enormous importance to Wittgenstein, and he was obsessed with the possibility that he had lied to himself about self-deception in his own work. In that sense, his concern with style is deeper than Kierkegaard's.

In the fourteenth essay, 'Advice to Philosophers who are Christians', I argue that the kind of attention philosophy calls for is threatened by the view that philosophers who happen to be Christians should not be content until they become Christian philosophers with a Christian philosophy. For example, the threat appears in the appeal to external considerations to determine whether the course philosophy has taken is beneficial or not. Thus it does not follow that something called Christian philosophy 'is on the move' because Christians are now in the philosophical establishment in America and are not ashamed to declare their allegiance. Everything depends on the character of the philosophical enquiry.

In the growth of Reformed epistemology in America, we often find the assumption that any common enquiry into religious belief or unbelief *must* involve an appeal to a common rationality by which they are assessed. But enquiry may show that no such standard exists. Nevertheless, a common method may still exist, namely, one which seeks for conceptual clarity. Reformed epistemologists argue that religious beliefs are not answerable to justification by some philosophical yardstick. I agree, but there is a difference between arriving at this view as a result of reflection and having it as a presumption from which one begins. At its most extreme Reformed epistemology states that a person may continue to embrace a Christian philosophy even if he cannot meet objections to it, since his religion may mean more to him than his inability to meet objections. In fact, his inability may be characterised as a reminder from God about his fallibility. I have no a priori objection to such an attitude. My difficulty is in seeing how it could be compatible with philosophical enquiry. Certainly, at that stage we seem far away from Wittgenstein's concern about integrity of style in philosophy.

In the fifteenth and final essay, 'Religion in Wittgenstein's Mirror', I show how Wittgenstein's concern is intimately connected with his conviction that philosophy leaves everything as it is. Many dismiss that remark as no more than a rhetorical flourish. In doing so, they are guilty of a grave disservice to Wittgenstein's work. Wittgenstein's appeal to *practice* has been badly misunderstood in contemporary philosophy of religion. No simple account can be given of what his appeal amounts to. Wittgenstein discusses the relation of philosophy to religion in at least five different contexts. First, he attacks the philosophical view that all religious beliefs are meaningless. Second, he criticises confused grammatical accounts of religious beliefs. Third, he discusses confusions in religious practices and the distinction between religion and superstition. Fourth, he discusses the variety in religious practices and how which we call higher and lower must be a personal matter. Fifth, he urges a certain kind of pragmatism in relation to religious practices, in trying to persuade philosophers that it is not incumbent on them to give a verdict on *every* phenomenon which confronts them.

In all five contexts Wittgenstein is not changing anything that lies before him, but is endeavouring to be clear about it. He pays religion the compliment, in all the diverse examples he considers, of leaving it where it is. That should be our ideal, too, in the philosophy of religion. It is one which is extremely difficult to achieve. I do not claim to have done so in this collection, but I hope, at least, to be travelling in that direction.

1

Philosophy, Theology and the Reality of God

What kind of philosophical and theological account does the concept of divine reality call for? To answer this question one must determine the grammar of the concept to be investigated. All too often in the case of the reality of God this requirement has been overlooked or taken for granted. Because the question of divine reality can be construed as 'Is God real or not?' it has often been assumed that the dispute between the believer and the unbeliever is over *a matter of fact*. The philosophical investigation of the reality of God then becomes the philosophical investigation appropriate to an assertion of a matter of fact. That this is a misrepresentation of the religious concept is made obvious by a brief comparison of talk about facts with talk about God.

When do we say, 'It is a fact that . . .' or ask, 'Is it a fact that . . .?'? Often, we do so where there is some uncertainty. For example, if the police hear that a wanted criminal has died in some remote part of the world, their reaction might be, 'Check the facts'. Again, we often say that something is a fact in order to rule out other possibilities. A student asks, 'Is the professor coming in today?' and receives the reply, 'No, as a matter of fact he never comes in on Monday.' A fact might not have been: it is conceivable that the wanted criminal had not died, just as it is conceivable that it had been the custom of the professor to come in on Mondays. On the other hand, the religious believer is not prepared to say that God might not exist. It is not that as *a matter of fact* God will always exist, but that it *makes no sense* to say that God might not exist.

We decide the truth or falsity of many matters of fact by taking account of the truth or falsity of other matters of fact. What is to count in deciding whether something is a fact or not is agreed upon in most cases. Refusal to admit that something is a fact in certain situations might be cause for alarm, as in the case of someone who sees chairs in a room which in fact is empty. Is this akin to the

1

dispute between the believer and the unbeliever; one sees God, but the other does not? The believer is not like someone who sees objects when they are not there, since his reaction to the absence of factual evidence is not at all like that of the man suffering from hallucinations. In the case of the chairs there is no dispute over *the kind of evidence* needed to settle the issue. When the positivist claims that there is no God because God cannot be located, the believer does not object on the grounds that the investigation has not been thorough enough, but on the grounds that the investigation fails to understand the grammar of what is being investigated – namely, the reality of God.

It makes as little sense to say, 'God's existence is not a fact' as it does to say, 'God's existence is a fact.' In saying that something either is or is not a fact, I am not describing the 'something' in question. To say that *x* is a fact is to say something about the grammar of *x*; it is to indicate what it would and would not be sensible to say or do in connection with it. To say that the concept of divine reality does not share this grammar is to reject the possibility of talking about God in the way in which one talks about matters of fact. I suggest that more can be gained if one compares the question, 'What kind of reality is divine reality?' not with the question, 'Is this physical object real or not?' but with the different question, 'What kind of reality is the reality of physical objects?'. To ask whether physical objects are real is not like asking whether this appearance is real or not where often one can find out. I can find out whether unicorns are real or not, but how can I find out whether the physical world is real or not? This latter question is not about the possibility of carrying out an investigation. It is a question of whether it is possible to speak of truth and falsity in the physical world; a question prior to that of determining the truth or falsity of any particular matter of fact. Similarly, the question of the reality of God is a question of the possibility of sense and nonsense, truth and falsity, in religion. When God's existence is construed as a matter of fact, it is taken for granted that the concept of God is at home within the conceptual framework of the reality of the physical world. It is as if we said, 'We know where the assertion of God's existence belongs, we understand what kind of assertion it is; all we need do is determine its truth or falsity.' But to ask a question about the reality of God is to ask a question about *a kind of reality*, not about the reality of *this* or *that*, in much the same way as asking a question about the reality of physical objects is not to ask about the reality of this or that physical object.

What then is the appropriate philosophical investigation of the reality of God? Suppose one asks, 'His reality as opposed to what?'. The possibility of the unreality of God does not occur *within* any religion, but it might well arise in disputes *between* religions. A believer of one religion might say that the believers of other religions were not worshipping the same God. The question how he would decide the identity of God is connected in many ways with what it means to talk of divine reality.

In a dispute over whether two people are discussing the same person there are ways of removing the doubt, but the identity of a god is not like the identity of a human being. To say that one worships the same God as someone else is not to point to the same object or to be confronted with it. How did Paul, for example, know that the God he worshipped was also the God of Abraham? What enabled him to say this was not anything like the method of agreement one has in the case of two astronomers who check whether they are talking of the same star. What enabled Paul to say that he worshipped the God of Abraham was the fact that although many changes had taken place in the concept of God, there was nevertheless a common religious tradition in which both he and Abraham stood. To say that a god is not the same as one's own God involves saying that those who believe in him are in a radically different religious tradition from one's own. The criteria of what can sensibly be said of God are to be found *within* the religious tradition. This conclusion has an important bearing on the question of what account of religion philosophy and theology can give. It follows from my argument that the criteria of meaningfulness cannot be found *outside* religion, since they are given by religious discourse itself. Theology can claim justifiably to show what is meaningful in religion only when it has an internal relation to religious discourse. Philosophy can make the same claim only if it is prepared to examine religious concepts in the contexts from which they derive their meaning.

Some theologians have claimed that theology gives a justification of religion. E. L. Mascall, for instance, says: 'The primary task of rational theology is to ask what grounds can be found for asserting the existence of God.'[1]

Mascall implies that theology is external to religion and seeks a rational justification of religious truth. This view differs sharply from what I claim to be the internal role of theology in religion. This role can be explained as follows.

One cannot have religion without religious discourse. This is taught to children through stories by which they become acquainted with the attributes of God. As a result of this teaching the child forms an idea of God. We have far less idea than we sometimes suppose of what the nature of the child's idea is, but for our purposes its content is irrelevant. What is relevant to note is that the child does not listen to the stories, observe religious practices, reflect on all this, and then form an idea of God out of the experience. The idea of God is being formed in the actual story-telling and religious services. To ask which came first, the story-telling or the idea of God, is to ask a senseless question. Once one has an idea of God, what one has is a primitive theology. This is in many ways far removed from the theology of the professional theologian, but what makes it far removed is a difference in complexity or maturity, not a difference in kind or function. In each case theology decides what it makes sense to say to God and about God. In short, theology is the grammar of religious discourse.

There is a limited analogy between the relation of theology to religious discourse and the relation of logic to language. One cannot have a language without a logic, although one can have a language without explicitly formulated logical principles. On the other hand, logical principles can have no meaning apart from the language in which they are found. This is not refuted by the fact that the meaning of a formal system can be explained in terms of the rules of that system. The question remains whether the possibility of any such system is dependent on the existence of language. The argument appears circular and contradictory if one thinks of either logic or language as being prior to the other. But as in the case of the child's stories and the concept of God, to ask which came first is to ask a senseless question. As soon as one has language one has logic which determines what can and what cannot be said in that language without being prior to it. As soon as one has religious discourse one has a theology which determines what it will be sensible to say and what it will be nonsensical to say within that religious discourse without being prior to it.

The limited nature of the analogy is evident when we want to talk of alternative theologies. To understand the need for a new theology, the need for a revised grammar of religious discourse, it is more helpful to consider an analogy with the development of scientific laws. In the course of scientific experimentation, in order to account for new phenomena, scientific laws have to be modified or

changed. One would not say that the old laws are wrong, or that the
new ones are nearer the truth, but simply that they differ in their
range of application. There is an analogy here with the way in which
old ideas of God are supplanted and new ones take their place. This
will not seem arbitrary if one remembers that the need for a new
theology, for a different idea of God, does not occur *in vacuo*. The
development of scientific laws can only be understood by reference
to the tradition of scientific enquiry, and the changes in the idea of
God can only be understood in terms of a developing religion. This
is not to say that the role of the concept of God is akin to the role of
a scientific model, for the analogy with developing scientific laws,
like the analogy with logic and language, is a limited one. I use it
simply to re-emphasise the internal relation of theology to religion.

Theology cannot impose criteria of meaningfulness on religion from
without. Neither can philosophy. Mascall, on the other hand, main-
tains that like theology, philosophy has a special role to play, namely
to seek rational grounds for asserting the existence of God. This view
misrepresents the relation of philosophy to religion. The role of
philosophy in this context is not to justify, but to understand. Mascall
says of the Christian: 'He knows what he means by God because the
Bible and the Church have told him. He can then institute a purely
rational enquiry into the grounds for asserting that God exists.'[2]

Why not remain with an understanding of what the Bible and the
Church teach? What extra is this rational enquiry supposed to
achieve? This question might be answered by indicating the problems connected with the existence of a plurality of religions. If one
accepts the internal relation of theology to religion and the religious
tradition as the means of identifying God, what is one to say of the
conflicting claims of different religions? In much the same spirit in
which I have been talking about the relation of theology to religion,
Peter Winch says:

criteria of logic are not a direct gift of God, but arise out of, and are
only intelligible in the context of, ways of living or modes of social
life. It follows that one cannot apply criteria of logic to modes of
social life as such. For instance, science is one such mode and
religion is another; and each has criteria of intelligibility peculiar
to itself. So within science or religion actions can be logical or
illogical . . . in religion it would be illogical to suppose that one
could pit one's strength against God's . . . But we cannot sensibly

say that either the practice of science itself or that of religion is either illogical or logical; both are non-logical.[3]

But can this thesis hold in face of a plurality of religions? The problem is brought out if one considers the way in which the analogy between theology, logic and scientific laws which we have considered breaks down. In the development of scientific laws there is eventual agreement that such development is desirable. The same could be said, roughly speaking, of the development of the idea of God in the Old Testament. But this need not be true of modern developments in theology: opposing theologians will stick to their respective positions and declare the others to be wrong. This brings up the question of authority or reference to an authoritative system. Both logic and science are *public* in so far as it can be decided whether a statement is logical or illogical, or whether a given practice is scientific or not. Illogical and non-scientific statements are refutable. But because of the nature of theology one may only say that a religious statement is refuted by *a* theology. There is no analogy here with either logic or science. This is due to what might be called *the personal element* in theology.[4] In the formulation of logical and scientific principles there is no personal element involved. This is not true of theology.

As I have already said, the systematic theology is a sophistication of that theology which is necessarily present in so far as religious language is present. The theological system is often constructed to answer certain questions and problems which may arise. But the foundation of a theological system is based on the non-formalised theology which is within the religious way of life carried on by the person who is constructing the theological system. In so far as this is true, theology is personal, since it is based on one's own experience of God. Where the connection between theology and experience is missing, there is a danger of theology becoming an academic game.

It is extremely difficult to steer a course between the personal and the public in this whole question. Theology must be personal in so far as it is concerned with one's own idea of God, and in this context religion must always be personal. On the other hand, in so far as religious language must be learnt, religion is public. One cannot have *any* idea of God. Once one has embraced a theology, one has established 'what can be said' in that particular religion, but what can be said does not depend on the fact that an *individual* is saying it.

Some philosophers have held that in face of theological differences *within* religions and the more pronounced theological differences *between* religions, philosophy itself must decide what are the meaningful religious assertions. This view is expressed in no uncertain terms by Peter Munz in his book, *Problems of Religious Knowledge*. In face of the plurality of religious traditions Munz thinks it foolish to identify the truth with any *one* of them. On the other hand, he also objects to saying that religious truth is *the sum* of religious traditions. One of Munz's aims is ' . . . to enquire whether it is not possible to find a criterion of religious truth which would enable us to avoid the identification of religious truth with any one provincial or with the alleged cosmopolitan tradition.'[5]

Munz thinks that such a criterion can be found in philosophy: ' . . . the philosophy of religion imposes its own criterion of what is good theological reasoning and what is bad theological reasoning. And in doing this, it ceases to be purely descriptive of religious knowledge and begins to be normative.'[6]

Munz's disagreement with Winch is obvious. He thinks that the norm of truth and falsity is not to be found within religion, but *outside* it. One reason why he thinks that philosophical criteria of theological reasoning are needed is the absence of real discussion between adherents of different religions. He describes the contact that does occur as follows: 'These arguments are therefore no more than affirmations of positions. They are monologues. A real argument must be a dialogue, an exchange of opinions and a weighing of evidence. Only a *real* argument can be more than an exercise in self-assertion. But to argue *really*, one must be clear as to the things one is arguing about.'[7]

Munz says more than he realises in the last sentence of the above quotation. In order for adherents of different religions to talk to each other, they must have something to talk about! But this is a religious matter, not a philosophical one. Philosophical speculation may help to distinguish religion from superstition, but where *religions* are concerned, whether they have enough in common to promote discussion depends on the content of their beliefs. No general answer is possible. In some cases, for instance between Christians and Jews, a wealth of discussion is possible. Between others – Christians and Buddhists, say – discussion is more difficult. When one considers tribal religions, one wonders whether one is talking about the same thing at all; whether here religion has a different meaning. The possibility of discussion then depends, not as Munz suggests on the intervention of philosophy from without, but on the theologies of the religions in question. If there were a union of religions this would be because of changes within the religions united. One might object to my analysis on the grounds that it stresses religious meaning at the expense of religious truth. The analysis does not indicate which religion is the true one. But why should anyone suppose that philosophy can answer that question?

One final objection. An opponent of religion might claim that far from leaving the question of religious truth unanswered, I have guaranteed that any possible answer is favourable to religion by insisting that the criteria of intelligibility in religious matters are to be found within religion. The objection confuses my epistemological thesis with an absurd religious doctrine. To say that the criteria of truth and falsity in religion are to be found within a religious tradition is to say nothing of the truth or falsity of the religion in question. On the contrary, my thesis is as necessary in explaining unbelief as it is in explaining belief. It is because many have seen religion for what it is that they have thought it important to rebel against it. The rebel sees what religion is and rejects it. What can this 'seeing' be? Obviously, he does not see the point of religion as the believer does, since for the believer seeing the point of religion is believing. Nevertheless, the rebel has knelt in the church even if he has not prayed. He has taken the sacrament of Communion even if he has not communed. He knows the story from the inside, but it is not a story that captivates him. Nevertheless, he can see what religion is supposed to do and what it is supposed to be. At times we stand afar off saying, 'I wish I could be like that.' We are not like that, but we know what it must be like. The rebel stands on the threshold of religion seeing what it must be like, but saying, 'I do not want to be like that. I rebel against it all.' It is in this context, as Camus has said, that 'every blasphemy is, ultimately, a participation in holiness'.

Notes

1. *Existence and Analogy* (London: Longmans, 1949) p. 1.
2. *Ibid.*, p. 17.
3. *The Idea of a Social Science* (London: Routledge, 1958) pp. 90–1.
4. An issue I return to in the final essay in the collection.
5. *Problems of Religious Knowledge* (London: SCM Press, 1959) p. 9.
6. *Ibid.*, p. 28.
7. *Ibid.*, p. 11.

2

Sublime Existence

Anselm wanted to understand what he *already* believed. He did not want to understand *in order to* believe. But he wanted to understand all the same. What kind of understanding was he seeking? What kind of understanding did he achieve? It has been suggested by Norman Malcolm, with good reason, that Anselm sought and achieved a grammatical, that is to say conceptual, insight![1] He wanted to clarify for himself, as well as for others, the *kind* of concept we are dealing with when we speak of God's existence. Anselm was elucidating, not proving.

Malcolm's suggestion may result in a loss of interest. We seem to be offered less than we were promised. We were promised a proof of God's existence such that the fool, or anyone else, who denied God's existence, would be silenced forever. Indeed, anyone who says God does not exist, it was said, is contradicting himself. To think clearly is to see that God necessarily exists. That conclusion, it might be thought, is one worth waiting for. Indeed, the ontological argument may *sound* good to us, even when we are convinced it does not work: God is the sum of perfections. Existence is a perfection. To think of God as not existing is to think of him as lacking a perfection. Therefore, whatever we thought about could not have been God. To think of God is, of necessity, to think that God exists. So runs one familiar version of the argument. But we are equally familiar with Kantian criticisms of the argument. 'Existence' is not a perfection. We would not list 'existence' among the properties or qualities of anything. No matter how many properties or qualities of a thing we enumerate, whether the thing exists is always a further question. One may list its properties and qualities and go on to say, without contradiction, that the thing does not exist. Unfortunately, for religious apologetics, this applies as much to God's existence as to the existence of anything else. Even if God is the sum of all perfections, the question remains whether such a being exists.

Such is the nature of the dispute with which undergraduates have become overfamiliar. Still, it might be said, the issue is a real one:

whether there is a God. By contrast, it may be thought, all philosophers offer us in Malcolm's version of the argument are truths
about language rather than truths about reality; or, as Alvin Plantinga
might say, mere moves in a language game instead of the sober truth
about the world.[2] We want to know whether there is a God or not,
not what it *means* to ask whether there is a God or not.

But let us pause a little at this point. If I ask whether an island
exists, my question gets its sense from the cluster of considerations,
interests and procedures which would enter into the determination
of whether the island exists. It is our acquaintance with these factors
which leads us to conclude that it makes no sense to say that islands
necessarily exist or necessarily do not exist. Gaunilo, Anselm's contemporary, thought that the same can be said of the existence of
God. He thought that the sense we talk about islands should save us
from the nonsense Anselm talked about God. If we talk like Anselm,
Gaunilo thought, we are led to talk nonsense about islands. From the
fact that we can think of the most perfect island, we would not
dream of concluding that such an island exists.

Gaunilo's objection is remembered with respect, but not much
attention is paid to Anselm's reply. Anselm did not quarrel with
what Gaunilo said about islands, but he wondered why on earth this
should apply to what he had said about God. Perhaps Anselm's
reply is neglected because it is assumed that its essence consists in
saying that, whereas the ideal island is perfect of its kind, God is the
sum of *all* perfections. Whereas an ideal island may lack a perfection,
such as existence, God cannot. But since 'existence' is not a perfection anyway, Anselm's distinction between being perfect of its kind
and being the sum all perfections is thought to be of little consequence.

I have no objections to these criticisms of Anselm's reply, but do
they exhaust the point of it? What if we emphasise, not the distinction between perfections of a kind and the sum of perfections, but
the conceptual distinction between talk of physical objects, such as
islands, and talk of God? Anselm is insisting that we cannot talk
about them in the same way.

This insistence is the main feature of Malcolm's argument. He
finds the grammatical distinction Anselm is emphasising in *Proslogion*
3, where he finds Anselm saying not that 'existence' is a perfection,
but that 'necessary existence' is. 'Necessary existence' is an internal
property of the concept of God; that is, it is part of its grammar. It
determines what it does and does not make sense to say where the

existence of God is concerned. For example, we cannot speak of God's existence in the way we speak of the existence of things that come to be and pass away. We cannot ask how long God has existed, what caused his existence, whether he still exists, and so on. God is not an object among objects, an individual among individuals, a phenomenon among phenomena. As Rush Rhees has said, we do not point and say, 'That's God', and if we want to find out whether two people mean the same by 'God', nothing is involved which is even remotely like determining whether we mean the same by 'the Queen', 'St Mary's Church', or a planet.[3]

Our talk and behaviour show that we recognise these differences when not philosophising, but we ignore them when we philosophise. Why do we do this? Much of the answer can be found in what Wittgenstein called, the tendency to sublime the logic of our language,[4] to take language out of its contexts of application. My contention in this essay is that we often misunderstand the notion of God's sublime existence because we sublime the logic of our language when we reflect on it. I shall consider eight examples of how we do this.

First: philosophers of very different persuasions have said that it is not *fitting* to speak of the existence of God. Think of Wittgenstein's discussion of the example that we can only check the King in chess. It would be highly misleading, he argues, to seek to explain or justify this by saying that it is fitting that the King should have this role. Such an explanation or justification is quite vacuous, since it is only within the game that the King can be said to have this role. An abstract notion of 'fittingness' does not determine which moves in the game are possible. A particular game may become pointless when we discover that an early move of a certain kind determines its outcome. This happens, not because it fails to correspond to a notion of what is fitting, which is beyond all games, but because the game, given its purposes, has been badly designed. Applying this to God's existence, how can it be determined in abstraction, whether it is fitting to speak of God's existence? This is an example of subliming the logic of 'what is fitting'.

Second: philosophers of very different persuasions have said that it is not fitting to speak of God's existence since it contradicts *the* logic of existence. Some have said this in order to emphasise the grammatical distinctions Anselm is making. They have said that talk of 'existence' does not do justice to religious usage concerning the reality of God. For this reason, we find Kierkegaard saying that God does not exist, he is eternal.[5] Simone Weil says that anything that exists is unworthy of absolute, unconditional love. In saying this she believes religion is rescued from anthropomorphism and idolatry; a god who is no more than man writ large, a natural god. She says that we need a purifying atheism. In loving God, she concludes, we love something that does not exist. God is more important than anything that exists.[6] John Wisdom asks us to reflect on what it means to come to God or to find him. No matter how impressive an individual or object we come across, no matter how magnificent the surroundings, it would not be that Spirit in which we live and move and have our being. It would simply be another individual, another object, another phenomenon, which we might or might not be able to make anything of.[7] What it would not be is the Creator of heaven and earth, an eternal God. For reasons such as these, Malcolm concludes that the proposition 'God exists' is no more than an idle philosophical construction.[8] Even if we answered the question, 'How long has God existed?' by saying, 'Always', this still would not do justice to the notion of God's eternity. Malcolm says that the moon could have endless duration, but not eternity.[9] On the other hand, R. F. Holland has argued forcefully that the notion of endless duration is unintelligible.[10] In any event, the essential distinction is between duration and eternity. To mark it, as we see, some philosophers insist that an eternal God should not be said to exist.

Yet, granting the importance of these grammatical distinctions, why should we tidy up ordinary language? People do wonder whether there is a God. In certain circumstances, they say they believe that God exists. Must we substitute 'belief in' for 'belief that'? Probably the former is the more natural use in religious belief. But as long as 'exist' is used in the same way as 'eternal', and 'belief that' is used in the same way as 'belief in', why should we object to the words? The point is in the practice. To think otherwise is to sublime the logic of 'existence' and 'belief'.

Yet, it is because of this very religious application of 'exists' in 'God exists' that philosophers of a very different persuasion say that God, logically, cannot exist. J. N. Findlay concedes that Anselm does justice to what he calls 'the religious attitude'. God must be thought of as absolute, unlimited, and independent. But, he adds, there is one difficulty about this: nothing thought of in this way can be said to exist. Existence is contingent. Anselm's argument, on this view, achieves the exact opposite of its intention. Anselm's aim is to show that we cannot say, without self-contradiction, that God does not exist. What he actually achieves, it is argued, is to show that we cannot say, without self-contradiction, that God does exist.[11] We are faced with two radical claims: that anyone who says 'God does not exist' and anyone who says 'God does exist' is contradicting himself. There is a strong smell of fish in the air.

Critics sympathetic to religion say that God does not exist, but has 'necessary existence'. Critics unsympathetic to religion say that God necessarily does not exist. Both sets of critics talk in this way because talk of God, they say, contradicts the conditions of talk about 'existence'. But what conditions are these? Presumably, the way we speak of things which come to be and pass away. But it is admitted *on all sides* that one cannot speak of God in that way, so why claim that one way of talking should be answerable to another? One would expect philosophers to look to see what is involved in talk of God's existence before reaching the conclusion that it *must* be answerable to some other way of talking. What they have done, in fact, is to sublime the logic of 'existence', assuming that we can only ascribe 'existence' to things which come to be and pass away.

The same tendency can be found among many philosophers who reacted to Malcolm's paper, 'Anselm's Ontological Arguments'. Interestingly, they take for granted that they have grasped his grammatical observations. Yet, they continue to speak in ways ruled out by those observations. Agreeing that Malcolm has delineated the formal requirements of the notion of 'God', they insist that we can then ask whether it happens to be the case that God exists. Questions of real existence, they insist, cannot be put aside. It is these real questions which all ontological arguments seek to by-pass.[12] But if these critics had grasped Malcolm's grammatical conclusions, they would have appreciated that to say 'There is a God' is not to say, 'There is a God, but there might not have been one'. Similarly, to say, 'There is no God' is not to say 'There is no God, but there might have been one'. Such ways of talking fail to do justice to atheism and belief.

The third example I want to mention of philosophers subliming the logic of our language is when they address so-called questions of real existence in the context of a metaphysical realism. 'Existence', they claim, the question of 'what is so', cannot be settled within any context of discourse but must be asked of these contexts themselves. No matter how much we elucidate the meanings which prevail in these contexts, the question remains, 'But is it really so?'.[13]

On such a view, the grammatical parameters of our forms of discourse are treated as descriptions of reality. The philosopher then asks whether these descriptions correspond to reality. But, as Peter Winch has argued, the grammatical parameters of our forms of discourse are *not descriptions of anything*.[14] Rather, they determine what it *means* to offer a description or to make an existential claim in that context. But the metaphysical realist wants to ask, independently of any context, 'But is it really so?'. In abstracting the question from all contexts of application he sublimes the logic of our language. So we should not take Plantinga's advice and exchange talk of what he calls 'mere moves in language games' for talk of 'the sober truth about the world', since until we know what games we are engaged in, we have no idea what is meant by 'the sober truth'. The moves we make, in various contexts, to determine what is so are not 'mere moves'. I make moves to determine whether there is a chair in the next room, whether I am in credit at the bank, whether someone loves me, whether a theory in physics is verified, etc. Saying something does not make it so, as the reference to 'mere moves' seems to suggest. Determining what is so involves *doing* something, but what that comes to cannot be appreciated apart from the context in which the question arises. To think otherwise is to sublime the logic of 'what is so', and to create a metaphysical realm in which the question 'But is it really so?' *does* become a mere move, an idle abstraction. A move is a 'mere move' not when it is in a language game, but when it is said to be outside all language games.

Once we create this metaphysical realm, the tendency to sublime the logic of our language increases alarmingly. This has happened in the case of the notion of 'necessity' giving us our fourth example. The metaphysical realm, it is said, contains the ultimate explanation of our present condition. Since we have no direct access to this realm, what we say about it, so the argument runs, must be speculative. According to Robert Adams, we are in this position with respect to the concept of necessity.[15] Apparently, we simply do not understand the nature of necessity. Why are we in this state? Because, it is said, we have no definition of necessity which covers all our uses of the word. Such definitions as we have, it is argued, are circular and thus give us no real understanding. For example, if we say that the proposition 'All bachelors are unmarried' is necessarily true because it cannot be contradicted, we are then asked what 'contradiction' is. It is said that contradictions *cannot* make sense. So far from explaining the notion of necessity, it is concluded, the reference to contradiction presupposes the very notion we are seeking to explain.

We can only get out of this conceptual muddle if we see that what we need is not a 'something' called 'necessity' which is supposed to lie beneath the allegedly baffling variety of our uses, but an elucidation of what lies open to view. The nature of necessity is supposed to explain why, in various language games, we would be contradicting ourselves if we drew certain conclusions or tried to say certain things. But this is to put matters entirely the wrong way round. It is not 'necessity' which explains the various ways in which we speak, but the various ways in which we speak which show the status of necessary propositions within them and how certain statements and conclusions are ruled out as contradictory. This is not a matter of explanation, but of elucidation. If I want to understand why I cannot speak of married bachelors, I need to get acquainted with families, marriages, etc. In short, what I need is not a metaphysical realm, but the familiar family round.

Once we take metaphysical flight, further philosophical fictions have to be created. We have to sublime the logic of our language further to explain why, if we do not understand necessity, we can nevertheless recognise necessities and contradictions. This gives us our fifth example. Do we call certain propositions necessary or contradictory, it is asked, because it is pragmatically useful to do so? Such pragmatic success would give us some reason to suppose that our concepts correspond to reality. But, the argument continues, why should we rely on this supposition? Why trust our feeble minds in so important an assumption? Surely, there is a better explanatory hypothesis available to us. What if the mind of God is such that he understands all necessary propositions? It would then be natural for God to so construct human beings that they can, within their limits, recognise these necessities. Of course, it is concluded, we cannot be sure of any of this, but at least it makes theism an attractive hypothesis. Its attraction lies in its ability to explain what is otherwise hard to explain.

But the difficulties are of the philosophers' own making. They look away from what lies open to view. Our understanding of our concepts is shown in the use we make of them. This is as true of the notion of divine necessity as of any other. We must reject the negative apologetic which merely says that, since we do not understand the nature of necessity, the possibility of divine necessity cannot be ruled out. We must locate the notion of divine necessity in its natural surroundings.

What are these surroundings? Here are some indications of them.[16] God's love is said to be a *necessary love*. To say that God loves is not to say that he could be malicious but, as a matter of fact, is loving. The 'is' in 'God is love' is not an 'is' of predication. 'God is love' gives us a rule for the use of the word 'God'. The judgement of God's love is said to be a *necessary judgement*. It makes no sense to speak of avoiding it. Separation from God is not the contingent consequence of sin. Sin *is* separation from God. The relation between sin and separation is a necessary one. The eternal destiny of the human soul is said to be determined by the relation in which it stands to the divine. The last judgement is not contingently last. It is not the judgement that follows the last but one.

The reactions of many philosophers to these suggestions provide a sixth example of subliming the logic of our language. They say that talk of necessary love or judgement presupposes the necessary existence of God and thus does not explain or elucidate it. John Searle has said that people would not engage in religious language games unless they had a prior belief in the existence of God.[17] The belief, it is said, explains the engagement. But I am not offering explanations. I offer elucidations. Consider the following analogy. We do not first believe in the reality of physical objects so that, with confidence, we may sit on chairs, set tables, climb stairs, etc. Rather, what we mean by the reality of physical objects is shown in such activities. Similarly, we do not presuppose God's necessary existence in order to talk of his love and judgement. Rather, it is such talk which gives sense to talk of God's necessary existence.[18] God's reality is synonymous with his divinity; God is divinely real. What we are investigating is not whether God exists, in some sublime sense of 'existence', but rather the grammar of 'sublime existence', 'the existence of the sublime'.

What follows from our grammatical conclusions? In the conclusions Malcolm wishes to draw he is sometimes in danger of subliming the logic of denial, a seventh example of subliming the logic of our language. On the one hand, Malcolm argues, if talk of God's necessary existence cannot be shown to be self-contradictory or logically absurd, it follows that God necessarily exists. On the other hand, Malcolm argues that an atheist could follow Anselm's argument, accept its conclusion, and yet remain an atheist.

An atheist is someone who says that there is no God. He may think that religious belief is self-contradictory because, in relation to

God, it tries to combine 'existence' and 'necessity'. But, as we have seen, the religious notion of divine existence is not the notion of contingent existence with 'necessity' added to it. It is a different concept. God's necessary existence is synonymous with the eternity of the divine. How can atheism call this concept self-contradictory? Only by subliming the logic of self-contradiction; that is, claiming to know what constitutes a self-contradictory use of language without specifying any linguistic context.

But Malcolm thinks this conclusion has implications for any atheist. He says that the fool can no longer say in his heart 'There is no God'. But, as O. K. Bouwsma has shown, Anselm turned the fool in the psalm into a literate fool.[19] The fool in the psalm never said 'There is no God' to himself. It is his heart that speaks. In other words, his life shows that God has no place in it. There are plenty of atheists of this kind. They need not hold any views on whether religious belief is self-contradictory or logically absurd. If they did, Anselm's argument may show such atheism to be untenable. But they hold no such views. Must their atheism be touched by the argument? Can't they still say in face of it, 'There is no God'? If Malcolm denies this, he is subliming the logic of denial, since denial may not take the form to which he and Anselm object.

Does Malcolm also provide us with an eighth example of subliming the logic of our language, in which the logic of religious affirmation is sublimed? The answer depends on whether Malcolm assents to his own summary of Anselm's conclusions: 'So if God exists His existence is necessary. Thus God's existence is either impossible or necessary. It can be the former only if the concept of such a being is self-contradictory or in some way logically absurd. Assuming that this is not so, it follows that He necessarily exists'.[20] The crucial question is: from whose mouth are these words, 'it follows that He necessarily exists' supposed to come? If they are philosophical, grammatical remarks, should they not be reformulated? What follows, it should be said, is not that He necessarily exists, but that in this concept of God, he is said to necessarily exist. The words, 'it follows that He necessarily exists', if taken naturally, sound like a religious declaration, almost a confession. On the other hand, Malcolm also insists that it is possible to give logical assent to the argument without being touched religiously. The problem is that if Malcolm assents to Anselm's conclusion, it looks as if God's necessary existence is being acknowledged, quite independently of any context of religious belief. Anselm's proof ends in praise: 'And this thou art, O Lord our God'. But grammatical clarification need not end in this praise. Acknowledgement of God is a religious acknowledgement. Elsewhere, Malcolm has argued that belief in God makes no sense apart from some affective state or attitude. These states and attitudes range from reverential love to blasphemy and rebellion.[21] For similar reasons, Kierkegaard said that proof in religion is from the emotions.[22] This is a grammatical remark. It is an indication of the contexts in which non-philosophical belief and atheism have their life. The view that these various forms of belief and atheism need to be underwritten by philosophy is a confusion shared by philosophical theism and philosophical atheism. Thus, the question, 'Is there an eternal God?' is idle if unrelated to practice, unrelated to actually affirming or denying a spiritual reality.[23]

In this essay I have discussed eight examples of our tendency to sublime the logic of our language:

1. The claim that it is not *fitting* to speak of God's existence.
2. The claim that to speak of God's existence contradicts *the* logic of 'existence'.
3. The claim that we can ask 'But is it really so?' independently of the criteria, in any context, for determining what is so.
4. That in endeavouring to understand necessary propositions we are speculating hypothetically about the nature of that necessity which is in a metaphysical realm beyond the limits of our knowledge.
5. That our ability to recognise necessary propositions and contradictions is explained best by the hypothesis that God has constructed us in such a way that we are able to do this.
6. The talk of the necessity of divine love and judgement implies prior belief in the existence of a God of whom this love and judgement can be predicated.
7. That if the grammatical insights of Anselm's argument are recognised, atheism cannot take the form of saying, 'There is no God'.
8. That a recognition of Anselm's insights could lead to an acknowledgement that God exists which is independent of the context of religious belief.

In my attempts to expose the untenability of these eight claims, one moral is constant: as long as we sublime the logic of 'existence', we shall never appreciate what it means, in religion, to speak of the existence of the sublime.

Notes

1. N. Malcolm, 'Anselm's Ontological Arguments', in *Knowledge and Certainty* (Englewood Cliffs, NJ: Prentice-Hall, 1963).
2. A. Plantinga, 'Advice to Christian Philosophers', *Faith and Philosophy*, vol. I, No. 3 (July 1984) p. 419. See Essay 14 in this collection.
3. R. Rhees, 'Religion and Language', in *Without Answers* (London: Routledge, 1969) see pp. 127–8.
4. L. Wittgenstein, *Philosophical Investigations*, trans. G. E. M. Anscombe (Oxford: Blackwell, 1988) see paras 38, 89, 94.
5. S. Kierkegaard, *Concluding Unscientific Postscript*, trans. D. F. Swenson, (Princeton: Princeton University Press 1944) p. 296.
6. S. Weil, *Gravity and Grace*, introduction by G. Thebon, trans. by E. Craufurd (London: Routledge & Kegan Paul, 1952) p. 99.
7. J. Wisdom, 'The Logic of God', in *Paradox and Discovery* (Oxford: Basil Blackwell, 1965) p. 11.
8. N. Malcolm, 'Is it a Religious Belief that "God Exists"?', in *Faith and the Philosophers*, ed. J. Hick (London, 1964). But compare his 'Anselm's Ontological Arguments', p. 153.
9. N. Malcolm, 'Anselm's Ontological Arguments', p. 148.
10. R. F. Holland, 'For Ever?', in *Against Empiricism* (Oxford: Blackwell, 1980).
11. J. N. Findlay, 'Can God's Existence Be Disproved?', in *New Essays in Philosophical Theology*, ed. A. Flew and A. MacIntyre (London: SCM Press, 1955).
12. See, for example, R. E. Allen, 'The Ontological Arguments'; T. Penelhum, 'On the Second Ontological Argument'; A. Plantinga, 'A Valid Ontological Argument?'; P. Henle, 'Uses of the Ontological Argument'; all in *The Philosophical Review*, Jan. 1961; T. Patterson Brown, 'Professor Malcolm on Anselm's Ontological Arguments', *Analysis*, vol. 22 (1961–2).
13. See Essays 3 and 4 in this collection.
14. P. Winch, 'Language, Belief and Relativism', in *Trying To Make Sense* (Oxford: Blackwell, 1987) p. 195f.
15. The speculations which follow are taken, in the main, from Robert Adams, 'Divine Necessity', in *The Concept of God*, ed. T. V. Morris, Oxford: Readings in Philosophy (OUP, 1987).
16. For more detailed discussion see my *The Concept of Prayer* ((London: Routledge & Kegan Paul, 1965; Oxford: Basil Blackwell, 1981).
17. J. Searle, 'Wittgenstein: dialogue with Bryan Magee', in *The Great Philosophers* (BBC Books, 1987). For my discussion see Essay 3.
18. See my *Faith After Foundationalism* (London: Routledge, 1988) Part One.

19. O. K. Bouwsma, 'Anselm's Argument', in *Without Proof or Evidence*, ed. and introduced by J. L. Craft and R. E. Hustwit (Lincoln and London: University of Nebraska Press, 1984) p. 53f.
20. N. Malcolm, 'Anselm's Ontological Arguments', p. 150.
21. N. Malcolm, 'Is it a Religious Belief that God Exists?'.
22. S. Kierkegaard, *The Journals*, trans A. Dru (New York: OUP, 1938) para. 926.
23. I have attacked the notion of the minimal belief thought to be presupposed by any religious affective state or attitude in Essay 4.

3

Searle on Language-Games and Religion

The public lectures and seminars I gave as the 1988 Cardinal Mercier lecturer at the University of Leuven, were concerned with different aspects of the influence of Ludwig Wittgenstein on contemporary philosophy of religion. It is possible to show some of the bearings these different aspects have on one another, I believe, by a discussion of recent remarks made by John Searle in this context.

In his discussion with Bryan Magee on the philosophy of Ludwig Wittgenstein, Searle makes brief comments on Wittgenstein's remarks on religious belief.[1] Despite their brevity, there are two reasons why they merit discussion. First, they are characteristic of a frequent reaction to Wittgenstein's influence on the philosophy of religion. Second, they illustrate what happens frequently when, after acceptable expositions of Wittgenstein, philosophers turn to consider his remarks on religion. In relation to religion, even more than elsewhere, many fail to appreciate how radical a challenge Wittgenstein makes to our philosophical assumptions.

When Searle comments on Wittgenstein's remarks on religion, he contradicts what he says when expounding Wittgenstein's conception of a language-game. It may be said that the contradiction is only apparent, since whereas Searle's comments are critical, in elucidating Wittgenstein's notion of a language-game, he is simply concerned with exposition, not criticism. While this distinction is true, it does not avoid the charge of contradiction, since this is internal to what Searle says about language-games.

I shall begin by quoting in full Searle's critical comments on Wittgenstein's remarks on religion:

> Wittgenstein's aversion to theory and his insistence that philosophy should be purely descriptive and not critical leads him to a kind of waffling in certain crucial areas. Consider religious discourse, for example. I believe Wittgenstein himself obviously had

a deep religious hunger. He did not have the middle-class Anglo-American attitude towards religion, that it was just a matter of something for Sunday mornings. There are frequent references in his more personal writings to God and to the problems of getting right with God. None the less, I think most people who knew him would say that he was an atheist. Now in a way, when you read his remarks about God, you almost feel that he wants to have it both ways. He wants to talk about God and still be an atheist. He wants to insist that to understand religious discourse we need to see the role it plays in people's lives. And that is surely right. But of course, you would not understand the role that it plays in their lives unless you see that religious discourse refers beyond itself. To put it bluntly, when ordinary people pray it is because they think there is a God up there listening. But whether or not there is a God listening to their prayer isn't itself part of the language game. The reason people play the language game of religion is because they think there is something outside the language game that gives it a point. You have to be a very *recherché* sort of religious intellectual to keep praying if you don't think there is any real God outside the language who is listening to your prayers (pp. 344–5).

The first problem in these remarks is closely connected with Wittgenstein's critique of realism in epistemology and in the philosophy of mind. According to realist theories, we first believe in the reality of various states of affairs, and then, as a result, act and behave in the characteristic ways we do. Thus, in the context under consideration, Searle says: 'The reason people play the language game of religion[2] is because they think there is something outside the language game that gives it its point.' This comment is open to an objection Wittgenstein brings against all realist theories. If the point of playing a language-game is given in a prior belief, what does this 'believing' amount to? 'Believing' is itself a language-game. But in what language-game is *this* 'believing' supposed to occur? Thus, Wittgenstein's objection is directed against a realist analysis of *any* kind of belief, not simply against a realist analysis of religious belief.[3] The realist, by placing 'belief' outside all possible language-games, places it beyond all possible techniques of application in which it could have any sense. The belief would have to tell you what it is without any such context – an incoherent supposition. As Searle says: 'For literally hundreds of paragraphs in his later work [Wittgenstein] goes through a discussion of how we use psychological verbs . . . an examination of the depth grammar shows how the use of the vocabulary is grounded in actual situations' (p. 345). But if the belief that the religious language-game has a point is *itself* placed in an actual situation, it would be an instance of believing in God. This religious believing, however, would have its meaning within the religious language-game and could not, therefore, be a reason *outside* the game for playing it.

Is the belief in the existence of a state of affairs, in this case the existence of God, supposed to be the foundation of the language-game? Surely, Searle cannot mean this, since, earlier, he had said:

> Wittgenstein insists that we shouldn't look for the *foundations* of language games any more than we should look for foundations of games such as football or baseball. All of these are just human activities . . . . A characteristic philosophical mistake is to think that there must be some foundation, some transcendental justification, for each language game. (p. 330)

But, in his critical remarks, Searle *does* speak as though a transcendent state of affairs is the *external* justification for playing the religious language-game. Once again, in his expository remarks, Searle had said:

> Wittgenstein is anxious to insist that there isn't any point of view from outside the language games where we can, so to speak, stand back and appraise the relationship between language and reality. He doesn't think that we can get outside of language to look at the relation between language and reality from the outside and see whether or not language is adequately representing reality. There isn't any non-linguistic Archimedean point from which we can appraise the success or failure of language in representing, coping with or dealing with the real world. We are always operating within some language game or other. So there can't be any transcendental appraisal of the adequacy of language games because there isn't any non-linguistic, transcendental point of view from which they can be appraised. (p. 331)

In his critical comments on Wittgenstein's remarks on religion, however, Searle is himself invoking an external relation between the language-game and reality. He is trading in a non-linguistic, transcendental point of view which, earlier, he has said makes no sense.

We have to reach the conclusion that Searle cannot maintain his exposition of Wittgenstein *and* say in criticism: 'The reason people play the language game of religion is because they think there is something outside the language game that gives it a point' (p. 345).

We also need to note that Searle is not consistent even in the critical comments he makes. As we have seen, he says that people play the religious language-game because they first believe that a transcendent state of affairs obtains. But Searle also says that Wittgenstein

> wants to insist that to understand religious discourse we need to see the role it plays in people's lives. And this is surely right. But of course, you would not understand the role that it plays in their lives unless you see that religious discourse refers beyond itself. To put it bluntly, when ordinary people pray it is because they think there is a God up there listening. (pp. 344–5)

Here, Searle is *not* saying that we know what is meant by the reality of God *prior* to playing the religious language-game. He is saying that *in* the context of this game, reference *is* made to the reality of God. This is certainly true. There is a conception of an independent reality in religion. Yet, to see what this conception of an independent reality amounts to, we must pay attention to the grammar of the religious concepts involved.

Searle's expository remarks would lead us to expect him to agree with this conclusion. For example, at one point in the discussion, Magee expresses the following misgiving:

> But you seem to be saying that according to Wittgenstein's later philosophy, we are never able to make any comparison between language and something which is not language, because we can never occupy any position which is not embedded in language – not, so to speak, inside language. All our conceptual structures – our conceptions of the everyday world, of science, of the arts, of religion – everything – are built up by us in linguistic terms that we can never get outside of it. On this showing, either there is no external reality at all or, if there is, it is something that we can never have independent knowledge of or contact with. Is this really what the later Wittgenstein is saying? (p. 331)

But Searle is quick to assure Magee that this is not so:

No, I think, in fact the way you have stated the position is a characteristic way in which Wittgenstein is misunderstood. Many people think: Surely this view leads to some kind of idealism, perhaps a kind of linguistic idealism. It leads to the view that the only things that exist are words . . . On Wittgenstein's view, we are always working inside language, even when we describe the workings of language. . . . Wittgenstein is not for one moment denying the existence of reality, he is not denying the existence of the real world, or the fact that we can make true claims about the real world. What he is anxious to insist on, though, is that if we have expressions in our language like 'real world', 'reality', 'truth', then they must have a use in language games that is just as humble, just as ordinary, as the use of the words 'chair' and 'table', or 'dog' and 'cat'. For Wittgenstein, our task as philosophers is not to sit back and contemplate the sublime nature of reality and truth, but rather to get busy and describe how we actually use expressions like 'real' and 'true'. (pp. 331–2)

If we apply these remarks to religion, we shall see that Wittgenstein is insisting that, in this context too, philosophy's task is a humble one. Here, too, we have uses of 'real' and 'true'. The philosopher must get busy and show what the applications of these terms amount to. This is precisely what Wittgenstein is doing in his remarks on religion. It is not my purpose to expound these remarks here, except to say that, in the course of them, Wittgenstein explores the deep differences between talking of the reality of God, and talking about the reality of physical objects. These differences are brought out by considering how issues concerning identity would be settled in the two contexts. Consider how we would go about settling whether we are talking about the same bus, the same building, the same star, the same person, etc. The methods for settling these questions clarify the grammar of 'the same' in the respective contexts. But how would we find out whether two people believe in the same God? The way we do this has little in common with criteria used in the other contexts. In the religious case we would have to look at the role religious belief plays in the lives of the people concerned. The issue could not be settled without considering the presence or the lack, and the content of spirituality in their lives. If that which surrounds the uses of 'the same' differs, it follows that the grammar of 'the same' differs too. It is in this way that we come to see that the grammar of 'the same God' differs from the grammar of 'the same object'.

Magee and Searle seem to agree with these conclusions, when, in their discussion, they point out striking differences between Wittgenstein and many other philosophers, in their respective treatment of religion. Magee says:

> The old-style logical positivists, who were extremely influenced by their reading of Wittgenstein's early philosophy, were also extremely dismissive of any form of religious utterance. Because religious utterances are characteristically unverifiable they took them to be, literally, meaningless. But the later Wittgenstein would have had a quite different attitude. He would have said that there is, and has been in every known form of society, religious utterance, and if we want to understand it we must pay close attention to the way concrete examples of it function within given forms of life. Every mode of discourse has its own appropriate logic, and it's simply no good appraising religious utterances as one would appraise scientific utterances – which is what the logical positivists had been doing. (p. 334)

Searle agrees, pointing out that Wittgenstein

> thinks it is ridiculous to suppose that we should take religious utterances as if they were some sort of second-rate scientific utterances, as if they were theories for which we have inadequate evidence . . . He hated the idea that we should over-intellectualise these matters, and try to make everything into some sort of theoretical enterprise. (pp. 334–5)

Nowhere is this over-intellectualisation more grotesque than the attempt to apply it to human suffering. Apologists for religion try to devise a science of suffering: a theodicy by means of which they hope to show that every conceivable and actual evil must be a means to a higher good. Wittgenstein had no time for such tendencies in the philosophy of religion. For him, they are failures to take either humanity or divinity seriously.[4]

Wittgenstein's attack on over-intellectualisation is relevant, however, not simply to the philosophical treatment of religious language, but to the way in which philosophers think of language in a wide variety of contexts. As Searle points out, one of the most powerful aspects of Wittgenstein's last work, *On Certainty*, is its attack on the long-standing philosophical tradition 'according to

which all our meaningful activities must be the product of some
inner theory. . . . But Wittgenstein points out that for a great deal of
our behaviour, we just do it' (p. 346). In this connection, Wittgenstein
emphasised the importance of primitive reactions, reactions which
play a crucial role in concept-formation in our language. It is
unsurprising, therefore, that to understand the role of religious
beliefs in human life, here, too, we need to take account of our
primitive reactions. Only then are we able to appreciate what
concept-formation comes to in this context (see Essay 7).

Why, given this general background of his exposition of
Wittgenstein's philosophy, should Searle, in his critical remarks,
suggest that Wittgenstein spoke of religion as if the existence of God
were of no importance? Why should Searle suggest that Wittgenstein
speaks of prayer as if it were of no importance that God hears
prayers? These are puzzling questions, and we can only speculate as
to why Searle does this.

The first suggestion we might consider is simply that Searle is
dissatisfied with the analysis Wittgenstein gives of religious belief.
But this dissatisfaction itself may have two different aspects. Searle
may be claiming that what Wittgenstein says about religion does not
accord well with what many religious believers, atheists and
philosophers say about religion *when asked*. This disagreement
undoubtedly exists, but what of it? Wittgenstein is critical of these
other accounts. The *mere* fact that they disagree with him need not
impress him. Wittgenstein knows that many argue for and against
religious belief in terms of what they call 'the theistic hypothesis'.
But why should Wittgenstein be more impressed by that fact, than
Searle would be by the fact that many give Cartesian answers when
asked about the nature of thinking? We would not dream of answering issues in the philosophy of mind by counting heads and concluding 'The Cartesians have it!' Why do we contemplate such a
procedure in the philosophy of religion?

But Searle may have more than this in mind. He may be saying
that Wittgenstein's analyses do not do justice to the role religious
beliefs play in people's lives. That *is* a serious criticism. It would
amount to saying that Wittgenstein is confused about the grammar
of religious concepts. Such disagreements can only be explored by
discussion. We can only proceed by endeavouring to produce perspicuous representations of the contexts in which religious concepts
have their life. As with the basic propositions Wittgenstein discusses
in *On Certainty* the task in the philosophy of religion is to show how

the basic propositions of religious belief are held fast by what surrounds them. This task does not involve treating that belief as a hypothesis. It also takes us beyond the Calvinist epistemologist's claim that, in epistemology, we simply have a negative confrontation between non-theistic and theistic epistemologists, each failing to deny the other's right to exist. Wittgenstein's methods invite us to engage in a *common* discussion of religious belief.[5] The trouble is that, so often, in the philosophy of religion, this is precisely what philosophers will not do. They prefer to discuss *philosophical* concepts, rather than the religious beliefs which are important in people's lives, and which often occasion our puzzlement.

My purpose, at the moment, is not to further this discussion, but to point out a move which Searle tries to make within it, but which cannot, in fact be made. Searle says: 'You have to be a very recherché sort of religious intellectual to keep praying if you don't think there is any real God outside the language who is listening to your prayers' (p. 345). But this cannot be a remark *against* Wittgenstein's analyses, because *everyone*, Wittgenstein included, would say that it is futile to pray to God unless there is a God to pray to. *The conceptual disagreement is precisely over what saying that amounts to.* Some think Wittgenstein's analyses are penetrating. Others disagree with them, but think that religious belief is meaningful. Again, others disagree and think that religious belief is meaningless. It is unnecessary to determine where Searle stands in this spectrum of reactions. Wherever he stands, he cannot say, as though it were an *argument* against Wittgenstein: 'when ordinary people pray it is because they think there is a God up there listening' (p. 345), since it is precisely the grammar of such ordinary language that is being discussed. Searle cannot take its grammar for granted.

Grammar is often taken for granted when philosophers of religion indulge in what I call *philosophy by italics.* In objecting to Wittgenstein's remarks on religion, philosophers are prone to say, 'After all, God *exists*'; 'God is *real*'; 'God is *there*'; '*Someone* must *listen* to prayers'; etc. but what these philosophers seem not to realise is that *no* grammatical work has been done simply by italicising these terms. As Searle said earlier, philosophy's humble task is the clarification of these concepts in their natural settings. Such clarity is as essential for an understanding of atheism, as it is for an understanding of religious belief.

The second suggestion which might explain Searle's dissatisfaction with Wittgenstein's remarks on religion, is the tension he perceives between them and the fact that many who knew Wittgenstein said he was an atheist. What *kind* of tension does Searle have in mind? It is difficult to know. The tension could be attributed to personal or philosophical considerations. First, the personal considerations about which I want to say very little. Why should it be surprising if an atheist talks a lot about God, or if a believer talks a lot about objections to religious belief? If something is deeply important to one, one may want to make sure that one has done justice to opposing points of view. Searle says that Wittgenstein had 'a hunger for God', but did not call himself a believer. I am not confirming these facts, but, if true, why should they create a puzzle? A person, out of respect for religion, realising the nature of its demands, may refuse to call himself a believer. As Searle says, the *last* thing religion was for Wittgenstein was a matter of respectability.

Second, what of the philosophical considerations which might have led Searle to see a tension between Wittgenstein's remarks on religion and his alleged atheism? These are of greater importance. What does the tension amount to? To be a participant in the religious language-game, to be a believer, is to make a confession. There are times when Wittgenstein in his *Lectures and Conversations on Aesthetics, Psychology and Religious Belief* and in *Culture and Value* speaks of what it would mean to make a confession before God. But that is not the same as actually making a confession. I am not at all sure that Wittgenstein did call himself an atheist. He certainly did not if, by atheism, we mean the opposite philosophical stance to philosophical theism. *That* kind of philosophy, with its arguments for and against religion, was anathema to him. Wittgenstein was interested in the clarification of religious concepts. That philosophical task may be performed better by someone who does not call himself a believer than by someone who calls himself a believer.

Two separate theses are often confused in discussing these issues. The first is rightly attributed to Wittgenstein: to understand religious belief one must take account of the use of religious concepts in people's lives. The second thesis, often confused with the first, is attributed to an aberration which has been called Wittgensteinian fideism: that religious belief can only be understood by those who play the religious language-game. Wittgenstein did not hold this view, and neither is it held by those influenced by him in the philosophy of religion.[6] If one did hold this view, there would be a tension between saying that one understood the grammar of religious belief and calling oneself an atheist. But since Wittgenstein held the first, not the second thesis we have mentioned, there is no tension between trying to clarify religious concepts while refusing to call oneself a believer.

As we have seen, Wittgenstein's philosophical method is open to believer and non-believer alike. We have also seen that it is not a method which appeals to a common assessment, from allegedly neutral evidence, of claims for and against the existence of God. Wittgenstein's method also avoids the totalitarian epistemologies of post-Enlightenment thought. It is well-known that writers such as Feuerbach, Freud, Marx and Durkheim treat religious beliefs, not as false beliefs, but as ideologies.[7] Recently, it has been claimed by Calvinist epistemologists that it is unbelievers who are in the grip of ideology.[8] The aim of Wittgenstein's work, on the other hand, is to find our way from conceptual puzzlement to conceptual clarity. This aim, if achieved, would clarify the grammar of belief and unbelief, and also the grammar of the disagreement between them. It is in this sense that philosophy's task is a humble one, and it is in this sense, too, that philosophy leaves everything where it is.

Notes

1. 'Wittgenstein: Dialogue with John Searle', in *The Great Philosophers*, Bryan Magee (BBC Books, 1987). All quotations are from this volume.
2. I would not speak myself of 'the language game of religion'. Religious belief involves many language-games. Similarly, I would not speak of religion as a form of life, but as existing in a form of life. The significance of religious belief could not be elucidated without bringing out how it illuminates *other* features of human life. But in the context of this essay I'll continue to use Searle's phrase, 'the language game of religion'.
3. This was the theme of my Cardinal Mercier seminar, 'On Really Believing'. See Essay 4.
4. I explored this theme in the Cardinal Mercier lecture, 'On Not Understanding God'. See Essay 10.
5. I explored these issues in the Cardinal Mercier lecture and seminar in 'Can There Be A Christian Philosophy?' (see Essay 14) and 'Religion and Epistemology: Plantinga's Reformed Epistemology and Wittgenstein's *On Certainty*' respectively. The comparisons and contrasts between Wittgenstein and Calvinist epistemology are explored at length in my book *Faith After Foundationalism*, Part One (Routledge, 1988).
6. In fact, none of the theses connected with Wittgensteinian fideism are held by Wittgenstein or by those influenced by him in the philosophy of

religion. I have shown this in *Belief, Change and Forms of Life* (Macmillan and Humanities Press, 1986).

7. I have discussed most of these writers in *Religion Without Explanation* (Basil Blackwell, 1976).

8. See Nicholas Wolterstorff, 'Is Reason Enough?', in *The Reformed Journal*, vol. 34, no. 4.

4
On Really Believing

It is widely assumed in contemporary philosophy of religion that if a philosopher wishes to give an analytic account of religious belief, one which seeks to clarify the grammar of that belief, he must choose between realism and non-realism. These, it is thought, are the only philosophical alternatives open to him. According to Terence Penelhum, 'Most atheists and agnostics are theological realists, and obviously most defenders and apologists for faith are also.'[1] Most, but not all, for, it is said, on the margins of the dispute between belief and unbelief are those philosophers and theologians who give non-realist accounts of these alternatives. According to realists, the non-realist analyses fail to capture the essence of belief and atheism.

What is the theological realist's account of believing in God? According to Penelhum, anyone committed to realism

> would hold that the supernatural facts which he thinks faith requires must indeed *be* facts for faith to be true, so that if they are not facts, but fantasies (or, even worse, not coherently expressible), then faith is unjustified. (p. 151)

The realist admits that faith, believing, has consequences which constitute the commitments which make up living religiously, but he insists, to use Roger Trigg's words, that 'The belief is distinct from the commitment which may follow it, and is the justification for it.'[2] The non-realist's sin, it is said, is to conflate believing with the consequences of believing, so making the realist's conception of belief redundant.

For the realist, the non-realist analyses of religious belief are reductionist in character. These analyses have been arrived at as a result of the alleged difficulties created for belief in the existence of God by the demands of verificationism. Many non-realists concur with this view. They are prepared to admit that realism portrays what faith once meant for people, but argue that this conception of faith cannot be sustained today. In this respect, non-realists are revisionists. As Penelhum says, 'Neither Hare nor Cupitt is claiming that theological realism *has not been* integral to the faith "as it is"' (p. 163). The same could be said of R. B. Braithwaite and the late Bishop of Woolwich. They all dispense with something, which they admit was once integral to faith, 'in the interest of preserving and revitalising the rest of it' (p. 163). The realist claims that what the non-realist dispenses with is logically indispensable for any notion of belief.

In contemporary philosophy of religion there has been a Wittgensteinian critique of realism. Given the assumption that philosophers have to choose between realism and non-realism, it is not surprising to find this critique discussed in these terms. The criticisms, and mine more than most, are placed firmly in the non-realist camp. According to Penelhum, however, there is one important difference between my work and that of the non-realists we have mentioned. As we have said, they admit that realism had once been integral to faith. But, Penelhum says, 'What Phillips has sought to do, if I understand him correctly, is to present an understanding of religious thought and practice that shows faith *as it is* to be a non-realist phenomenon' (p. 163). Clearly, for Penelhum, this is an audacious claim, and he is astonished and puzzled, I suspect, as to how anyone can advance it. It is bad enough, in his eyes, to claim that we can dispense with theological realism in faith as we know it today. To say that such realism was *never* applicable to faith seems, to Penelhum and Trigg, plainly absurd.

What I shall show in this essay is that Wittgenstein's critique of realism is far more radical than Penelhum and Trigg suspect. They assume, throughout, that realism and non-realism are intelligible alternatives. Their concern is simply with which one gives the correct analysis of religious belief. They are confident about the answer. They do not realise that, for Wittgenstein, realism and non-realism are equally confused. Further, what Wittgenstein is saying, is not that realism is a correct analysis of ordinary beliefs, but not of religious beliefs. His view is that realism is a confused account of *any* kind of belief: believing that my brother is in America, that a theorem is valid, that fire will burn me. In short, realism is not coherently expressible.

I

Consider the following remarks by Wittgenstein:

One man is a convinced realist, another a convinced idealist and teaches his children accordingly. In such an important matter as the existence or non-existence of the external world they don't want to teach their children anything wrong . . .

But the idealist will teach his children the word 'chair' after all, for of course he wants to teach them to do this and that, e.g. to fetch the chair. Then there will be the difference between what the idealist-educated children say and the realist ones. Won't the difference only be one of battle cry? (*Zettel*, 413–14)

Rightly or wrongly, Wittgenstein is accusing realism and non-realism of being idle talk; talk which takes us away from the directions in which we should be looking if we want to clarify the grammar of our beliefs concerning chairs. Similarly, the accusation against theological realism is that it is idle talk. If this accusation is a just one, realism has never been integral to faith. This does not mean that we must embrace non-realism. Penelhum and Trigg are wrong in thinking that I have done so in my work. Theological non-realism is as empty as theological realism. Both terms are battle-cries in a confused philosophical and theological debate, which is not to deny that these slogans may cause all sorts of trouble for believers and unbelievers alike.

Why have Penelhum and Trigg failed to appreciate the radical character of Wittgenstein's critique? A large part of the answer lies in their neglect of the grammatical issues involved in 'believing'. They take themselves to be reflecting, philosophically, a straightforward relation between belief and its object. Similarly, theological realism takes itself to be the expression of a truism: we cannot believe in God unless we believe there is a God to believe in. If that were denied, it seems belief would be robbed of its object. Aren't we all realists? What we need to realise is that, as yet, *no* grammatical work has been done to elucidate the relations between belief and its object.

Instead of elucidating these relations, theological realism often indulges in philosophy by italics. We are told that we would not worship unless we believed that God *exists*. We are told that we cannot talk to God unless he is *there* to talk to. We are told that, for the believer, God's existence is a *fact*. And so on. But nothing is achieved by italicising these words. The task of clarifying their grammar when they are used remains. Realists speak of the relation between belief and its object as though the character of that relation can be taken for granted. But is the relation between belief and its object the same no matter what the character of what is believed? Realism prevents us from answering this question by ignoring the very circumstances which would enable us to answer it; the circumstances in which 'really believing' has its sense.

The realist accuses the non-realist of conflating 'believing' with the fruits of believing. The fruits of believing, the role belief plays in human life, are said to be the consequences of believing. What, then, is 'believing'? According to Trigg, it is a mental state, as a result of which, certain consequences follow. There are, of course, occasions where an assertion gives us information about the state of mind of the asserter. For example, 'He's coming! I can't believe it!' (Wittgenstein, *Remarks on the Philosophy of Psychology*, vol. I, para. 485). But if I say, 'I believe it will rain'. I am not referring to my state of mind. 'I believe it will rain' can be replaced by 'It'll rain'. Wittgenstein writes:

> What does it mean to say that 'I believe p' says roughly the same as 'p'? We react in roughly the same way when anyone says the first and when he says the second: if I said the first, and someone didn't understand the words 'I believe'. I should repeat the sentence in the second form and so on. As I'd also explain the words 'I wish you'd go away' by means of the words 'Go away' (*R. P. P.*, vol. I, para. 477).

'I believe' is not a report or description of a mental state. It is doing something, making an assertion. But, according to Trigg and Penelhum, the essence of 'believing' cannot be found in action, in doing anything, since, according to them, action is itself based on something called 'belief'. But, once again, what does this conception of belief amount to? Is it not entirely vacuous? Wittgenstein imagines someone saying, '"If I look outside, I see that it's raining; if I look within myself, I see that I believe it." And what is one supposed to do with this information?' (*R. P. P.*, vol. I, para. 819). Would it make sense to wonder what the odds are that actions will in fact follow as a consequence of my mental state of believing? (see *R. P. P.*, vol. I, para. 823). Wittgenstein is challenging this whole way of thinking:

> How does such an expression as 'I believe . . .' ever come to be used? Did a phenomenon, that of belief, suddenly get noticed? Did we observe ourselves and discover this phenomenon in that way? Did we observe ourselves and other men and so discover the

phenomenon of belief? (*R. P. P.*, vol. I, paras. 62–4). Compare these remarks with the following:

> Someone says: 'Man hopes'. How should this phenomenon of natural history be described? – One might observe a child and wait until one day he manifests hope: and then one could say 'Today he hoped for the first time.' But surely that sounds queer! Although it would be quite natural to say 'Today he said "I hope" for the first time.' And why queer? One does not say that a suckling hopes that . . . but one does say it of a grown-up. – Well, bit by bit daily life becomes such that there is a place for hope in it (*R. P. P.*, vol. II, para. 15. Cf. Z. para. 469).

But the realist divorces 'believing' and 'hoping' from the situations in human life in which they have their sense. On the realist's view, our actions are based on the trustworthiness of our beliefs. This means, as Wittgenstein says:

> I should have to be able to say: 'I believe that it's raining, and my belief is trustworthy, so I trust it.' As if my belief were some kind of sense-impression. Do you say, e.g., 'I believe it, and as I am reliable, it will presumably be so'? That would be like saying: 'I believe it – therefore I believe it'. (*R. P. P.*, vol. I, paras. 482–3).

One way of referring to the criticisms Wittgenstein makes of realism, is to say that the realist wishes to speak of the relation of belief to its object,without specifying the context of application which specifies what the relation comes to. As a result, what Penelhum and Trigg mean by the relation of belief to its object remains completely obscure. Wittgenstein asks,

> How do you know that you believe that your brother is in America? . . . Suppose we say that the thought is some sort of process in his mind, or his saying something, etc. – then I could say: 'All right, you call this a thought of your brother in America, well, what is the connection between this and your brother in America? Why is it that you don't doubt that it is a thought of your brother in America?, (*Lectures on Religious Belief*, p. 66)

If we simply say that the thought pictures the fact, this obscures the fact that it is only within a context of application that the distinction between successful and unsuccessful picturing has any application. For example, where photographs are concerned, 'having a likeness' is obviously a central feature of the method of projection by which we speak of photographs and their subjects. Wittgenstein comments, 'If I give up the business of being like [as a criterion], I get into an awful mess, because anything may be this portrait, given a certain method of projection . . .' (*L. R. B.*, pp. 66–7). But Trigg robs us of any reference to a method of projection when he says, 'It is a great mistake to confuse the meaning of a concept with the occasions on which it is learnt' (p. 20). Wittgenstein describes the realist's dilemma as follows:

> The first idea [you have] is that you are looking at your own thought, and are absolutely sure that it is a thought that so and so. You are looking at some mental phenomenon, and you say to yourself 'obviously this is a thought of my brother being in America'. It seems to be a super-picture. It seems, with thought, there is no doubt whatever. With a picture, it still depends on the method of projection, whereas here it seems you get rid of the projecting relation, and are absolutely certain that this is a thought of that. (*L. R. B.*, p. 66)

This is exactly how it seems when Trigg says, 'The fact that our commitments can never be "free-floating" but are always directed means that there must be a propositional element lurking behind every commitment' (p. 42). The sense of the proposition seems to be given independently of any context of application. What Trigg is left with is a free-floating concept of a proposition. Lewy suggested that the connection between belief and its object is given via a convention. He said, 'The word designates.' Wittgenstein replies, 'You must explain "designates" by examples. We have learnt a rule, a practice, etc.' (*L. R. B.*, p. 57).

Trigg's attempts to separate our beliefs and concepts from our practices are doomed to failure. To illustrate the possibility of such separation he says, 'There is no contradiction in supposing that none of the things by means of which we were taught "red" are red any more (because they have all been repainted some other colour)' (p. 21). Trigg operates with a simple picture of words as labels we attach to objects. Of course, a labelling procedure is itself a method of projection. The attaching of the label to an object is not simply given independent of the procedure. Our beliefs about colours also have their sense within practices and situations with which we are familiar. Trigg's suggestion, on the other hand, is wholly unfamiliar. He suggests that his opponents are committed to saying that if some object is believed to be red, that object cannot change its colour! Of course, they are committed to no such view. They know, like Trigg, what it means to talk of changing colours, fading colours, renewing colours, etc. But such talk has its sense within our practices. Trigg, like the rest of us, from an early age, saw things being painted over, sometimes with a different colour, sometimes with the same one. He saw colours fade in the sun. He came to appreciate the marvellous changes of colour in the natural world which the seasons bring. Our beliefs about colours are not confined to any *one* of these situations, but Trigg's reaction is to sever 'believing' from them all! But unless we agreed in our colour reactions, we would not know what it means to entertain beliefs about colours changing, fading or being renewed. But our reactions are what we do. They are not the consequences of our beliefs. Without agreement in reactions there would be nothing to have beliefs about.

Wittgenstein's critique of realism, then, is not confined to theological realism. If it were, the suggestion might be that religious beliefs, unlike beliefs of other kinds, are rooted in our practices and our commitments. Sometimes, it is easy to give this impression in emphasising differences between religious beliefs and other kinds of beliefs. For example, in *The Concept of Prayer*, I said:

> To say 'This is the true God' is to believe in Him and worship Him. I can say 'This theory is true, but I couldn't care less about it' and there is nothing odd in what I say. On the other hand, if I say 'This is the true God, but I couldn't care less' it is difficult to know what this could mean. Belief in the true God is not like belief in a true theory.[3]

Without denying grammatical differences between religious beliefs and theoretical beliefs, my remarks in this instance create the impression that whereas belief in God is internally related to practice and commitment, belief in a theory is not. But why take indifference to a theory as the paradigm of believing it? Similarly, when Trigg says, 'No philosopher worries about the difference a belief that there are elephants in Africa could make to a person' (p. 38), his words, like mine, do not get to the root of the issue concerning the relation of belief to its object.

The theological realist argues, as Trigg does: 'It must be recognised that there are two distinct parts in religious commitment, the acceptance of certain propositions as true, and, as a result, a religious response, expressed in both worship and action' (p. 42). The realist argues that the same distinction can be made with respect to all our beliefs. On the one hand we believe certain things are true, and on the other hand we commit ourselves and act accordingly. But what is involved in believing something to be true? The realist can give no intelligible answer to this question. His failure is due to his exclusion of the mode of projection within which the relation of belief to its object has its sense. So when the theological realist seeks to divorce the meaning of believing from our actions and practices, he effects a divorce between belief and practice which would render *any* kind of believing unintelligible.

We cannot, as the realist supposes, give the same kind of account of belief in every context. To say that the relation between belief and its object varies is to say that contexts of application vary. Wittgenstein gives us numerous examples to illustrate this. Here are some of them:

What are the criteria that we believe something? Take a particular theory of Eddington's about the end of the world: in 10^{10} years, the world will shrink, or expand, or something. He might be said to *believe* this. How does he do this? Well, he says that he believes it, he has arrived at it in a certain way, is rather pleased that he has reached this knowledge, and so on. But what could be called actions in accordance with his belief? Does he begin to make preparations? I suppose not – Compare believing something in physics and the case where someone shouts 'Fire!' My saying 'I believe' will have different properties and different consequences, or perhaps none. (*Lectures on the Foundations of Mathematics*, p. 136)

Again:

Ask yourself: What does it mean to *believe* Goldbach's theorem? What does this *belief* consist in? In a feeling of certainty as we state, hear, or think of the theorem? (That would not interest us.) And what are the characteristics of this feeling? Why I don't even know how far the feeling may be caused by the proposition itself.

Am I to say that belief is a particular colouring of our thoughts? Where does this idea come from? Well, there is a tone of belief, as of doubt.

I should like to ask: how does the belief connect with this proposition? Let us look and see what are the consequences of this belief, where it takes us. 'It makes me search for a proof of the proposition.' – Very well: and now let us look and see what your searching really consists in. Then we shall know what belief in the proposition amounts to. (*Philosophical Investigations*, I, para. 578).

But now, contrast these examples with the following:

A man would fight for his life not to be dragged into the fire. No induction. Terror. That is, as it were, part of the substance of the belief. (*L. R. B.*, p. 56)

The differences in the character of these beliefs is shown by the practices of which they are a part. The practices cannot be cut off from the beliefs in the way suggested by the realist's account of 'believing'. What would 'believing' be after such a divorce? Consider the following example:

One would like to say: 'Everything speaks for, and nothing against the earth's having existed long before . . .'. Yet might I not believe the contrary after all? But the question is: What would the practical effects of this belief be? – Perhaps someone says: 'That's not the point. A belief is what it is whether it has any practical effects or not.' One thinks: It is the same adjustment of the human mind anyway. (*On Certainty*, para. 89)

But it is to practice, what a man does, that one would look to determine whether he believes something or not. What kind of example would one have to think of to imagine a severe dislocation between a man's words and his beliefs? Consider the following:

Imagine an observer who, as it were automatically, says what he is observing. Of course he hears himself talk, but, so to speak, he takes no notice of that. He sees that the enemy is approaching and reports it, describes it, but like a machine. What would that be like? Well, he does not act according to his observation. Of him, one might say that he speaks what he sees, but that he does not *believe* it. It does not, so to speak, get inside him. (*R. P. P.*, vol. I, para. 813).

Notice that Wittgenstein does not object to saying that the belief does not get inside this man. He might also have said that the man had not made the words he spoke his own. But it is what surrounds the words, or rather, in this case, the absence of expected surroundings, which leads to his characterisation of the words. Again, it is the absence of certain surroundings which leads to our refraining from attributing certain beliefs to animals. For example, 'A dog believes his master is at the door. But can he also believe his master will come the day after tomorrow? – And *what* can he not do here? – How do I do it? – How am I supposed to answer this' (*P.I.*, p. 174). As we have seen, the answer is found by looking at what we do in connection with such expectations. These activities do not play any part in a dog's life. That being so, we cannot attribute beliefs to the dog which have their sense within such activities.

In all these examples, it can be seen that what the relation between belief and its object amounts to can only be seen within the context of application within which the belief has its sense. The reason why I have dwelt on so many non-religious examples is that the theological realist speaks as though, in relation to religion, philosophers of religion, influenced by Wittgenstein, have introduced a way of discussing what believing amounts to which departs from the ordinary meanings of believing. It has been said that Wittgensteinian philosophers had a motive for doing this, namely, their desire to protect religious beliefs from the stringent tests to which beliefs are subject in other spheres. As we have seen, these tests vary. To see what our beliefs come to, we must turn to the very contexts which the realists want to rule out of consideration, namely, the actions and practices we engage in. We cannot appreciate the relation between belief and its object while ignoring the appropriate context of application. These contexts vary. In bringing out differences between them, we can also bring out the grammatical differences between various beliefs. This is the philosopher's task where religious belief is concerned, not because it is a distinctive kind of belief, true though that is, but because this is the philosopher's task in endeavouring to understand what is involved in *any* kind of believing.

II

Let us suppose that someone says that 'I believe in God' pictures the object of belief, or refers to it. How is the 'picturing' or 'referring' to be understood? As we have seen, this involves exploring the context of application involved. This context cannot be taken for granted.

We have yet to explore the relation between 'I believe in God' and the object of the belief. The relation can be explored by asking how we would set about deciding whether two people believe in the same God. Rush Rhees has shown how *not* to answer this question:

> If one lays emphasis . . . on the fact that 'god' is a substantive, and especially if one goes on . . . to say that it is a proper name, then the natural thing will be to assume that meaning the same by 'God' is something like meaning the same by 'the sun' or meaning the same by 'Churchill'. You might even want to use some such phrase as 'stands for' the same. But nothing of that sort will do here. Questions about 'meaning the same' in connexion with the names of physical objects are connected with the kind of criteria to which we may appeal in saying that this is the same object – 'that is the same planet as I saw in the south west last night', 'that is the same car that was standing here this morning'. Supposing someone said 'the word "God" stands for a different object now.' What could that mean? I know what it means to say that 'the Queen' stands for a different person now, and I know what it means to say that St. Mary's Church is not the St. Mary's Church that was here in So-and So's day. I know the sort of thing that might be said if I were to question either of these statements. But *nothing* of that sort could be said in connexion with any question about the meaning of 'God'. It is not by having someone point and say 'That's God'. Now this is not a trivial or inessential matter. It hangs together in very important ways with what I call the grammar of the word 'God'. And it is one reason why I do not think it is helpful just to say that the word is a substantive.[4]

Another way of making the same point is to say that 'I believe in God' does not picture its object as a photograph does. In the latter relation, the criterion of likeness is central. For example, Wittgenstein says, 'I could show Moore the picture of a tropical plant. There is a technique of comparison between picture and plant' (*L. R. B.*, p. 63). Believing that a particular picture is in fact a picture of the plant has its sense from the technique in which likenesses and comparisons play a central role. But such techniques have nothing to do with belief in God even when religious pictures are involved. Wittgenstein gives the following example:

> Take 'God created man'. Pictures of Michelangelo showing the

creation of the world. In general, there is nothing which explains the meanings of words as well as a picture, and I take it that Michelangelo was as good as anyone can be and did his best, and here is the picture of the Deity creating Adam. (*L. R. B.*, p. 63)

Wittgenstein is saying, ironically, that if we did think this was a photograph or the representation of a likeness, we could trust Michelangelo to have made a good job of it! But, of course, we do not treat it in this way. 'If we ever saw this, we certainly wouldn't think this the Deity. The picture has to be used in an entirely different way if we are to call the man in that queer blanket "God", and so on. You could imagine that religion was taught by means of these pictures' (*L. R. B.*, p. 63). To say that God is in the picture, is not to say that it is a picture of God. To believe in the truth of such a picture is to adopt what it says as one's norm of truth. To say God is in the picture is a confession of faith.

The realist will not wait on the language of religion. Even when some of its central features are pointed out to him, he draws the wrong conclusions from them. Wittgenstein provides the reminder: 'The word "God" is amongst the earliest learnt – pictures and catechisms, etc. But not the same consequences as with pictures of aunts. I wasn't shown [that which the picture pictured]' (*L. R. B.*, p. 59). The realist takes this to mean that we *could* have been shown that which the picture pictures, but, as it happens, we were not. It is as if one said, 'We *could* have had a picture of God creating Adam (after all, it must have looked like something) but Michelangelo's picture does not represent it.' Perhaps the realist will say that because God is transcendent, it is hardly surprising that this should be so. Wittgenstein imagines someone saying: 'Of course, we can only express ourselves by means of these pictures . . . I can't show you the real thing, only the picture', and he responds, 'The absurdity is, I've never taught him the technique of using this picture' (*L. R. B.*, p. 63).

The realist does not appreciate that when Wittgenstein says we were not shown that which the picture pictured, he is not referring to an omission which ought to be rectified. He is not referring to an omission at all. Rather, he is remarking on the *kind* of picture he is talking about, namely, one which does not have its sense in a context of application in which the important criterion is the likeness of the picture to what it pictures. If the latter relation is what we are looking for, Wittgenstein's point is that there is nothing for the picture to be compared or likened to – that is part of the grammar of the picture.

What, then, is involved in believing the picture? Wittgenstein replies:

> Here believing obviously plays much more this role: suppose we said that a certain picture might play the role of constantly admonishing me, or I always think of it. Here, an enormous difference would be between those people for whom the picture is constantly in the foreground, and the others who just didn't use it at all. (*L. R. B.*, p. 56)

But this is precisely what Trigg denies. He argues: 'The important thing about talk of God is that it is about God. The place it holds in the life of an individual must be a secondary consideration' (pp. 74–5). But, as we have seen, on this view we are unable to give a coherent account of what believing in God amounts to. Further, no way could be found of determining whether two people are worshipping the same God, since, here, too, what we would refer to is what belief comes to in the believer's life, to what spiritual matters amount to for him.

Why are realists so reluctant to embrace these conclusions? They fear that the fruits of belief are emphasised in such a way as to neglect, or even ignore, the object of the belief, namely, God. Some non-realist accounts of religious belief have fuelled these fears. The most well-known of these is R. B. Braithwaite's notorious suggestion that it is unnecessary for believers to assent to the truth of religious beliefs.[5] Braithwaite characterises these religious beliefs as stories, the essential function of which is to give psychological aid to moral endeavour. It is conceivable that this endeavour should be aided by stories and beliefs other than religious ones. Little wonder, then, that this leads the realist to conclude that, on this view, religious belief could be dispensed with altogether. What is essential is the efficacy of moral endeavour. The non-realist gives a reductionist account of religious belief. Religious concepts are explained away in non-religious terms. This is the root of the realist's fears.

According to Penelhum, my views, too, give rise to similar misgivings. He refers to my remark in *Death and Immortality*:

> that eternal life for the believer is participation in the life of God, and that this has to do with dying to the self, seeing that all things are a gift from God, that nothing is ours by right or necessity . . . In learning by contemplation, attention, renunciation, what forgiving, thanking, loving, etc. mean in these contexts, the believer

is participating in the reality of God: *this is what we mean by God's reality.*[6]

Penelhum argues that I am advancing a view of religious beliefs 'as expressions of certain preferred religious attitudes', a view which, he argues, 'eliminates suggestion of supernatural facts' (p. 180). But this is certainly not my view. On the contrary in *Religion Without Explanation*,[7] in an explicit criticism of Braithwaite, I emphasised the internal relations between religious belief and the endeavour it informs. Penelhum and other realists fear that belief in God is being reduced to ways of talking about forgiveness, thankfulness and love. What I was saying, however, is that, in these contexts, we cannot understand what forgiveness, thankfulness and love amount to without recognising that these are *religious* conceptions. We are talking of God's forgiveness, God's love, thankfulness to, and love of God.

Ironically, it is Penelhum who divorces belief in God from these matters. For him, belief in God is one thing, the fruits of belief are its consequences. On this view there is no internal relation between belief and its consequences. This much is clear from Penelhum's treatment of the following example:

> While faith should issue in serenity and spiritual liberation, it in no way follows from this that serenity and liberation can only come from faith, or that everyone who seeks or achieves those conditions must *have* faith. I do not wish to enquire here what alternative courses might produce some of the affective elements in faith, but possible candidates are alternative sets of belief (such as those of Freudianism and Marxism), brainwashing, music, and drugs. To call spiritual liberatedness faith is to identify faith with one of its fruits or manifestations (p. 180).

For Penelhum, then, the *same* serenity can be a consequence of quite different beliefs.

Penelhum does not ask himself how we would decide whether a certain disposition is of God, or whether it is a case of bad faith explicable in Freudian or Marxist terms, a case of drug-induced behaviour, the result of brainwashing, or a case of non-religious absorption in music. How would Penelhum obey Paul's injunction to test the spirits to see whether they are of God? Of course, when not philosophising, Penelhum, like the rest of us, would consider the character of the disposition. He would consider the place and surroundings of the disposition in the person's life. But, philosophically, it is this very context that his realism declares an irrelevance. As we have seen, the essence of belief is said to be presupposed by such dispositions. Believing is thought of as a mental state. I have already discussed the confusions which come from such a philosophical dichotomy.

Yet, what if one gives a closer examination to the notion of a mental state? Wittgenstein comments: 'Is "I believe . . ." a description of my mental state? – Well, what *is* such a description? "I am sad", for example, "I am in a good mood", perhaps "I am in pain"' (*R. P. P.*, para. 470). Clearly, if we go on to speak of what is involved in sadness, good and bad moods, we will be led, once again, to those contexts of action and practice which realism ignores. Ascribing mental states, like ascribing beliefs, does not happen *in vacuo*. It, too, has its sense within human practices. Without this mediation of sense, the notion of a mental state becomes as metaphysically isolated as the realist's conception of believing.

What if we do take proper account of the place believing in God has in human life? Then we find the possibility of speaking of Penelhum's example of serenity in a way far beyond the reaches of realism. For example, if a believer is in a state of serenity, someone may say of him that he is possessed by the spirit of God. God, it is said, is in the serenity. It might well be part of what Brother Lawrence called, 'the practice of the presence of God'. It is hard for Penelhum and Trigg to take these claims seriously, because, for them, anything called an affective state or attitude is merely a consequence of a belief said to be logically independent of it. But, we ask again: what *is* the belief? Do not religious believers speak of God at work in men's thoughts and deeds, at work in what Penelhum and Trigg call the fruits of belief? But if the essence of belief is not to be found in its so-called fruits, how can God be said to be present in them? *In this way, realism cannot take seriously the central religious conviction that God is at work in people's lives. The reductionism which the realist finds in non-realism, is all too prevalent in the realist's account of believing in God.*

Trigg believes that Wittgenstein, too, gives an account of religious belief in terms of attitudes from which the essence of believing is missing. On this view, religious beliefs are simply one way of expressing attitudes which can also be expressed in other ways. But Wittgenstein holds no such view. He asks us to consider the following example: 'Suppose someone, before going to China, when he might never see me again, said to me: "We might see one another after death" – would I necessarily say that I don't understand him? I might say [want to say] simply, "Yes. I *understand* him entirely."' At this point, Lewy suggests that Wittgenstein's reaction is a way of expressing a certain attitude. This is precisely the way Trigg wants to describe what Wittgenstein is doing. But Wittgenstein rejects this account of what he is saying: 'I would say "No, it isn't the same as saying I'm very fond of you" – and it may not be the same as saying something else. It says what it says. Why should you be able to substitute anything else?' (*L. R. B.*, pp, 70–1) Wittgenstein is insisting on the irreducibility of religious pictures. He is not giving a reductionist account of them. With some pictures matters are different: 'Of certain pictures we say that they might just as well be replaced by another – e.g. we could, under certain circumstances, have one projection of an ellipse drawn instead of another. [He may say]: 'I would have been prepared to use another picture. It would have had the same effect . . ."' But in other cases, religious cases included, he says. 'The whole *weight* may be in the picture" (*L. R. B.*, pp. 71–2). For example, belief in the Last Judgement is not the expression of an attitude concerning morality which, as it happens, is expressed on this occasion in this way. On the contrary, belief in the Last Judgement makes morality something different from what it would be otherwise.[8]

Wittgenstein's remarks show how different he is from those non-realists, such as the late Bishop of Woolwich, who argue that religious beliefs are simply the outward forms of attitudes which can survive their demise. The forms of the religious beliefs may change, but, it is claimed, the attitude which the successive beliefs express remains the same. Wittgenstein, on the other hand, is insisting that the whole weight may be in the picture. In that case, the loss of the picture may constitute the loss of what is essential in a belief. When a picture is lost, a truth may be lost which cannot be replaced. This is a far cry from the view of Wittgenstein as a non-realist who sees religious beliefs as expressive attitudes which have no necessary relation to the object of the belief. It is in the use of the picture that the relation of belief to its object is to be understood. It is this use, this context of application, which the realist ignores. What Wittgenstein is trying to do is not to get the realist to embrace non-realism. Rather, he is trying to get him to look in a certain direction, to our actions and practices, where religious belief has its sense. For example, Wittgenstein says:

Religion teaches us that the soul can exist when the body has disintegrated. Now do I understand this teaching? – Of course I understand it – I can imagine plenty of things in connexion with it. And haven't pictures of these things been painted? And why should such a picture be only an imperfect rendering of the spoken doctrine? Why should it not do the *same* service as the words? And it is the service which is the point. (*P.I.*, p. 178)

III

For the realist, as we have seen, belief in God is presupposed by the religious life which is seen as the fruits of the belief. The belief is said to be cognitive, and the religious life is said to be its expressive consequences. The challenge to realism is to give an account of its conception of belief. It must be remembered that the realist is claiming to show what *the essence* of believing in God is. The religious life, it is suggested, desirable though it may be, is secondary by comparison.

In one attempt to show that it makes sense to speak of believing in God without reference to any affective state or attitude in the believer, realists refer to the belief that devils are supposed to have. Clearly, the devils do not worship. So here, it seems, we have a case of belief without the fruits of belief. In relation to God, however, affective states and attitudes range from love and worship, to hate and rebellion. In the case of the devils, although the affective state present is not that of worship, an affective state is clearly present nevertheless. As Penelhum has to admit, the devils believe and *tremble*. This is not the kind of example the realist is looking for.

Let us remind ourselves, again, of the realist's claim. He is arguing that belief must not be equated with its fruits. Believing in God, on his view, is logically independent of any role it plays in the religious life. My criticism has been that this is tantamount to trying to give an account of the relation of belief to its object, without reference to *any* context of application. It may be argued, however, that this conclusion is premature.[8] What the realist is urging, it may be said, is not that the essence of religious belief can be understood without reference to a context of application, but that the context involved does not feature the characteristic commitments of the religious life. As we have seen, this is too generous to the philosophical implications of realism, but let us suppose the objection stands.

What then? The essence of religious belief may then be compared with those *minimal* beliefs which can be found in every walk of life. Notice, however, that 'I believe in God', in its essence, is said, by the realist, to be presupposed by what believing in God amounts to *in the religious life*. Thus, the *essence* of believing in God would, on this view, be a *minimal* belief. Let us examine the implications of this suggestion.

If we forge too close a link between belief and commitment, it is argued, we shall find ourselves denying a host of ordinary beliefs. Consider, for example, 'I believe that "elm" is the name of a tree'. It certainly does not follow from this that I can pick out an elm. To say that 'I believe in God' involves some affective state or attitude, is like arguing that 'I believe "elm" is the name of a tree' involves the ability to pick out an elm. Is this so? The aim of the argument is to show that just as we should not deny that someone believes that 'elm' is the name of a tree, just because he cannot pick out an elm, so we should not deny that the indifferent and the apathetic believe in God, when they say they believe in him, simply because their belief involves no affective state or attitude of a religious kind. In short, you can have belief without commitment.

In replying to this argument, the first thing to remember is that, in relation to each example of belief, there is an appropriate context of application which gives it its sense. 'I believe "elm" is the name of a tree' is not a watered-down version of 'I believe this is an elm'. It need involve little more than believing what one has been told about trees. It must be remembered, however, that this involves one's acquaintance with trees and conventions of naming. The grammar of talk about trees and naming operates as a background to the belief, minimal though it is. The person would have to be able to pick out trees. One has not dispensed with a method of projection. One cannot do that with *any* kind of belief. This is true of a belief which is even more minimal. Suppose someone says, 'I believe there are trees' when he is entirely unacquainted with trees. He is looking forward to seeing his first tree, or his first picture of a tree. Here, what his belief amounts to has its sense within the context of his acquaintance with physical objects, with descriptions of physical objects, and with acquiring knowledge of new physical objects. Someone may say, 'I believe there's something called "trees", but I don't know what it is'. This is simply a confession that there is something the person believes he can find out about, but its grammar, as yet, is unspecified. As a result, what believing in it would amount to is, as yet, also unspecified.

When we try to apply these examples to religious belief, we see how differences emerge. If someone says, 'I believe in God', we still have to ask what the belief amounts to in his life. I knew a person who became upset if someone called him an atheist, or when he heard that someone else was an atheist. But what did that amount to? Nothing more, in this case, than a kind of feeling of respectability which was shocked from time to time in the way described. This is hardly the essence of 'believing' which the realist seeks for, one said to be presupposed by religious commitment. What if someone says 'I believe in God but, as yet, I am completely unacquainted with him'? I suppose that could be construed as meaning that I believe there is something in religion which is there to become acquainted with. Once again, however, in this case, the grammar of the 'something' in question and what becoming acquainted with it would involve is, as yet, entirely unspecified. Again, this cannot be the essence of belief the realist is searching for. Of course, in the case of trees, someone may believe they exist and be entirely indifferent to the fact. But that does not mean that the sense of the belief is unmediated in a method of projection. On the contrary, the belief has its sense in our talk about physical objects, a familiar feature of which is our indifference to the existence of many of them. But if we want to treat 'I believe in God, but I couldn't care less' in *this* way, that presupposes treating 'God' as a substantive and saying that one is indifferent to the existence of the 'something' it 'stands for'. We have already seen, however, that this is to import an alien grammar into our language concerning God. To make *this* assertion of God's existence the essence of believing, the realist would have to show otherwise; he would have to show that grammar is appropriate.

When we turn from the futile search for this minimal sense of belief, back to the paradigm of religious belief, which has its home in religious life, we see that to say 'I believe in God' is to make a confession. Believing is called a virtue, and failing to believe a sin. Believing is something capable of growth, and this growth is said to be the increasing presence of God in one's life. Yet, this is what the paradigm realists ignore. The realist would like to say, that whether believing plays any significant role in a person's life or not, he can simply believe that there is a God. But this 'simply believing' has, as yet, been given no application. One recalls Wittgenstein's response we have already quoted: 'But the question is: What would the practical effects of this belief be? – Perhaps someone says: "That's not the point. A belief is what it is whether it has any practical effects or not." One thinks: It is the same adjustment of the human mind anyway' (*O. C.*, para. 89). For Trigg, to emphasise 'the practical effects' implies that 'beliefs are not really beliefs at all. They are the frills on a commitment to a certain way of life, instead of the justification for it' (p. 36). What we have seen is that by ignoring the role of belief in human life, realism is left either with its conception of belief as a mental state, a philosophical chimera, or with a minimal conception of belief which provides, not the essence of believing the realist seeks, but, at best, deviations, distortions, and approximations, when compared with what really believing in God involves.

The realist offers a further consideration in favour of denying that we find what is involved in believing in God by looking to the role the belief plays in people's lives. Trigg seems to think that emphasising this role entails denying that God existed before men. Trigg says:

> The existence of God is in no way dependent on our individual or collective thoughts of Him. This is an indispensable part of the concept of the Christian God. Part at least of the notion of God as Creator must involve the belief that God existed when men did not. It is obvious, too, that the very idea of God being limited by being dependent on anything or anybody must be incoherent (p. 69).

But where does Trigg have to turn to find out what is meant by calling God our Creator, or to find out what is meant by saying that God existed before men? To that very context of Christian thought and practice which he seems to think does not allow us, by appealing to it, to say these things. But Trigg must not take for granted the grammar of believing in God as a Creator, or the sense of saying that God existed before men. That grammar has to be explored.

It is part of our talk about mountains that we say that they existed before men. It is not part of our talk about banking to say that it existed before men. Banking is a human institution created by men. Within religion, things are said about God of a time which precedes man's existence. That does not mean that God existed before men in the sense in which mountains, rainbows or rivers did. These are all empirical phenomena and my beliefs concerning their prior existence allow me to ask questions about what they looked like, how long they had existed, whether some of these empirical phenomena have ceased to exist, and so on. Nothing of this sort makes any sense where God's reality is concerned. That being the case, these examples cannot throw any light on the religious beliefs. What kind of language do we hear in these beliefs? Here is an example: 'the earth was without form, and void: and darkness was upon the face of the deep . . . the Spirit of God moved upon the face of the waters.' That is not like saying that any kind of object moved on the face of the waters. We know that from the way we might speak *now* of a place being filled with God's presence, or of God being found in the deep. Ask yourself what might lead you to speak in this way, or what disagreement about this way of talking might amount to. What is it to curse God's presence in all things, and why is it that if we spit in his face we can't miss? If these religious utterances can be said with meaning, why not the words in Genesis? True, those words, referring to the time they do, have an added dimension, as do Simone Weil's words when, drawing a contrast with perceived beauty, she said, 'The forest is at its most beautiful when there is no one looking at it.' It is important to note, however, one further major difference in the religious example of God being before man. The 'before' involved, unlike the case of mountains, rivers, etc. is not a temporal 'before'. We are told: 'Before the mountains were brought forth, or ever thou hadst formed the earth and the world, from everlasting to everlasting, thou art God.' All things have their meaning in God, for the believer. That is why God is not a maker, but a creator. The sense of these religious beliefs is not given independently of the mode of projection in which they have their natural home. Realism distorts that natural setting.

One concluding point. Philosophers who are realists think of themselves as the defenders of the real. The final irony is that they, like some of their non-realist opponents, can give no account of the assurance often found in real belief. Realists are foundationalists, for whom beliefs never yield certainty. Belief is a second best to knowledge. But it has always been an embarrassment to foundationalists that their analyses obviously fail to capture the primary language of faith.[10] They cannot capture the conviction involved in a confession of faith. Penelhum and Trigg, along with other foundationalists, turn the conviction into mere probability. Wittgenstein illustrates the ludicrous result:

> Suppose someone were a believer and said: 'I believe in a Last Judgement,' and I said: 'Well, I'm not so sure. Possibly.' You would say that there is an enormous gulf between us. If he said 'There is a German aeroplane overhead,' and I said 'Possibly. I'm not so sure,' you'd say we were fairly near (*L. R. B.*, p. 53).

Wittgenstein points out that if their ideal conditions were real-ised, so that foundationalists would not be dependent on probabil-ities any longer, what comes to pass would not be what is expressed in the religious belief.

> Suppose, for instance, we know people who foresaw the future; make forecasts for years and years ahead; and they described some sort of Judgement Day. Queerly enough, even if there were such a thing, and even if it were more convincing than I have described, belief in this happening wouldn't be at all a religious belief. Suppose that I would have to forego all pleasures because of such a forecast. If I do so and so, someone will put me in fires in a thousand years, etc. I wouldn't budge. The best scientific evidence is just nothing. (*L. R. B.*, p. 56)

Penelhum and Trigg play with probabilities. Penelhum admits that the lack of the epistemic certainty he seeks affects the character of religious believing:

> But it is quite clear, I think, that if one lacks certainty, even if one considers the beliefs one has to have a good measure of probabil-ity, this lack cannot fail to have the result of making trust less *unreserved,* and making the faith to a marked degree a matter of acting-as-if, that is, a matter of resolution. (p. 179)

Trigg speaks in the same way, and makes similar admissions. He says:

> a faith does not imply certainty. It is much more a determination to remain committed in spite of apparent difficulties . . . There is no contradiction in my facing up to the possibility that my beliefs may be mistaken, while in the meantime holding firmly to my faith. I can be totally committed and at the same time admit that I might be wrong. I am however basing my life on the assumption that I am not. (p. 55)

Contrast with this Wittgenstein's remarks:

> Also, there is this extraordinary use of the word 'believe'. One talks of believing and at the same time one doesn't use 'believe' as one does ordinarily. You might say (in the normal use): 'You only

believe – oh well . . .' Here it is used entirely differently: on the other hand it is not used as we generally use the word 'know'. (*L. R. B.*, pp. 59–60)

Here is one central expression of religious belief: 'He that loveth not knoweth not God; for God is love . . . No man hath seen God at any time. If we love one another, God dwelleth in us, and his love is perfected in us. Hereby know we that we dwell in him, and he in us, because he hath given us of his Spirit.' In Penelhum's and Trigg's hands, this testimony becomes merely the consequences of belief, not to be confused with the essence of belief. That essence of belief, in turn, is said to be devoid of certainty, being a matter of acting as if there were a God, or acting on the assumption that one is not mistaken about this. What has happened to the God who is said to dwell in men and in whom they are said to dwell? It is the realist who severs belief from its object. Such severance is unavoidable, since realism ignores the context in which the relation between religious belief and its object has its sense.

Notes

1. Terence Penelhum, *God and Skepticism* (Reidel, 1983) p. 161.
2. Roger Trigg, *Reason and Commitment* (CUP, 1973) p. 75. All quotations from Penelhum and Trigg are from the two works cited.
3. D. Z. Phillips, *The Concept of Prayer* (1965) (Basil Blackwell, 1981) pp. 149–50.
4. Rush Rhees, 'Religion and Language', in *Without Answers* (Routledge, 1969) pp. 127–8.
5. R. B. Braithwaite, 'An Empiricist's View of the Nature of Religious Belief', in *The Philosophy of Religion*, ed. B. Mitchell (OUP, 1971).
6. D. Z. Phillips, *Death and Immortality* (Macmillan, 1970) pp. 54–5.
7. See D. Z. Phillips, *Religion Without Explanation* (Blackwell, 1982) pp. 140–5.
8. Cf. Peter Winch, 'Wittgenstein: Picture and Representation', in *Trying To Make Sense* (Blackwell, 1987). I have benefited a great deal from this paper and from discussing its wider implications for the philosophy of religion with Peter Winch.
9. The consideration of this argument was necessitated by probing questions put to me by my colleague, H. O. Mounce.
10. See D. Z. Phillips, *Faith After Foundationalism* (Routledge, 1988), Chapter One.

5

Religious Beliefs and Language-Games

Many philosophers of religion have protested against the philosophical assertion that religious beliefs must be recognised as distinctive language-games. They feel that such an assertion gives the misleading impression that these language-games are cut off from all others. This protest has been made by Ronald Hepburn, John Hick, and Kai Nielsen, to give but three examples. Hepburn says, 'Within traditional Christian theology . . . questions about the divine existence cannot be deflected into the question, "Does 'God' play an intelligible role in the language-game?"'[1] Hick thinks that there is something wrong in saying that 'The logical implications of religious statements do not extend across the border of the *Sprachspiel* into assertions concerning the character of the universe beyond that fragment of it which is the religious speech of human beings.'[2] Nielsen objects to the excessive compartmentalisation of modes of social life involved in saying that religious beliefs are distinctive language-games, and argues that 'Religious discourse is not something isolated, sufficient unto itself'.[3] 'Although "Reality" may be systematically ambiguous . . . what constitutes evidence, or tests for the truth or reliability of specific claims, is not completely idiosyncratic to the context or activity we are talking about. Activities are not that insulated.'[4] I do not want to discuss the writings of these philosophers in this chapter. I have already tried to meet some of their objections elsewhere.[5] Rather, I want to treat their remarks as symptoms of a general misgiving about talking of religious beliefs in the way I have indicated which one comes across with increasing frequency in philosophical writings and in philosophical discussions. I write this chapter as one who has talked of religious beliefs as distinctive language-games, but also as one who has come to feel misgivings in some respects about doing so.

What do these misgivings amount to? Partly, they amount to a feeling that if religious beliefs are isolated, self-sufficient language-games, it becomes difficult to explain why people *should* cherish religious beliefs in the way they do. On the view suggested, religious beliefs seem more like esoteric games, enjoyed by the initiates but of little significance outside the internal formalities of their activities. Religious beliefs begin to look like hobbies – something with which men occupy themselves at week-ends. From other directions, the misgivings involve the suspicion that religious beliefs are being placed outside the reach of any possible criticism, and that the appeal to the internality of religious criteria of meaningfulness can act as a quasi-justification for what would otherwise be recognised as nonsense.

There is little doubt that talk about religious beliefs as distinctive language-games has occasioned these misgivings. As I shall try to show later, to some extent there is good reason for these misgivings. It is also true, however, that these misgivings must be handled with great care. Some attempts at removing them lead to confusions about the logical grammar of certain religious beliefs. In the first two sections of this essay I shall consider some of these.

I

In face of the misgiving that talk of religious beliefs as distinctive language-games may make them appear to be self-contained eso-teric games, some philosophers of religion have denied that such talk is legitimate. What must be established, they argue, is the im-portance of religious beliefs. People must be given reasons why they ought to believe in God. In this way, religious beliefs are given a basis; they are shown to be reasonable. My difficulty is that I do not understand what is involved in this enterprise.

In his 'Lecture on Ethics', Wittgenstein emphasises the difference between absolute judgements of value and relative judgements of value. Such words as 'good', 'important', 'right' have a relative and an absolute use. For example, if I say that this is a *good* chair, I may be referring to its adequacy in fulfilling certain purposes. If I say it is *important* not to catch a cold, I may be referring to the unpleasant consequences of doing so. If I say that this is the *right* road, I may be referring to the fact that it would get me to my destination if I follow it.[6] Now, in these instances, I can reverse my judgement as follows: 'This is not a good chair, since I no longer want to relax, but to work.' 'It is not important that I do not catch a cold, since I don't care about the consequences. Doing what I want to do will be worth it.' 'This is not the right road for me, since I no longer want to get to where it would take me.' But as well as a relative use of words like 'good', 'important', 'right', or 'ought', there is an absolute use of the words. Wittgenstein illustrates the difference where 'ought' is concerned in the following example:

> Supposing that I could play tennis and one of you saw me playing and said, 'Well, you play pretty badly,' and suppose I answered, 'I know I'm playing badly, but I don't want to play any better,' all the other man could say would be: 'Ah, then that's all right.' But suppose I had told one of you a preposterous lie and he came up to me and said, 'You're behaving like a beast,' and then I were to say, 'I know I behave badly, but then I don't want to behave any better,' could he then say, 'Ah, then that's all right'? Certainly not; he would say, 'Well, you *ought* to want to behave better.' Here you have an absolute judgement of value, whereas the first instance was one of a relative judgement.[7]

Many religious apologists feel that if religious beliefs are not to appear as esoteric games they must be shown to be important. This is true as far as it goes. What remains problematic is the way in which the apologists think the importance of religion can be established. When they say it is important to believe in God, how are they using the word 'important'? Are they making a relative or an absolute judgement of value? Sometimes it seems as if relative judgements of value are being made. We are told to believe in God because he is the most powerful being. We are told to believe in God because only those who believe flourish in the end. We are told to believe in God because history is in His hand, and that, despite appearances, the final victory is His. All these advocacies are founded on relative judgements of value. As in the other cases we mentioned, the judgements are reversible. If the Devil happened to be more powerful than God, he would have to be worshipped. If believers are not to flourish in the end, belief becomes pointless. Belief in God is pointless if historical development goes in one direction rather than another.

But need religious beliefs be thought of in this way? Belief in God is represented as a means to a further end. The end is all-important, the means relatively unimportant. Belief in God has a point only if certain consequences follow. This seems to falsify the absolute character which belief in God has for many believers. They would say that God's divinity cannot be justified by external considerations. If we can see nothing in it, there is nothing apart from it which will somehow establish its point. Rush Rhees made a similar observation when he compared an absolute judgement of value in morality with a relative judgement of value:

> 'You ought to make sure that the strip is firmly clamped before you start drilling.' 'What if I don't?' When I tell you what will happen if you don't, you see what I mean.
>   But 'You ought to want to behave better.' 'What if I don't?' What more could I tell you?[8]

We cannot give a man reasons why he should be good. Similarly, if a man urges someone to come to God, and he asks, 'What if I don't?', what more is there to say? Certainly, one could not get him to believe by telling him that terrible things will happen to him if he does not believe. Even if it were true that these things are going to happen, and even if a person believed because of them, he would not be believing in God. He would be believing in the best thing for himself. He would have a policy, not a faith. Furthermore, if religious beliefs have only a relative value, one can no longer give an account of the distinction between other-worldliness and worldliness, a distinction which is important in most religions. The distinction cannot be accounted for if one assumes that the value of religious beliefs can be assessed by applying them to a wider common measure. Consider the following arguments:

(1) We should believe in God. He is the most powerful of all beings. We are all to be judged by Him in the end. He is to determine our fate. In this argument there is only one concept of power: worldly power. *As it happens,* God is more powerful than we are, but it is the same kind of power.
(2) Many battles are fought. At times it looks as if the good is defeated and evil triumphs. But there is no reason to fear: the ultimate victory is God's. Here a common measure is applied to God and the powers of evil, as if God's victory is demonstrable, something recognised by good and evil alike. The man who says God is not victorious would be contradicting the man who says He is victorious.

These apologetic manoeuvres remind one of Polus in Plato's

Gorgias. Polus did not understand Socrates when the latter said that goodness is to a man's advantage. He pointed to Archelaus the Tyrant of Macedonia. Surely, here was a wicked man who flourished. Is it not easy for even a child to show that Socrates is mistaken? But the fallacy in Polus's argument is his supposition that he and Socrates can only mean one thing when they speak of advantage – namely, what he, Polus, means by it. For Socrates, however, it is not the world's view of advantage which is to determine what is good, but what is good which is to determine what is to count as advantage. In what way are some apologists similar to Polus? In this way: when someone shows them how much power the forces ranged against religion have, they reply, 'But our God is more powerful!' But they use the same concept of power. Their idea of power is not qualitatively different from that of their opponents. On the contrary, on their view the world and God share the same kind of power, only God has more of it. But, like Polus, they need to realise that for many believers it is not the outcome, the course of events, which is to determine whether God is victorious, but faith in God which determines what is regarded as victory. If this were not so, there would be no tension between the world's ways of regarding matters and religious reactions to them. The same tension exists in ethics. There are those for whom justice, to be worth pursuing, must be acceptable to a thousand tough characters. Others, like Socrates, recognising that in Athens or any other city anything may happen to one, can say without contradiction that all will be well. In the eyes of the world, all cannot be well if anything will happen to one. Things must go in one way rather than another. Since, for many believers, love of God determines what is to count as important, there will be situations where what the believer calls 'success' will be failure in the eyes of the world, what he calls 'joy' will seem like grief, what he calls 'victory' will seem like certain defeat. So it was, Christians believe, at the Cross of Christ.[9] In drawing attention to this tension between two points of view, my aim is not to advocate either, but to show that any account of religious beliefs which seems to deny that such a tension exists falsifies the nature of the beliefs in question.

What we have seen in the first section of the essay is how, if philosophers are not careful, misgivings about treating religious beliefs as esoteric games can lead to an attempt to show why religious beliefs are important which distorts the nature of the values involved in such beliefs.

II

Misgivings about the philosophical characterisation of religious beliefs as distinctive language-games not only lead to attempts to give
an external justification of religious values, but also to attempts both
by philosophers who are sympathetic and by philosophers who are
unsympathetic to religion to show that their conclusions are reached
by criteria of rationality which their opponents do or ought to accept. Unless believers and non-believers can be shown to be using
common criteria of rationality, it is said, then the misgivings about
religious beliefs being esoteric games cannot be avoided.

Wittgenstein raised the question whether, in relation to religion,
the non-believer contradicts the believer when he says that he does
not believe what the believer believes.[10] If one man contradicts another, they can be said to share a common understanding, to be
playing the same game. Consider the following examples: The man
who says that the sun is 90 million miles away from the earth
contradicts the man who says that the sun is only 20 million miles
away from the earth. The man who says that the profit from a
business venture is £100,000 is contradicted by the man who says
that the profit is £50,000. The man who says that there are unicorns
contradicts the man who says that there are no unicorns. In these
examples the disputants participate in a common understanding.
The disputants about the distance of the sun from the earth share a
common understanding – namely, methods of calculation in as-
tronomy. The disputants about the business profit share a common
understanding – namely, business methods of calculating gain and
loss. The disputants about the unicorns share a common understanding – namely, methods of verifying the existence of various
kinds of animals. The disputants differ about the facts, but they are
one in logic – that is, they appeal to the same criteria to settle the
disagreement. But what if one man says that handling the ball is a
foul and another says that handling the ball is not a foul? Are they
contradicting each other? Surely they are only doing so if they are
playing the same game, referring to the same rules.

In the light of these examples, what are we to say about the man
who believes in God and the man who does not? Are they contradicting each other? Are two people, one of whom says there is a God
and the other of whom says he does not believe in God, like two
people who disagree about the existence of unicorns? Wittgenstein

shows that they are not.[11] The main reason for the difference is that God's reality is not one of a kind; He is not a being among beings. The word 'God' is not the name of a thing. Thus, the reality of God cannot be assessed by a common measure which also applies to things other than God. But these are conclusions for which reasons must be given.

If I say that something exists, it makes sense to think of that something ceasing to exist. But religious believers do not want to say that God might cease to exist. This is not because, as a matter of fact, they think God will exist for ever, but because it is meaningless to speak of God's ceasing to exist. Again, we cannot ask of God the kinds of questions we can ask of things which come to be and pass away: 'What brought Him into existence?' 'When will He cease to exist?' 'He was existing yesterday. How about today?' Again, we find religious believers saying that it is a terrible thing not to believe in God. But if believing in God is to believe in the existence of a thing, an object, one might wonder why it is so terrible to say that the thing in question does not exist. Or one might be puzzled as to why there is such a fuss about these matters, anyway, since religious believers only *believe* them to be true. We might say, as we would normally in such cases, 'You only believe – Oh, well . . .'[12] But is this the way in which the word 'belief' is used in religion? Is it not queer to say of worshippers, 'They only believe there is a God'?

What is the reaction of philosophers to these differences? They are not unaware of them. On the contrary, we have quarterly reminders of their multiplicity. But most philosophers who write on the subject see these differences as an indication that serious blunders have been committed in the name of religion for some reason or another. Once the differences are seen as blunders, it is assumed that what are sometimes called 'the logical peculiarities' of religious discourse are deviations from or distortions of non-religious ways of speaking with which we are familiar. Thus, the reality of God is made subject to wider criteria of intelligibility. Like the particular hypotheses about the distance of the sun from the earth, the profit in business, or the existence of unicorns, beliefs about God are thought to have a relative reality – that is, the reality of a hypothesis which is relative to the criteria by which it is assessed. In the case of religious beliefs, it is said that when they are brought into relation with the relevant criteria of assessment they are shown to be mistakes, distortions, illusions, or blunders. If I understand Wittgenstein, he is saying that this conclusion arises, partly at least, from a deep philo-sophical prejudice. One characteristic of this prejudice is the craving for generality, the insistence that what constitutes an intelligible move in one context must constitute an intelligible move in all contexts. The insistence, to take our examples, that the use of 'existence' and 'belief' is the same in all contexts, and the failure to recognise this as an illegitimate elevation of *one* use of these words as a paradigm for *any* use of the words. What Wittgenstein shows us in his remarks on religious belief is why there is good reason to note the different uses which 'belief' and 'existence' have, and to resist the craving for generality.

One of the ways of generalising which has serious implications, and leads to a host of misunderstandings in philosophical discus-sions of religion, is to think that nothing can be believed unless there is evidence or grounds for that belief. Of course, where certain religious beliefs are concerned – for example, belief in authenticity of a holy relic – grounds and evidence for the belief are relevant. But one cannot conclude that it makes sense to ask for the evidence or grounds of every religious belief. Wittgenstein considers belief in the Last Judgement. Now, one way of proceeding is to ask what evi-dence there is for believing in the Last Judgement. One could ima-gine degrees of belief concerning it: some say they are sure about it, others say that possibly there will be a Last Judgement, others do not believe in it. But, despite these disagreements, we can say, as we did of our earlier examples, that the disputants are one in logic. The Last Judgement seems to be thought of as a future event which may or may not occur. Those who feel sure it will occur, those who think it might possibly occur, and those who do not think it will occur are all, logically, on the same level. They are all playing the same game: they are expressing their belief, half-belief, or unbelief in a hypo-thesis. So this religious belief is taken to be a hypothesis.

But need religious beliefs always be hypotheses? Clearly not. Wittgenstein points out that the word 'God' is amongst the earliest learnt. We learn it through pictures, stories, catechisms, etc. But, Wittgenstein warns us, this does not have 'the same consequences as with pictures of aunts. I wasn't shown (that which the picture pic-tured)'.[13] Later, Wittgenstein illustrates the point as follows:

Take 'God created man'. Pictures of Michelangelo showing the creation of the world. In general, there is nothing which explains the meanings of words as well as a picture, and I take it that

> Michelangelo was as good as anyone can be and did his best, and
> here is the picture of the Deity creating Adam.
>   If we ever saw this, we certainly wouldn't think this the Deity.
> The picture has to be used in an entirely different way if we are to
> call the man in that queer blanket 'God', and so on. You could
> imagine that religion was taught by means of these pictures. 'Of
> course we can only express ourselves by means of pictures.' This
> is rather queer. . . . I could show Moore the pictures of a tropical
> plant. There is a technique of comparison between picture and
> plant. If I showed him the picture of Michelangelo and said, 'Of
> course, I can't show you the real thing, only the picture' . . . The
> absurdity is, I've never taught him the technique of using this
> picture.[14]

So the difference between a man who does and a man who does not
believe in God is like the difference between a man who does and a
man who does not believe in a picture. But what does believing in a
picture amount to? Is it like believing in a hypothesis? Certainly not.
As Wittgenstein says, 'The whole *weight* may be in the picture.'[15] A
man's belief in the Last Judgement may show itself in the way a man
has this before his mind when he takes any decisions of importance,
in the way it determines his attitude to his aspirations and failures,
or to the fortunes or misfortunes which befall him. In referring to
these features of the religious person's beliefs, Wittgenstein is stressing the grammar of belief in this context. He is bringing out what
'recognition of a belief' amounts to here. It does not involve the
weighing of evidence or reasoning to a conclusion. What it does
involve is seeing how the belief regulates a person's life. 'Here
believing obviously plays much more this role: suppose we said that
a certain picture might play the role of constantly admonishing me,
or I always think of it. Here an enormous difference would be
between those people for whom the picture is constantly in the
foreground, and the others who just didn't use it at all.'[16] What, then,
are we to say of those who do not use the picture, who do not believe
in it? Do they contradict those who do? Wittgenstein shows that they
do not:

> Suppose someone is ill and he says: 'This is a punishment', and I
> say: 'If I'm ill, I don't think of punishment at all.' If you say, 'Do
> you believe the opposite?' – you can call it believing the opposite,
> but it is entirely different from what we would normally call
> believing the opposite.

I think differently, in a different way. I say different things to myself. I have different pictures.

It is this way: if someone said, 'Wittgenstein, you don't take illness as punishment, so what do you believe?' – I'd say: 'I don't have any thoughts of punishment.'[17]

Those who do not use the picture cannot be compared, therefore, with those who do not believe in a hypothesis. Believing in the picture means, for example, putting one's trust in it, sacrificing for it, letting it regulate one's life, and so on. Not believing in the picture means that the picture plays no part in one's thinking. Wittgenstein brings out the difference between this and dispute over a hypothesis very neatly when he says, 'Suppose someone were a believer and said: "I believe in a Last Judgement," and I said: "Well, I'm not so sure. Possibly." You would say that there is an enormous gulf between us. If he said "There is a German aeroplane overhead," and I said "Possibly. I'm not so sure," you'd say we were fairly near.'[18]

Beliefs, such as belief in the Last Judgement, are not testable hypotheses, but absolutes for believers in so far as they predominate in and determine much of their thinking. The absolute beliefs are the criteria, not the object of assessment. To construe these beliefs as hypotheses which may or may not be true is to falsify their character. As Wittgenstein says: 'The point is that if there were evidence, this would in fact destroy the whole business.'[19] The difficulty is in seeing what might be meant in saying that absolute religious beliefs would turn out to be mistakes or blunders. As Wittgenstein points out, 'Whether a thing is a blunder or not – it is a blunder in a particular system. Just as something is a blunder in a particular game and not in another.'[20] Some blunders may be pretty fundamental. Others may be elementary. We can see what has gone wrong if, when asked to go on in the same way, someone continues the series 2, 4, 6, 8, 10 . . . by repeating it. But, Wittgenstein says, 'If you suddenly wrote numbers down on the blackboard, and then said, "Now, I'm going to add," and then said, "2 and 21 is 13," etc., I'd say: "This is no blunder".'[21] We do not say that the person has made a blunder in adding. We say that he is not adding at all. We may say that he is fooling, or that he is insane. Consider now the view that evidence for religious beliefs is very slender. Wittgenstein considers the example of a man who dreams of the Last Judgement and then says he knows what it must be like.[22] If we think of this as we think of attempts to assess next week's weather, it is queer to think of the dream as slender evidence. 'If you compare it with anything in science which we call evidence, you can't credit that anyone could soberly argue: "'Well, I had this dream . . . therefore . . . Last Judgement." You might say, "For a blunder, that's too big."'[23] As in the other case, you might look for other explanations. You might say that the believer is joking or insane. But this brings us precisely to the heart of the misgivings I mentioned at the outset. How do we know that religious practices are not forms of disguised nonsense which, for some reason or another, believers do not recognise as such? This question brings us to the final section of the essay.

III

So far I have been stressing how certain philosophers, because they have feared the implications of describing religious beliefs as distinctive language-games, have tried to show why religious beliefs are important in much the same way as one might show a certain course of action to be prudential; or have tried to show the rationality of religious beliefs by assuming that the existence of God is to be established by reference to criteria under which it falls as *one* appropriate instance among many. Such attempts, I argued, falsify the absolute character of many religious beliefs and values.

Against this it might be urged that, on my view, religious believers can say what they like. Such a reaction is strengthened when philosophers talk of language-games as having criteria of intelligibility within them, and of the impossibility of rendering one language-game unintelligible in terms of criteria of intelligibility taken from another. It is important, however, not to confuse the view I have argued for with another which has superficial resemblances to it. The view I have in mind was once put forward by T. H. McPherson: 'Religion belongs to the sphere of the unsayable, so it is not to be wondered at that in theology there is much nonsense (i.e. many absurdities); this is the natural result of trying to put into words – and to discuss – various kinds of inexpressible "experiences", and of trying to say things about God.'[24] J. A. Passmore comments on this observation: 'One difficulty with this line of reasoning, considered as a defence of religion, is that it "saves" religion only at the cost of leaving the door open to any sort of transcendental metaphysics – and indeed to superstition and nonsense of the most arrant sort.'[25] One difference between calling religious beliefs distinctive language-games and McPherson's observations is that there is no talk of incomprehensibility in the former. On the contrary, within religious practices there will be criteria for what can and cannot be said. So a believer can commit blunders within his religion. But this observation might not satisfy the critics, since they might argue that a set of pointless rules could have an internal consistency. People can follow, and therefore fail to follow, pointless rules. In that way they may make mistakes. But the possibility of their being correct or incorrect would not of itself confer a point on a set of pointless rules. To argue, therefore, that religious beliefs are distinctive language-games with rules which their adherents may follow or fail to follow does not, of itself, show that the rules have any point.

I think the misgivings I have outlined are justified. They point to a strain in the analogy between religious beliefs and games. The point of religious beliefs, why people *should* cherish them in the way they do, cannot be shown simply by *distinguishing between* religious beliefs and other features of human existence. What I am saying is that the importance of religion in people's lives cannot be understood simply by distinguishing between religion and other modes of social life, although, as we have seen, there are important distinctions to be made in this way. I had said elsewhere that if religion were thought of as cut off from other modes of social life it could not have the importance it has, but I had not realised the full implications of these remarks.[26] I have been helped to see them more clearly by Rush Rhees's important paper, 'Wittgenstein's Builders'.[27]

In the *Tractatus* Wittgenstein thought that all propositions must, simply by being propositions, have a general form. Rhees says that, although Wittgenstein had given up the idea of 'all propositions' in the *Investigations*, he was still interested in human language and in what belonging to a common language meant:

> When he says that any language is a family of language-games, and that any of these might be a complete language by itself, he does not say whether people who might take part in several such games would be speaking the same language in each of them. In fact, I find it hard to see on this view that they would *ever* be speaking a language.[28]

Why does Rhees say this? One important reason, as he says, is that Wittgenstein takes it for granted that the same language is being spoken in the different language-games. But if this is so the sameness or unity of that language cannot be explained by describing the way in which any *particular* language-game is played. The problem becomes acute when Wittgenstein says that each language-game could be a complete language in itself. One reason why Wittgenstein said that each language-game is complete is that he wanted to rid us of the supposition that all propositions have a general form. The different language-games do not make up one big game. For the most part, this is what I have been stressing in relation to religious language-games in this essay, but it gives rise to new problems. The different games do not make up a game, and yet Wittgenstein wants to say that a language, the same language, *is* a family of language-games – that is, that this is the kind of unity a language has. At this point there is a strain in the analogy between language and a game.

In the example of the builders at the beginning of the *Investigations*, Wittgenstein says that the language of orders and response, one man shouting 'Slab!' and another bringing one, could be the entire language of a tribe. Rhees says: 'But I feel that there is something wrong here. The trouble is not to imagine a people with a language of such limited vocabulary. The trouble is to imagine that they spoke the language only to give these special orders on this job and otherwise never spoke at all. I do not think it would be speaking a language.'[29]

As Rhees points out, Wittgenstein imagines the children of the tribe being taught these shouts by adults. But such teaching would not be part of the technique of order and response on the actual job. Presumably, men go home and sometimes discuss their work with their families. Sometimes one has to discuss snags which crop up in the course of a job. Those things are not part of a technique either. What Wittgenstein describes, Rhees argues, is more like a game with building stones and the correct methods of reacting to signals than people actually building a house. What Rhees is stressing is that learning a language cannot be equated with learning what is generally done: 'It has more to do with what it makes sense to answer or what it makes sense to ask, or what sense one remark may have in connection with another.'[30] The expressions used by the builders cannot have their meaning entirely with the job. We would not be able to grasp the meaning of expressions, see the bearing of one expression on another, appreciate why something can be said here but not there, unless expressions were connected with contexts other than those in which we are using them now. Rhees says that when a child comes to learn the differences between sensible discourse and a jumble of words, this

> is not something you can teach him by any sort of drill, as you might perhaps teach him the names of objects. I think he gets it chiefly from the way in which the members of his family speak to him and answer him. In this way he gets an idea of how remarks may be connected, and of how what people say to one another makes sense. In any case, it is not like learning the meaning of this or that expression. And although he can go on speaking, this is not like going on with the use of any particular expression or set of expressions, although of course it includes that.[31]

What Rhees says of the builders can also be said of worshippers. If the orders and responses of the builders are cut off from everything outside the technique on the job, we seem to be talking about a game with building blocks, a system of responses to signs, rather than about the building of an actual house. Similarly, if we think of religious worship as cut off from everything outside the formalities of worship, it ceases to be worship and becomes an esoteric game. What is the difference between a rehearsal for an act of worship and the actual act of worship? The answer cannot be in terms of responses to signs, since the responses to signs may be correct in the rehearsal. The difference has to do with the point the activity has in the life of the worshippers, the bearing it has on other features of their lives. Religion has something to say about aspects of human existence which are quite intelligible without reference to religion: birth, death, joy, misery, despair, hope, fortune and misfortune. The connection between these and religion is not contingent. A host of religious beliefs could not be what they are without them. The force of religious beliefs depends, in part, on what is outside religion. Consider, for example, Jesus's words, 'Not as the world giveth give I unto you.' Here the force of the contrast between the teaching of Jesus and worldliness depends, logically, on both parts of the contrast. One could not understand the sense in which Jesus gives unless one also understands the sense in which the world gives. So far from it being true that religious beliefs can be thought of as isolated language-games, cut off from all other forms of life, the fact is that religious beliefs cannot be understood at all unless their relation to other forms of life is taken into account. Suppose someone were to object to this, 'No. What you need to understand is religious language,' what would one think of it? One could not be blamed if it reminded one of those who think that all will be well if an acceptable liturgy is devised – a piece of empty aestheticism. Religion could then be described literally as a game, a neat set of rules with ever-increasing refinements in their interpretation and execution. It would be impossible to distinguish between genuine and sham worship. As long as the moves and responses in the liturgical game were correct, nothing more could be said. In fact, we should have described what religious practices often do become for those for whom they have lost their meaning: a charming game which provides a welcome contrast to the daily routine, but which has no relevance to anything outside the doors of the church. I suppose that Father Sergius knew more about religious language, the formalities of worship, than Pashenka. She was so absorbed in her day-to-day duties in cleaning the church that she never had time to read the Bible herself or to attend worship. But her devotion, sacrifice and humility were such that Sergius was led to say that she lived for God and imagined she lived for men, while he, versed in religious rite and language, lived for men and imagined he lived for God.

Religion must take the world seriously. I have argued that religious reactions to various situations cannot be assessed according to some external criteria of adequacy. On the other hand, the connections between religious beliefs and such situations must not be fantastic. This in no way contradicts the earlier arguments, since whether the connections are fantastic is decided by criteria which are not in dispute. For example, some religious believers may try to explain away the reality of suffering, or try to say that all suffering has some purpose. When they speak like this, one may accuse them of not taking suffering seriously. Or if religious believers talk of death as if it were a sleep of long duration, one may accuse them of not taking death seriously. In these examples, what is said about suffering and death can be judged in terms of what we already know and believe about these matters. The religious responses are fantastic because they ignore or distort what we already know. What is said falls under standards of judgement with which we are already acquainted. When what is said by religious believers does violate the facts or distort our apprehension of situations, no appeal to the fact that what is said is said in the name of religion can justify or excuse the violation and distortion.

Furthermore, one must stress the connection between religious beliefs and the world, not only in bringing out the force which these beliefs have, but also in bringing out the nature of the difficulties which the beliefs may occasion. If religious beliefs were isolated language-games, cut off from everything which is not formally religious, how could there be any of the characteristic difficulties connected with religious beliefs? The only difficulties which could arise would be akin to the difficulties connected with mastering a complex technique. But these are not the kind of difficulties which do arise in connection with religious beliefs. Is not *striving* to believe itself an important feature of religious belief? Why should this be so?

Consider, for example, difficulties which arise because of a tension between a believer's beliefs and his desires. He may find it difficult to overcome his pride, his envy, or his lust. But these difficulties cannot be understood unless serious account is taken of what pride, envy, and lust involve. Neither can the positive virtues be understood without reference to the vices with which they are contrasted.

Consider also difficulties of another kind, not difficulties in holding to one's beliefs in face of temptation, but difficulties in believing. The problem of evil occasions the most well-known of these.[32] One might have heard someone talk of what it means to accept a tragedy as the will of God. He might have explained what Jesus meant when He said that a man must be prepared to leave his father and mother for His sake by pointing out that this does not imply that children should forsake their parents. What Jesus was trying to show, he might say, is that for the believer the death of a loved one must not make life meaningless. If it did, he would have given the loved one a place in his life which should only be given to God. The believer must be able to leave his father and mother – that is, face parting with them – and still be able to find the meaning of his life in God. Listening to this exposition, one might have thought it expressed what one's own beliefs amounted to. But then, suddenly, one has to face the death of one's child, and one realises that one cannot put into practice, or find any strength or comfort in, the beliefs one had said were one's own. The untimely death of one's child renders talk of God's love meaningless for one. One might want to believe, but one simply cannot. This is not because a hypothesis has been assessed or a theory tested, and found wanting. It would be nearer the truth to say that a person cannot bring himself to react in a certain way; he has no use for a certain picture of the situation. The point I wish to stress, however, is that no sense can be made of this difficulty unless due account is taken of the tragedy. If religion were an esoteric game, why should the tragedy have any bearing on it at all? Why should the tragedy be a difficulty for faith or a trial of faith?

From the examples considered, it can be seen that the meaning and force of religious beliefs depend in part on the relation of these beliefs to features of human existence other than religion. Without such dependence, religion would not have the importance it does have in people's lives. It is an awareness of these important truths which in part accounts for the philosophical objections to talking of religious beliefs as distinctive language-games. But these objections are confused, the result of drawing false conclusions from important truths. Having recognised, correctly, that the meaning of religious beliefs is partly dependent on features of human life outside religion, philosophers conclude, wrongly, that one would be contradicting oneself if one claimed to recognise this dependence, and also claimed that religious beliefs are distinctive language-games. They are led to this conclusion *only because they assume that the relation between religious beliefs and the non-religious facts is that between what is justified and its justification, or that between a conclusion and its grounds.* This is a far-reaching confusion. To say that the meaning of religious beliefs is partly dependent on non-religious facts is not to say that those beliefs are justified by, or could be inferred from, the facts in question.

The main points I have been trying to emphasise in this essay can be summed up in terms of some examples:

A boxer crosses himself before the fight; a mother places a garland on a statue of the Virgin Mary; parents pray for their child lost in a wreck. Are these blunders or religious activities? What decides the answer to this question is the surroundings, what the people involved say about their actions, what their expectations are, what, if anything, would render the activity pointless, and so on. Does the boxer think that anyone who crosses himself before a fight will not come to serious harm in it? Does the mother think that the garland's value is prudential? Do the parents believe that all true prayers for the recovery of children lead to that recovery? If these questions are answered in the affirmative, the beliefs involved become testable hypotheses. They are, as a matter of fact, blunders, mistakes, regarding causal connections of a kind. We can say that the people involved are reasoning wrongly, meaning by this that they contradict what we already know. The activities are brought under a system where theory, repeatability, explanatory force, etc., are important features, and they are shown to be wanting, shown to be blunders. But perhaps the activities have a different meaning. Perhaps the boxer is dedicating his performance in crossing himself, expressing the hope that it be worthy of what he believes in, and so on. The mother may be venerating the birth of her child as God's gift, thanking for it, and contemplating the virtues of motherhood as found in the mother of Jesus. The parents may be making their desires known to God, wanting the situation which has occasioned them to be met in Him. The beliefs involved are not testable hypotheses, but ways of reacting to and meeting such situations. They are expressions of faith and trust. Not to use these objects of faith, not to have any time for the reactions involved, is not to believe. The distinction between religious belief and superstition is extremely important. I want to emphasise it by considering one of the above examples in a little more detail.

Consider again the example of two mothers who ask the Virgin Mary to protect their newly-born babies. Tylor would say that this is an example of 'a blind belief in processes wholly irrelevant to their supposed results'.[33] What I am stressing is that such a description begs the question as to what is meant by 'belief', 'processes', 'relevance', and 'results' in this context. For Tylor the supposed results would be the future material welfare of the child, and the irrelevant processes would be the bringing of the child to a statue of the Virgin Mary and the connections which might be thought to exist between this and the future fortunes of the child. How could the irrelevance be demonstrated? The answer seems to be simple. All one needs is a comparison of the material fortunes of babies for whom the blessing of the Virgin has been sought and the material fortunes of those who have received no such blessing. The results will be statistically random. One is reminded of the suggestion that the efficacy of prayer could be shown by observations of two patients suffering from the same ailment, one of whom is treated medically and the other of whom is simply prayed for. The idea seems to be that prayer is a way of getting things done which competes with other ways of getting things done, and that the superiority of one way over the other could be settled experimentally. Now, of course, I am not denying that a mother who brings her baby to the Virgin Mary could have the kind of expectations which Tylor would attribute to *any* mother who asks the Virgin to protect her baby. And I agree that, if these were her expectations, her act would

be a superstitious one. What characterises the superstitious act in
this context? Firstly, there is the trust in non-existent, quasi-causal
connections: the belief that someone long dead called the Virgin
Mary can, if she so desires, determine the course of an individual's
life, keep him from harm, make his ventures succeed, and so on.
Secondly, the Virgin Mary is seen as a means to ends which are
intelligible without reference to her: freedom from harm, successful
ventures, etc. In other words, the act of homage to the Virgin Mary
has no importance in itself; she is reduced to the status of a lucky
charm. What one *says* to the Virgin makes no difference. But someone may object to this. How can this be said? Surely what is said to
her makes all the difference in the world. If one worships before her
one is blessed with good fortune, but if one blasphemes one is
cursed with bad fortune. But this is precisely why I say that what
one says to the Virgin makes no difference. *As it happens*, freedom
from physical harm, fortune in one's ventures, are secured in this
way, but the way is only important in so far as these things are
secured. If they could be obtained more economically or more abun-
dantly by pursuing some other way, that way would be adopted.
What is said is only important as long as it leads to the desired end,
an end which can be understood independently of what is said. On this
view, the act of bringing one's child to the Virgin could be shown to
be valid or invalid in terms of future consequences.

But why is it confused to understand *all* acts of homage to the
Virgin in this way? The answer is: because the religious character of
the homage paid to the Virgin is completely ignored. Or, at least, it
is assumed that its religious character is reducible to its efficacy *as
one way among others* of securing certain ends. As I have said, bringing a child to a statue of the Virgin may be superstitious, but it may
not. A mother may bring her new-born baby to the mother of Jesus
in an act of veneration and thanksgiving; one mother greets another
at the birth of a child. Connected with this act of greeting are a
number of associated beliefs and attitudes: wonder and gratitude in
face of new life, humility at being the means of bringing a child into
the world, and, in this case, recognition of life as God's gift, the
givenness of life. But what about the protection sought for the child?
What is important to recognise is that the protection must be understood in terms of these beliefs and attitudes. These virtues and
attitudes are all contained in the person of Mary, the mother of Jesus.
For the believer she is the paradigm of these virtues and attitudes.
They constitute her holiness. Now, when her protection is sought,

the protection is the protection of her holiness: the mother wants the child's life to be orientated in these virtues. The first act in securing such an orientation is the bringing of the child to the Virgin. This orientation is what the believer would call the blessing of the Virgin Mary.

The difference between the two situations I want to contrast should now be clear. In the one case, the protection determines whether or not the act of bringing the child to the Virgin and the alleged holiness of the Virgin have been efficacious or not. In the other case, it is the holiness of the Virgin which determines the nature of the protection. In Tylor's account there is no need to refer to the religious significance which the Virgin Mary has for believers. But, on the view I am urging, you cannot understand the request for a blessing unless that is taken account of, or think of the blessing as one way among many of producing the same result.

The above remarks can be applied to one of Tylor's own examples. Tylor believes that the soul is migrant, 'capable of leaving the body far behind, to flash swiftly from place to place'.[34] He traces among various peoples the belief in the soul as breath or a ghost:

> And if any should think such expression due to mere metaphor, they may judge the strength of the implied connection between breath and spirit by cases of most unequivocal significance. Among the Seminoles of Florida, when a woman died in childbirth the infant was held over her face to receive her parting spirit, and thus acquire strength and knowledge for its future use. These Indians could have well understood why at the death-bed of an ancient Roman the nearest kinsman leant over to inhale the last breath of the departing. . . . Their state of mind is kept up to this day among Tyrolese peasants, who can still fancy a good man's soul to issue from his mouth at death like a little white cloud.[35]

Tylor thinks that the meaning of these examples is unequivocal: power is being transferred from one being to another by means of the transfer of a soul which he envisages as a non-material substance. Notice the neglect of the situations in which these actions take place. All Tylor sees is the alleged transfer of pseudo-power by odd means. If we asked Tylor why the mother's soul *should* be transferred to the baby rather than to anyone else, or why the ancient Roman's soul *should* be transferred to the nearest kinsman rather than to anyone else, I suppose he would answer that such a transfer was laid down by social rules. He might even say that such a transfer is natural. But the naturalness is not brought out at all by Tylor's analysis. On his view, the power, via the migrant soul, could have gone into *any* being, but as it happened it was decreed or thought natural that it should go where it did.

We get a very different picture if we take note of the situations in which these actions take place: the relationship between a dying mother and her child and the relationship between a dying man and his nearest kinsman. In these cases, why should Tylor find the symbolic actions odd? A mother has given her life in bringing her child into the world. The breath of life, her mother's life, her mother's soul, is breathed into the child. Surely this is an act of great beauty. But one cannot understand it outside the relationship between a dying mother and her child. Similarly, it is in terms of the relationship between a dying man and his next of kin that the symbolic act of passing on authority and tradition is to be understood. It would not make sense to say that *anyone* could be the object of these acts. If the wrong child were held over the dying woman's face, what would be terrible is not, as Tylor thinks, that power has been transferred to the wrong person, but that this child has not the relationship to the woman that her own child has: it is not the child for whom she gave her life. The expression of love and sacrifice expressed in the mother's parting breath is violated if it is received by the wrong child.

In the examples we have considered we have seen that the religious or ritualistic practices could not be what they are were it not for factors independent of them. The internal consistency of rules, something to which astrology could appeal, does not show that the rules have a point. To see this one must take account of the connection between the practices and other features of the lives people lead. It is such connections which enable us to see that astrology is superstitious and that many religious practices can be distinguished from superstition, while other so-called religious practices turn out to be superstitious.

But the main point I wish to stress is that it does not make sense to ask for a proof of the validity of religious beliefs, whatever that might mean. Consider, finally, the example of the mother who reacts to the birth of her baby by an act of devotion to the Virgin Mary. It is true that the act of devotion could not be what it is without the birth of the baby, which, after all, occasioned it. It is also true that the connection between the religious act and the baby's birth must not be fantastic.[36] It must be shown not to be superstition. But having made these points, it is also important to stress that the birth is not evidence from which one can assess the religious reaction to it. People react to the birth of children in various ways. Some may say that the birth of a child is always a cause for rejoicing. Others may say that whether one rejoices at the birth of a child should be determined by the physical and mental health of the child, or by whether the family into which it is born can look after it properly. Others may say that one should always give thanks to God when a child is born. Others may condemn the folly of those responsible for bringing a child into a world such as this. All these reactions are reactions to the birth of a child, and could not mean what they do apart from the fact of the birth. But it does not follow that the various reactions can be inferred from the birth, or that they are conclusions for which the birth of the baby is the ground. All one can say is that people *do* respond in this way. Many who respond in one way will find the other responses shallow, trivial, fantastic, meaningless, or even evil. But the force of the responses cannot be justified in any external way; it can merely be shown. This is true of religious responses, the religious beliefs which have an absolute character and value. Philosophy may clarify certain misunderstandings about them. It may show the naïvety of certain objections to religion, or that some so-called religious beliefs are superstitions. But philosophy is neither for nor against religious beliefs. After it has sought to clarify the grammar of such beliefs its work is over. As a result of such clarification, someone may see dimly that religious beliefs are not what he had taken them to be. He may stop objecting to them, even though he does not believe in them. Someone else may find that now he is able to believe. Another person may hate religion more than he did before the philosophical clarification. The results are unpredictable. In any case, they are not the business of philosophy.

Notes

1. R. W. Hepburn, 'From World to God', *Mind*, LXXII (1963), p. 41.
2. John Hick, 'Sceptics and Believers', in *Faith and the Philosophers*, ed. J. Hick (Macmillan, 1964) p. 239.
3. Kai Nielsen, 'Wittgensteinian Fideism', in *Philosophy*, July 1967, p. 207.
4. Ibid., p. 208.

5. See 'Religion and Epistemology: Some Contemporary Confusions' in *Faith and Philosophical Enquiry* (Routledge, 1970) ch. vii, pp. 123–45.

6. See Ludwig Wittgenstein, 'A Lecture on Ethics', *Philosophical Review*, January 1965, p. 8.

7. Ibid., p. 5.

8. Rush Rhees, 'Some Developments in Wittgenstein's View of Ethics', *Philosophical Review*, January 1965, pp. 18–19.

9. See 'Religious Belief and Philosophical Enquiry' in *Faith and Philosophical Enquiry* (Routledge, 1970) p. 75.

10. See Essay 8. See also, Ludwig Wittgenstein, *Lectures and Conversations on Aesthetics, Psychology, and Religious Belief*, ed. Cyril Barrett (Basil Blackwell, 1966) pp. 53–72. The lectures are selections from notes taken by Wittgenstein's students. They do not claim to be a verbatim report of his words.

11. I have tried to argue for a similar conclusion in *The Concept of Prayer* (Routledge & Kegan Paul, 1965). See chs 1 and 2. See Essay 1.

12. Wittgenstein's examples. See Wittgenstein, *Lectures and Conversations*, pp. 59–60.

13. Ibid., p. 59.

14. Ibid., p. 63.

15. Ibid., p. 72.

16. Ibid., p. 56.

17. Ibid., p. 55.

18. Ibid., p. 53.

19. Ibid., p. 56.

20. Ibid., p. 59.

21. Ibid., p. 62.

22. See ibid., p. 61.

23. Ibid., pp. 61–2.

24. T. H. McPherson, 'Religion as the Inexpressible', in *New Essays in Philosophical Theology*, ed. A. Flew and A. MacIntyre (SCM Press, 1955) p. 142.

25. J. A. Passmore, 'Christianity and Positivism' in the *Australasian Journal of Philosophy*, xxxv (1957), p. 128.

26. But see Essays 6 and 7 in this collection.

27. R. Rhees, 'Wittgenstein's Builders', *Proceedings of the Aristotelian Society*, 1959–60; reprinted in *Ludwig Wittgenstein: the Man and His Philosophy*, ed. K. T. Fann (Delta Books, 1967) and R. Rhees, *Discussions of Wittgenstein* (Routledge & Kegan Paul, 1970).

28. Ibid., p. 253.

29. Ibid., p. 256.

30. Ibid., p. 260.

31. Ibid., p. 262.

32. See Essay 10.

33. *Primitive Culture*, i, p. 133.

34. Ibid., i, pp. xi, 429.

35. Ibid., p. 433.

36. Of course, the matter may be further complicated by the fact that people may well disagree over whether a given 'connection' is fantastic or not.

6

Wittgenstein's Full Stop

In *Zettel*, §314, Wittgenstein describes what he calls

> a remarkable and characteristic phenomenon in philosophical investigation: the difficulty – I might say – is not that of finding the solution but rather of recognizing as the solution something that looks as if it were only a preliminary to it. 'We have already said everything. – Not anything that follows from this, no *this* itself is the solution!'
>
> This is connected, I believe, with our wrongly expecting an explanation, whereas the solution of the difficulty is a description, if we give it the right place in our considerations. If we dwell upon it, and do not try to get beyond it.
>
> The difficulty here is: to stop.

In Wittgenstein's work the difficulty of stopping, the urge to go beyond a certain point in a search for explanations, justifications and foundations is explored in a variety of contexts. The nature of the difficulties and temptations varies and does not form a neat unity. Nevertheless, the difficulties and temptations all involve in some way or other a failure to stop when one should stop.

We want to ask how we know that we are seeing a tree when we are directly confronting it, how we know we are in pain while we are experiencing it, how we know that others are happy when we see them smile and laugh, how we know that a certain number will not occur in a mathematical progression, how we know that we are justified in drawing a statistical curve, how we know that the colour we see is red, and so on. Many commentators on Wittgenstein's work have written penetratingly on these various topics. It is an interesting fact, however, that some of them are strangely silent regarding Wittgenstein's remarks on ethics and religion. Of course, there is no guarantee that what a philosopher says on various topics is equally worthwhile, and these commentators may feel that there were blind-spots in his work. When they themselves write on such topics they certainly do so as if Wittgenstein had never said a word on such matters. Yet I believe that there is a more adequate explanation of their silence, one that is philosophical in character. It has to do with Wittgenstein's insistence on the hold which certain philosophical tendencies have on us, tendencies to say what cannot be said. The hold of these tendencies is stronger than we realise. Thinking we are free of them we turn to some new field, in which philosophical difficulties arise, only to find that they reassert their hold on us with all their old force. Thus we may be prepared to say with Wittgenstein in *On Certainty* that to question certain propositions which are held fast by all that surrounds them is senseless. If our trust in these propositions were undermined, if we could not show in our actions that we took these things for granted, we would not say that we were mistaken, since we would not know any more what it would mean to speak of knowing, not knowing, believing, not believing, being right or being mistaken, about such things. At certain points we say, 'But this is what I mean by saying it's a tree, a person, or a certain colour.' Or in physics we say, 'This is what I mean when I say that the conclusion is justified.' Wittgenstein asks, 'Is it wrong for me to be guided in my actions by the propositions of physics? Am I to say that I have no good ground for doing so? Isn't precisely this what we call a "good ground"? (*On Certainty*, §608) Our request for justifications in our talk about physical objects, persons, colours and physics, comes to an end. Our assurance is shown in the way we do go on, in the way we act with respect to these things. But just as we are about to accept these conclusions Wittgenstein juxtaposes the following example which illustrates how deep are the tendencies to resist them:

> Supposing we met people who did not regard that as a telling reason. Now, how do we imagine this? Instead of the physicist, they consult an oracle. (And for that we consider them primitive.) Is it wrong for them to consult an oracle and be guided by it? – If we call this 'wrong' aren't we using our language-game as a base from which to *combat* theirs? (*On Certainty*, §609)

This resistance, Wittgenstein claims, is due to a misunderstanding of the nature of our language-games. There is a continuity between the questions raised in *On Certainty* and what Wittgenstein called 'the great question' in the *Philosophical Investigations* (*PI*) (§65), namely, the question of whether one ought, having noted the multiplicity of language-games, go on to search for something in common to them, some essence, which would make them all language. It is our desire to look beyond the language-games involved in religious beliefs and rituals which makes it difficult for us to see how Wittgenstein's full stop has any application here. We may be unable to see its application even when we can see its application elsewhere clearly.

It may be that Wittgenstein's influence on the philosophy of religion has aroused more hostility recently than any other aspect of his work. It has been said that 'the years since the Second World War have been a sorry time for the philosophy of religion in English-speaking countries', and that this is due, not least, to the disastrous influence of Wittgenstein.[1] The blame is not attributed so much to Wittgenstein himself as to his influence, and we have seen the growth of a philosophy by innuendo by which it is hinted that what Wittgenstein is said to have said about religion and rituals is not related closely to the rest of his work, cannot be found in his work, or is an aberration on the part of some of those influenced by him. Complaints such as these have been heard for more than a decade.[2] Their essential content can be summed up in terms of a recent version:

> The idea of autonomous language games, each of which can be understood only from within, by those who actually play the game in question, and which is therefore immune to all external criticism, seems to me open to objection . . . If it is carried to a point at which any fruitful dialogue between religious belief and critical philosophy is excluded, theology retreats into a kind of ghetto, cut off from the cultural life of which philosophy is one expression.[3]

Kenny quotes these remarks with approval. Clearly it is thought that to speak of Wittgenstein's full stop here puts a stop to many commendable activities, understanding, dialogue, criticism. Philosophical attempts at throwing light on the nature of religious beliefs or rituals have been seen as attempts to shield them against criticism. This alleged anti-intellectualism and conservatism has been given the name 'fideism', a term which, unfortunately, seems here to stay.[4] In this essay, I want to show how these misgivings are unjustified, do not follow from a proper reading of Wittgenstein's remarks, and take us away from the central questions which Wittgenstein was raising.

LANGUAGE-GAMES AND WITTGENSTEIN'S FULL STOP

First, I shall try to show how Wittgenstein's remarks on language-games give rise to some of the misgivings I have mentioned. Given Wittgenstein's use of the term, it makes no sense to speak of a confused language-game. H. O. Mounce reminds us that one of Wittgenstein's reasons for introducing the notion of a language-game,

> was to free us from the idea that logic constitutes what he called 'the *a priori* order of the world', the idea that logic is, as it were, 'prior to all experience'. He wished us to see rather, that logic – the difference between sense and nonsense – is learnt, when, through taking part in a social life, we come to speak a language. Logic is to be found not 'outside' language but only within the various language games themselves.

This implies ' . . . that the sense of any language game cannot itself be questioned; for one could do so only on the assumption which Wittgenstein rejects, that logic does lie "outside" it'.[5] In a footnote to the phrase 'the sense of any language game cannot itself be questioned', Mounce adds, 'the "cannot", of course, is logical. I do not mean that if one tried one would fail, but that it would be senseless to try' (p. 349). Now, if one argues that there are distinctive language-games involved in rituals or religious beliefs it follows that it makes no sense to question their sense. But, surely, people do respond to religious beliefs by saying, 'That belief makes no sense' or 'I no longer see anything in that belief'. So it seems that if one does say that there are distinctive language-games associated with rituals and religion, one at the same time protects those rituals and that religion from criticism. But religious practices and rituals *are* criticised, so it seems that to interpret Wittgenstein in this way is to indulge in conservatism and protectionism. Kenny says, 'The concept of language-games is an obscure and ambiguous one in Wittgenstein's own writings: in the hands of some of his religious admirers it has become a stone-wall defence against any demand for a justification of belief in God' (p. 145).

At this point, it is tempting to take a short-way-out of these difficulties. One could do so by suggesting that one must make a distinction between the notion of a language-game on the one hand, and the notion of modes of discourse or a practice on the other. By contrasting language-games with modes of discourse one might approach a normative view of language-games. Modes of discourse could be criticised because they might distort language-games in some way or other. Thus it would not be sufficient to appeal to the fact that these are moral or religious modes of discourse to avoid the charge of senselessness. Thus one might say that 'Language has a variety of uses, and people who speak a language frequently use that language for religious purposes.'[6] But what does it mean to speak of language being used for religious purposes? Is it like saying that an argument is being used for political or prudential purposes, where the status of the argument is quite distinct from the purposes for which it is employed?

Consider another contrast. Could we say that the only difference between moral and prudential commendation is in the different purposes for which the concept of commendation is employed? Wittgenstein would not have agreed with this way of putting the matter. In his 'Lecture on Ethics'[7] Wittgenstein wants to distinguish between what he calls absolute and relative uses of 'ought'. So if we compare 'You ought to keep your matches dry' and 'You ought to treat her decently' are we to say that we have here two instances of doing the same thing – of commending? The moral context makes a difference to what the commending comes to. Bell wants to say of religion, what he would probably say of ethics also, namely, that

> uses of language . . . do not convert the status of 'utterances', 'assertions' or 'expressions' to a different level of linguistic under-standing . . . Thus when 'religious' is used with 'language' it should draw our attention to the fact that certain concepts are being used for religious purposes, and not that some kind of semantic or substantive shift has been made to a new type of discourse. (p. 6)

But this cannot be said of the moral use of 'ought'. One cannot say that the concept is used for moral purposes, since it is these so-called purposes which give the concept its distinctive grammatical status. One cannot distinguish between the language-game and the moral issues about which commendations are made, since it is precisely the character of the issues which affect the character of the commen-dation. But do religious beliefs have a distinctive grammatical sta-tus? In fact Bell's article contains an admission of such grammatical distinctions, but he does not seem to realise its significance for his more general comments: '"Asking, thanking, cursing, greeting, pray-ing": In theological and religious behaviour these language-games usually have liturgical functions which only partially parallel their ordinary use' (p. 13). So this short-way with our difficulties does not succeed.

Another, more subtle, but equally unsatisfactory attempt at a short-way with our difficulties can be found in H. O. Mounce's attempt to distinguish between language-games and practices. This does not involve a normative view of language-games. It is not denied that distinctive language-games may be involved in modes of discourse or practices, but simply that one cannot identify every practice with a language-game. To do so would preclude the pos-sibility of speaking of confused practices. However pervasive a prac-tice, it may nevertheless be confused. The suggestion advanced is that Wittgenstein usually meant by language-games, not a practice, but a set of concepts which run through almost any conceivable practice:

> When we speak of our certainty that another person is in pain, for example, we play a different game from when we speak of our certainty that there is a table in the next room. Now . . . it would be difficult to suppose that what Wittgenstein here means by a language game is anything like a practice such as conducting scientific experiments or worshipping in church. For example, one may speak of people coming together to conduct a scientific experiment but hardly of their coming together to exercise the concept of pain; one may speak of a person giving up religious worship but not of his giving up the use of the notion of an object. What we here mean by a language game is not a practice or set of practices but a set of concepts which may enter into almost any practice we can imagine.[8]

There are difficulties, as we shall see, in Mounce's attempt to distinguish between language-games and practices in Wittgenstein, but in any case, how general a phenomenon is the distinction he draws of the examples Wittgenstein provides? Mounce suggests it is general:

> For example, one instance of a language game is giving an order. Now if a person gives an order one may say that he is performing an action but hardly that he is engaged in an activity or practice.

One may say, it is true, that an order can be given in the *course* of an activity. The point is, however, that in saying this, one does not have any particular activity in mind. Almost any activity can be the occasion for giving an order. Similar remarks apply to most of Wittgenstein's other examples.[9]

This is an overstatement and oversimplification of Wittgenstein's notion of language-games. That it is an overstatement can be seen from the examples of language-games Wittgenstein provides in *PI*, §23. While one has examples such as 'Giving orders and obeying them', 'Asking', 'Thanking', etc., one also has examples such as 'Presenting the results of an experiment in tables and diagrams' and 'Solving a problem in practical arithmetic.' Wittgenstein says that the instances are countless and extremely varied. Nor will it do to say that what giving an order amounts to always comes to the same thing. 'What the general commands,' 'What the gods command' and 'What the state commands' are importantly different. I mean that the grammar of 'command' is importantly different. This can be illustrated by Wittgenstein's own examples of language-games. He gives the following list: 'Asking, thanking, cursing, greeting, praying' (*PI*, §23).Clearly, praying, worshipping, is an example of an activity which is also called a language-game. It makes sense to speak of people coming together for this purpose, and of their giving up praying. But, more importantly, we cannot say without qualification of asking, thanking and cursing that whereas they can occur in the course of a wider activity one need not have any particular activity in mind. Failure to keep in mind the activity in question may lead to the ignoring of important conceptual differences. For example, it is obvious that one asks and thanks for things in prayer. It is also the case that people have cursed God. If the activity of praying made no conceptual difference to what asking and thanking amount to, its inclusion in the list of language-games would be superfluous. It cannot be said that the difference between asking God for something and asking another human being for something resides in the resources of him to whom the request is made, since this would not introduce any conceptual change into the nature of the asking. The presence of prayer in the list of language-games means that Wittgenstein thought some conceptual distinction is involved. I cannot explore this conceptual difference here, but I have suggested elsewhere that asking and thanking in prayer is to come to a certain kind of understanding of those features of our lives which prompt our gratitude and ingratitude and occasion our desires.[10] Similarly, conceptual differences would emerge from a comparison of cursing God with cursing another human being. Just as we can say, 'My friend forgives me, but I cannot forgive myself,' but not, 'God forgives me, but I cannot forgive myself,' so, in one context at least, one can curse another person and still find life meaningful, whereas to curse God is to curse the day that one was born.

For the above reasons I think Mounce's distinction between language-games and practices will not do. More importantly it obscures the importance of the notion of a practice in Wittgenstein. One cannot speak of conceptual distinctions as though they were logically or temporally prior to practices since, for Wittgenstein, the language-game is rooted in practice, in how we take things, in what we do. For example, we cannot separate the conceptual distinctions involved in the language-games we play with colours and pains from the ways in which we react and respond since the concepts are themselves rooted in these common reactions and responses, by these practices. Without the common practices, there would be no concepts concerning colours or pains.

So it seems as though our problem still remains. If we cannot seek short-cuts to our difficulties by distinguishing between language-games on the one hand and modes of discourse on the other, and if we say that rituals and religious beliefs are rooted in certain practices, does it follow that Wittgenstein has left no room for criticism of these practices? The difficulty remains.

RITUALS, BELIEFS AND APPLICATIONS IN HUMAN LIFE

Let us now try to approach the difficulty from another direction. Wittgenstein insisted that each language-game is complete. It is not a partial or confused attempt to indicate something else to which it approximates. But this very claim of completeness with respect to language-games involved with rituals or religion has again led people to feel that this puts a full stop to any interaction between religious practices and other features of human life. These practices begin to look more like esoteric games, just as, if one thought of building activity as similarly cut off from all that surrounds it it begins to look more like a game with building blocks.[11] Here the analogy between language and games begins to limp, since although we do not say that all games make one big game, we do say that people engaged in the various language-games are engaged in the same language. It would be misleading to ask how many language-games need to be played in order to describe what is going on as language, but, clearly, it is a fact that many of the language-games we do play would not make sense were there not language-games independent of them. This applies to rituals and religious practices. One could not have songs and dances concerning the harvest unless independently of such songs and dances one had activities concerning the harvest, sowing and reaping and notions concerning what constitutes a good or bad harvest, and so on. Similarly, there would be little point in prayers of thanks, confession and petition, if independently of them there were not purposive activities, successes and failures, hopes and frustrations, good acts and evil acts. Otherwise, what would be brought to God in prayer? The prayer would have no substance.

If, however, we admit all this, must we not also admit that there is two-way traffic involved? Just as various events and activities in human life can be celebrated in ritual or brought before God under the aspect of prayer, may not the aspects of rituals and prayers themselves be changed by these various events and activities? And if this is admitted, may not their aspect change for the worse, sometimes, may not confusion and distortion set in? May they not cease to be distinctive language-games? These questions must be answered in the affirmative, but there is no reason to think that Wittgenstein cannot allow such an answer. On the contrary, one cannot ascribe to Wittgenstein the view that anything that is called religious or ritualistic is free from confusion.[12] That much is clear from the following passage from 'Remarks on Frazer's *Golden Bough*' (RF):

> We should distinguish between magical operations and those operations which rest on a false, oversimplified notion of things and processes. For instance, if someone says that the illness is moving from one part of the body into another, or if he takes measures to draw off the illness as though it were a liquid or a temperature. He is then using a false picture, a picture that doesn't fit. (p. 31)

Wittgenstein, apparently, had in mind here quack doctors and certain kinds of faith-healing. But he *also* thought that confusion could be found in practices which did not purport to be substitutes for science. In a remark to Drury Wittgenstein said that myths and rites were closer to metaphysical than to scientific errors. To illustrate what Wittgenstein may have had in mind contrast acupuncture with sticking pins in an effigy. Acupuncture may have various consequences, some good, some bad. But whatever one's view of its status, it clearly aims at achieving ends similar to those of other medical methods. But sticking pins in an effigy may not have an aim in that sense, any more than a war dance in conducting a war. How, then, does a ritual tell us something? Here the distinction between a language-game and a form of life is important for Wittgenstein. How the language-game, certain ritualistic songs and dances, say, is taken, depends on its connection with other things. It does not convey its meaning in itself, any more than the act of pointing does. To think otherwise is to adopt what Wittgenstein would call a magical view of meaning. This larger context of human life in which we see how a language-game is taken Wittgenstein calls a form of life. The notion of a form of life is essential in seeing in what sense a ritual can say something.

The ritual may contain words and gestures peculiar to the ritual, but it will also contain words and gestures which have an application in the non-ritualistic contexts of life. Without this application the ritual could not have its power and its force. Without it, as we have seen, it becomes an esoteric game. And yet this notion of the power of the ritual may breed confusion: the idea that the power resides in the words themselves, a common idea where magic is concerned. The confusion involved may be akin to metaphysical confusion. Consider the following example:

> I point with my hand and say 'Come here'. A asks 'Did you mean me?' I say 'No, B' – What went on when I meant B (since my pointing left it in no doubt which I meant)? – I said those words, made that gesture. Must still more have taken place, in order for the language-game to take place? But didn't I already know, while I was pointing, whom I meant? Know? Of course – going by the usual criteria of knowledge. (*Zettel*, §22)

The confusion here is the desire to follow 'He meant B' with the question, 'How does he mean B?,' expecting an answer in terms of a process or power which somehow accompanies the words, or in terms of some inherent power in the act of pointing. Understanding lies in seeing that meaning here depends on the shared application that the words and the gestures have in this context. A similar confusion may arise in rituals in thinking that the power lies in the words or in the gestures: the curse is spoken, the wizard points, the man falls.

To see how the ritual speaks one must take account of its application in human life. Compare the following:

> For how can it be explained what 'expressive playing is'? Certainly not by anything that accompanies the playing – What is needed for the explanation? One might say: a culture – If someone is brought up on a particular culture – and then reacts to music in such-and-such a way, you can teach him the use of the phrase, 'expressive playing'. (*Zettel*, §164)

What we need to bring in to show how a ritual says something is its role in a culture. That role in magic and religion has much to do with the formal character of the ritual. Certain features of everyday life are formalised, set apart, celebrated at set times, solstices, equinoxes, phases of the moon, birth, death, harvest: the exact words are to be repeated in the exact order, surrounded by sanctions and responses of distinctive kinds.

It is this application in human life which is important, but which, as in the case of the gesture, 'Come here' or expressive playing, may be distorted if it is thought that the power is an inherent property of the words, something accompanying them, as it were. The temptation to think this is particularly strong if the ritual does contain gestures and words which, in non-ritualistic circumstances, *would* be instances of ways of attaining certain ends. Wittgenstein warns us of this as follows:

> The way music speaks. Do not forget that a poem even though it is composed in the language of information is not used in the language-game of giving information. (*Zettel*, §160)

What underlies the temptation to think otherwise in these examples may be akin to what underlies the temptation towards the metaphysical conclusion about the connection between words and meanings. This is *one* way in which a connection might be established between magic and metaphysics.[13]

Consider another example. Apparently, in an earlier manuscript than his 'Remarks on Frazer', Wittgenstein says that he finds the role of the scapegoat in rituals an inappropriate symbolism. It is not too difficult to understand the common enough conception in tribal societies of one man taking on himself the sins of another. The misdeeds of the fathers are visited on their children and on their children's children. Neither is it difficult to understand acts of self-immolation by which a priest may take on himself the sins and the guilt of his people. Neither is it hard to understand a longing on the part of people, through a ritual or sacrament, to be freed of the burden of their sins so that they may walk again with God. The difficulty is in seeing how any of this can be achieved through an animal. What does it mean to speak of an animal feeling remorse for his own misdeeds, let alone being able to remove the sins of a people? Consider the following comment which, to some extent, though not entirely, recognises the difficulty:

> On the ritual of the scapegoat, Matthew Henry observes that it 'had been a jest, nay an affront to God, if he himself had not ordained it' . . . But in these days can we any longer say that God ordained it? Ritual may be a substitute for true religion, or it may be its natural and spontaneous expression . . . Men may take a magical view of the sacraments, as of such rites as the scapegoat . . . It is obvious that sins could not really be transferred to a goat. But can sins be transferred at all? . . . Christ, as identified with man in his shame and sin, rejected by men and driven away bearing their sins and done to death for their forgiveness, is symbolically depicted, crudely and inadequately yet really, in the scapegoat.[14]

Notice that here one has the possibility of criticism within a tradition. The ritual concerning the scapegoat is called crude and inadequate. Wittgenstein might say that this crudity – and inadequacy – is partly connected, at least, with the confusion in the role attributed to an animal in the ritual. Thinking that the scapegoat can take away sins serves to obscure the perfectly legitimate longings of a people to be freed from the burdens of their sins; the sense which can be made of such longings changes, or what such longings amount to changes. Of course, the prophets criticised such magical conceptions of rituals. It might be instructive to compare how the belief, that one's sins are washed away connected with the practice of bathing in a holy river, may develop in diverse directions, some religious, others superstitious. A mechanistic view of what it is to lose one's sins may go hand in hand with conferring quasi-causal properties on the river. The power of baptism, let us say, in the river, for the remission of sins, may be partly confused in much the same way as the idea that the efficacy of a phrase resides in its inherent power: a baptism of meaning. In saying that the symbolism of the scapegoat jars, Wittgenstein is showing how reflection and criticism within religion may have affinities with the discussion of philosophical confusions.[15]

In the light of these considerations of how Wittgenstein shows that confusions of various kinds may enter into religions and rituals we can see that Coplestone's misgivings about a lack of fruitful dialogue between religious belief and critical philosophy are seen to be unfounded. Similarly we can see how Passmore's reaction to the distinction between modes of discourse is misplaced when he says that it 'has recently attracted a good many admirers, particularly amongst those who desire to be uncritically religious without ceasing to be critically philosophical'.[16] We have seen that Wittgenstein's views do not rule out criticism and that its possibility comes, not from distinguishing between language-games on the one hand, and modes of discourse and practices on the other, but from considering what may happen to certain language-games in the course of their application in human life.[17]

THE NON-DERIVABILITY OF LANGUAGE-GAMES AND THE DESIRE FOR EXPLANATION

In the previous section we saw how certain misunderstandings could arise from Wittgenstein's claim that language-games are complete in themselves. Yet, despite these misunderstandings which brought out certain limits in the analogy between language and games, this still does not affect the positive element in the analogy which was Wittgenstein's main purpose in using it; it does not affect his insistence on the non-derivability of language-games. Acknowledging the limitations in the analogy does not lead to the view put forward by Hepburn, Hick and Nielsen, namely, that distinctive language-games in rituals or religion require a further justification, foundation, or even verification. It is tempting to assume that since some practices may be confused, those which are not must be so by virtue of being well-founded. This temptation must be resisted. To say that the force of a religious or ritualistic response, cannot be appreciated in isolation from the form of life of which that response is a part, is not to say that there must be a further justification of the response; the response need not be related to that which surrounds it as a hypothesis is related to the evidence for it, a conclusion is related to its premises, or a belief to its reasons.[18] Once the response is elucidated one may say no more from within philosophy than, 'Human life is like that.' Our task is a descriptive one. In this task the big question about language will keep coming up, since there will always be the temptation to think that what we have before us are incomplete forms of expression awaiting completion in a wider system.

In his 'Remarks on Frazer', Wittgenstein was simply examining one form which the urge to regard expressions in ritual as incomplete may take. There are important connections between Wittgenstein's remarks on Frazer and his remarks on Schlick's *Ethics*. Although in 1930 he still speaks of ethics as thrusting against the limits of language, he also says that he regards it 'as very important to put an end to all the chatter about ethics'. What he meant by this principally was the various attempts to give values a foundation, an explanation. Speaking of such explanations he says, 'Whatever one said to me I would reject it; not indeed because the explanation is false, but because it is an explanation.'[19]

Similarly, Wittgenstein's reason for rejecting Frazer's explanations is not that they are false, but that they are explanations and as such take us away from the philosophically arresting features of the rituals he is discussing. In the earlier set of remarks on Frazer, written about 1931, Wittgenstein speaks as though we had in our possession, in the language, a principle by which all the different ritualistic practices could be ordered. But as Rhees points out in his introductory note, by the time he comes to the second set of remarks, at least five years later, this is not so. Here, to imagine a ritual is to imagine it in a form of life. Rhees says,

> It will in fact be helpful if we *do* hold on to the kinship between ritual and language here, not because ritual is a form of language, but because in order to understand *language* it is also necessary to look to the lives of the people who take part in it. What we call language, or what we call *'saying something'* is not determined by some 'knowledge of the language' which each of us carries 'within his own mind'. What I would call 'saying something', perhaps because it is correctly formed or constructed on every count, would *not* be 'saying something' unless it had what Wittgenstein called 'an application in our life'.[20]

When this application is considered, it should put an end to the chatter about rituals, just as it should put an end to the chatter about ethics. And when this is seen, philosophical clarity is achieved. Drury brings out the matter well:

> Frazer thinks he can make *clear* the origin of the rites and ceremonies he describes by regarding them as primitive and erroneous scientific beliefs. The words he uses are, 'We shall do well to look with leniency upon the errors as inevitable slips made in the search for truth.' Now Wittgenstein made it clear to me that on the contrary the people who practised these rites already possessed a considerable scientific achievement, agriculture, metalworking, building, etc., etc.; and the ceremonies existed alongside these sober techniques. They are not mistaken beliefs that produced the rites but the need to express something; the ceremonies were a form of language, a form of life. Thus today if we are introduced to someone we shake hands; if we enter a church we take off our hats and speak in a low voice; at Christmas perhaps we decorate a tree. These are expressions of friendliness, reverence, and of celebration. We do not believe that shaking hands has any mysterious efficacy, or that to keep one's hat on in church is dangerous! Now this I regard as a good illustration of how I understand clarity as something to be desired as a goal, as distinct from clarity as something to serve a further elaboration. For seeing these rites as a form of language immediately puts an end to all the elaborate theorising concerning 'primitive mentality'. The clarity prevents a condescending misunderstanding, and puts a full-stop to a lot of idle speculation.[21]

The urge for explanation is, however, deep-rooted. Having perhaps rid ourselves of the view of rites and rituals as theories or erroneous scientific beliefs, we can easily come to look for psychological explanations of the same phenomena. In Drury's remarks, for example, we find him talking of certain forms of behaviour as expressions of friendliness, reverence and celebration. But he also speaks of rites as the result of a need to express something. This too savours of an explanation. It makes it look as though the rites are the means by which something is expressed, as though there were a distinction between means and ends involved. Speaking of burning an effigy Wittgenstein says,

> Burning an effigy. Kissing the picture of a loved one. This is obviously *not* based on a belief that it will have a definite effect on

the object which the picture represents. It aims at some satisfaction and it achieves it. Or rather, it does not aim at anything; we act in this way and then feel satisfied. (RF, p. 31)

A man does not smash the portrait of his beloved *in order* to express his anger. This is the form his anger takes. Whether the rites are regarded as erroneous scientific beliefs or as psychologically instrumental, these explanations take us away from the philosophically important features of the rites. G. K. Chesterton comments as follows:

> even where the fables are inferior as art, they cannot be properly judged by science; still less properly judged as science. Some myths are very crude and queer like the early drawings of children; but the child is trying to draw. It is none the less an error to treat his drawing as if it were a diagram, or intended to be a diagram. The student cannot make a scientific statement about the savage, because the savage is not making a scientific statement about the world. He is saying something quite different; what might be called the gossip of the gods. We may say, if we like, that it is believed before there is time to examine it. It would be truer to say that it is accepted before there is time to believe it.[22]

Chesterton is bringing out the naturalness of religious responses, a naturalness which explanations obscure from us. But this naturalness is naturalness within a culture. To ignore this is to invite confusion. Thus, having said that 'The weeping-willow, taken by the Elizabethans as a symbol of unhappy love, does resemble in its lines the drooping and hanging hands,'[23] Edwyn Bevan goes on to say that 'if convention had once made a holly-bush instead of a weeping-willow the symbol of unhappy love, an association would in time be created in the mind between them, so that the sight of holly would immediately suggest the other'.[24] This makes it look as though the significance of the weeping-willow were a function of a rule of association consisting in no more than a constant conjunction decreed by convention. What this obscures completely is the naturalness of seeing a connection between the weeping-willow and the drooping gait. A failure to see this is not failure of knowledge of an associative rule, but a failure of imagination.

The misunderstandings in the urge for explanations of religious responses are well illustrated in Bevan's chapter on 'Height'. He tries to give various explanations of why divinity has often been expressed in terms of height. He speculates, for example, that since commanders needed to get on high land to see the sweep of the land, those in authority became associated with height, they were to be looked up to. The association between height and authority could have developed from these facts. It may be tempting to say that authority becomes connected with height because kings and thrones are placed on high. This simply postpones the issue. Why are they placed on *high*? Again, the explanation takes us away from the naturalness of the expression in a culture, a naturalness shown in the vision of the Divine Being which the prophet Isaiah expresses as 'sitting on a throne high and lifted up'. Here we have the language of exaltation. Bevan approaches a recognition of the naturalness of this way of talking when he says that 'the idea of height, as an essential characteristic of supreme worth, was so interwoven in the very texture of all human languages that it is impossible for us even today to give in words a rendering of what was meant by the metaphor. We are inevitably forced, if we try to explain the metaphor, to bring in the very metaphor to be explained.'[25] He is not content to rest with the expression as a natural response in a culture and proceeds, in some ways, absurdly, to try to explain it:

> Of those symbols which are taken from the outside material world the significance of height seems to have come to men everywhere immediately and instinctively. We may feel it today so obvious as not to call for any explanation. And yet if one fixes the attention on what height literally is, the reason for this universal instinct seems problematic. For height literally is nothing but the distance from the earth's surface or extension of something on the earth's surface in a direction at right angles outwards. The proposition: Moral and spiritual worth is greater or less in ratio to the distance outwards from the earth's surface, would certainly seem to be, if stated nakedly like that, an odd proposition. And yet that is the premiss which seems implied in this universal associaton of height with worth and with the Divine.[26]

Bevan does not realise the import of his own remarks when he speaks of the expressive uses of height in connection with divinity not calling for explanation. For Bevan these uses are problematic, whereas in fact what is problematic is his own insistence that one must fix one's attention on what height literally is. He was ignoring what Wittgenstein calls the mythology in our language. To be aware of this mythology and to see the naturalness of its connection with religious beliefs and rituals is to give up asking why these things happen, why they are believed, or whether these expressions in language correspond to reality. Such enquiries are brought to a full stop.

I hope we are now in a position to see why what I have called Wittgenstein's full stop has nothing to do with any attempt, subtle or otherwise, to shield religion from criticism. Not only have we seen how philosophical criticism may draw attention to confusion in rituals but criticism of another kind is left precisely where it is. Seeing what religious belief or rituals come to, someone may still wish to make moral criticisms of them. Nothing Wittgenstein says prohibits such criticism. Neither do Wittgenstein's remarks imply that one should or should not want to see these practices flourish or decline and work to that end. When he says that he would not call the consulting of oracles wrong, in the sense of mistaken, he would not deny that people may want to combat that practice. On the contrary, he says that is what they do when they oppose it. He asks us to think of what happens when missionaries convert natives.[27] He is not denying the fact of conversion from one view or belief to another. He is asking us to reflect on what that comes to. In particular he is asking us to see that it does not necessitate the postulation of a wider system in which the warring beliefs are contradictories. Think of the temptation to assume that when Callicles accused Socrates of passing off on his audience a low popular conception of what is fine, there must be a wider ethical system in which the views of Callicles and Socrates are contradictories. When Wittgenstein says that the language-games are complete he is resisting the postulation of a wider system of which they are the parts.

Similarly, nothing Wittgenstein says means that religious beliefs or rituals could not lose their sense for an individual or in a culture. Wittgenstein says that 'new language-games . . . come into existence, and others become obsolete and get forgotten' (*PI*, I, para. 23). But what loss of sense amounts to involves many things.[28] A man may lose his faith, fail to see the sense in it, because it proves too hard for him. Other things win his allegiance. He finds he cannot serve God and Mammon. The more Mammon interests him, the less sense he sees in serving God. Such loss of faith may become a pervasive feature of a society as the result of the things held to be prestigious within it. Nothing Wittgenstein has said denies these possibilities.

Neither would he deny that bad philosophy may bring about a loss of faith. A man may lose the sense of his faith because he comes to believe the stipulations of philosophers about the sense it must have. On the other hand, in other circumstances, shielding belief from intellectual enquiry may itself be a sign of religious, as well as intellectual, insecurity.

But it may be said, there is one kind of criticism of religious beliefs and practices which Wittgenstein will not allow, namely, the kind of criticism one finds in Frazer. He would also reject the kind of request for foundations and verifications found in Nielsen, Hick and others. Neither could he regard religious belief as an ideology or illusion awaiting explanation in the styles of Marx or Freud. Therefore, it may be said, he does not leave all criticism where it is. Even if this were true, it would not be because it is *criticism*, but because it is bad philosophy, bad philosophy concerning logic. But the charge is not even true, since it cannot be said that Wittgenstein rules out *any* genuine form of criticism. What he does not allow is something which purports to be criticism, but which is itself a species of philosophical confusion.[29] A philosopher can hardly be expected to leave bad philosophy where it is. What Wittgenstein does not leave where it is are certain forms of rationalism and scientism and the criticism, justification and explanation of religion emanating from them. But he does so by an appeal to what already lies before us.

EXAMPLES IN PHILOSOPHY

Wittgenstein, we say, appeals to what already is before us. The role of examples is crucial in the philosophy of religion as elsewhere in philosophy. If we want to show that there are a multiplicity of language-games which must be regarded as complete, and not as the incomplete parts of a wider system, the force of the example is essential. How else can the grammatical distinctions and the grammatical confusions be brought out? Yet, many, in face of Wittgenstein's examples, refuse to take them in the ways he wants us to, or cannot appreciate these ways. There have been similar reactions to Winch's discussion of witchcraft[30] and to the examples I gave in *The Concept of Prayer*. In another article Winch has discussed further the difficulty of trying to understand a practice in another culture which has no parallel in one's own.[31] He has in mind the consultation of the poison oracle among the Azande. We cannot assume that the English language is capable, without extension, of translating this concept. We have already seen that it will not do to say with Wittgenstein, in the first set of remarks on Frazer, that we already have in our minds a whole language by means of which these possibilities can be ordered. Neither will it do to say with Chesterton that all a student of folk-lore has to do in face of these examples is 'to look at them from the inside, and ask himself how he would begin a story',[32] for why should the way *he* would order such a story be the principle which governs all possibilities? Chesterton, on the other hand, does bring out how, in some respects, the strangeness of an example can be an advantage (*pace* Winch) whereas its cultural proximity may be a disadvantage. 'Things that may well be familiar as long as familiarity breeds affection,' he argues, 'had much better become unfamiliar when familiarity breeds contempt.'[33] Speaking as a Catholic, Chesterton says that 'the next best thing to being really inside Christendom is to be really outside it'.[34] In this latter context there is still the possibility of approaching the beliefs with the wonder and strangeness of a child. What is fatal, Chesterton claims, is a kind of half-way position characterised by rationalism and scientism: 'They suggest everywhere the grey gradations of twilight, because they believe it is the twilight of the gods. I propose to maintain that whether or no it is the twilight of the gods, it is not the daylight of men.'[35]

There is no doubt that Wittgenstein thought that the grey gradations of twilight in Frazer stood in the way of seeing what is in rituals. And so he produced his examples. But, as I have said, there may be difficulties in discussion of getting people to take them in a certain way.[36] The obstacles may be partly aesthetic, akin to the difficulty of getting someone to see why one development of a theme is more appropriate than another. The obstacles may be moral or psychological – a person may be unable to bring himself to think in a certain way. The obstacles may be philosophical – a person may not see the implications of the language he himself uses quite naturally when not philosophising. In all these cases an offered example will prove unacceptable; it will not be taken in the way one intended it to be taken. Speaking of the immortality of the soul, Wittgenstein says:

It might seem as though, if we asked such a question as 'Does Lewy *really* mean what so and so means when he says so and so is alive?' – it might seem as though there were two sharply divided

cases, one in which he would say he didn't mean it literally. I want
to say this is not so. There will be cases where we will differ, and
where it won't be a question at all of more or less knowledge, so
that we can come together.[37]

Examples will be offered in discussion, but they will not hit the
mark.[38] At this point, discussion itself may well come to a full stop.
But, then, if the arguments in this essay have anything in them, that
this is so should not be altogether surprising.

Nevertheless, that this is so has interesting consequences for
Wittgenstein's conception of philosophy as purely descriptive. Kenny,
in his book on Wittgenstein, says that,

> In saying that in philosophy there are no deductions Wittgenstein
> set himself against the type of philosophy which offers proofs, e.g.
> of the existence of God or immortality of the soul . . . Throughout
> his life he remained sceptical of and hostile to philosophy of that
> kind. 'We must do away with all explanations' he wrote 'and
> description alone must take its place'. The point of the description
> is the solution of philosophical problems: they are solved not by
> the amassing of new empirical knowledge, but by the rearrange-
> ment of what we already know (*PI*, I, para. 109).[39]

But do we all know the same things? O. K. Bouwsma has brought
out the difficulty as follows:

> In the works of Wittgenstein there is ordinary language we under-
> stand. That ordinary language is related to words or expressions
> that give us trouble. In ordinary language we discover the correc-
> tive of the language which expresses the confusion. In the work of
> Kierkegaard there corresponds to ordinary language in
> Wittgenstein the language of scriptures, which Kierkegaard un-
> derstands. Without this latter assumption Kierkegaard cannot be
> effective. And this is not how it is in Wittgenstein. There ordinary
> language is taken to be language which we all understand. Here
> there is agreement. But Kierkegaard's task is in that way more
> formidable. He has first to teach us the language of scripture.[40]

One might add that Kierkegaard's reflections often constitute a contribution to the language of religion, whereas Wittgenstein's do
not.[41] Yet, in discussing Wittgenstein's remarks on Frazer and his

lectures and conversations on belief, Bouwsma's sharp distinction between Kierkegaard and Wittgenstein cannot be maintained. Nevertheless, with regard to distinctively religious language-games, further difficulties have been indicated, difficulties which help us to see why, when one man sees that his spade is turned and a natural full stop has been reached, another wants to go on searching for proofs, foundations, explanations, justifications and verifications. So it is in contemporary philosophy of religion.

Notes

1. Anthony Kenny, 'In Defence of God', *Times Literary Supplement*, 7 Feb. 1975, p. 145.
2. See Ronald Hepburn, 'From World to God', *Mind*, LXXII (1963), 42, and John Hick, 'Sceptics and Believers', in *Faith and the Philosophers*, ed. J. Hick (London: Routledge & Kegan Paul, 1964) p. 238.
3. F. C. Coplestone, *Religion and Philosophy* (Dublin: Gill & Macmillan, 1974), p. viii.
4. See Kai Nielsen, 'Wittgensteinian Fideism', *Philosophy*, vol. 42 (1967).
5. H. O. Mounce, 'Understanding a Primitive Society', *Philosophy*, vol. 48 (1973) p. 349.
6. Richard H. Bell, 'Wittgenstein and Descriptive Theory', *Religious Studies*, vol. 5 (1969).
7. 'Wittgenstein's Lecture on Ethics', *Philosophical Review*, vol. 74 (1965).
8. Mounce, pp. 350–1.
9. Ibid., p. 350.
10. D. Z. Phillips, *The Concept of Prayer* (London: Routledge & Kegan Paul, 1965; in paperback, Oxford: Basil Blackwell, 1981).
11. For a perceptive statement and treatment of these problems, see Rush Rhees, 'Wittgenstein's Builders', *Proceedings of the Aristotelian Society*, 1959–60, reprinted in Rush Rhees, *Discussions of Wittgenstein* (London: Routledge & Kegan Paul, 1970).
    I have also benefited from a discussion with Norman Malcolm on questions concerning these issues. See also Essay 5.
12. I am indebted in the remainder of this section to a discussion with Rush Rhees. See also Essay 7.
13. Rhees put this forward simply as a suggestion of how Wittgenstein might have made the connection. On the other hand, he insisted that one could not rule out the possibility of this being rejected out of hand by Wittgenstein. In *Religion Without Explanation* (Oxford: Blackwell, 1976), Chapter 7, I was puzzled by the analogy between magic and metaphysics. There, however, I am attacking an attempt to identify them in general as part of a strategy to show that religion is the product of confusion.

14. *The Interpreter's Bible*, vol. II (New York, 1953) pp. 82–4.
15. Again, this is simply a suggestion as to how Wittgenstein might have developed the analogy.
16. John Passmore, *A Hundred Years of Philosophy* (London: Pelican Books, 1968), Chapter 18, 'Wittgenstein and Ordinary Language', pp. 450ff.
17. This is my disagreement with Mounce's paper which nevertheless does stress that religious beliefs though not mistakes may be confused, since not all confusion, including metaphysical confusion, can be called mistakes. Also Mounce would assign to the realm of confusion, I believe, too many examples of religious and magical practices which, I would argue, express various kinds of possibilities of meaning.
18. For a more detailed discussion see 'Religious Beliefs and Language-games', Essay 5 in this collection.
19. 'Lecture on Ethics', *Philosophical Review*, LXXIV, no. 1 (1965) pp. 15–16.
20. 'Remarks on Frazer's *Golden Bough*', pp. 27–8. By 'earlier' and 'later' I simply mean to refer to the division in the published text of the work indicated by Rhees in his Introductory Note.
21. M. O'C. Drury, *The Danger of Words* (London: Routledge & Kegan Paul, 1973) pp. x–xi.
22. G. K. Chesterton, *The Everlasting Man* (New York: Dodd, Mead & Co) pp. 110–11.
23. Edwyn Bevan, *Symbolism and Belief* (London: Fontana/Collins, 1962) p. 11
24. Ibid., p. 11.
25. Ibid., p. 25.
26. Ibid., pp. 26–7.
27. Cf. *On Certainty*, 612.
28. See Essays 8 and 9 in this collection and the final chapter of D. Z. Phillips, *Religion Without Explanation*.
29. This stronger way of expressing the matter was suggested to me by Gordon Graham in a discussion of this study at the University of St Andrews Philosophical Club.
30. Peter Winch, 'Understanding a Primitive Society', in *Ethics and Action* (London: Routledge & Kegan Paul, 1972).
31. Peter Winch, 'Language, Belief and Relativism', in *Contemporary British Philosophy*, fourth series, ed. H. D. Lewis (London: Allen & Unwin, 1977).
32. Chesterton, p. 112.
33. Ibid., p. xviii.
34. Ibid., pp. xi–xii.
35. Ibid., p. xvii.
36. These difficulties do not depend on whether or not the person one is arguing with is a religious believer. I say this because of the view attributed to myself and others, that one has to be a religious believer in order to understand religious belief. Despite the frequency of this claim it has little textual foundation. In my own work, for example, it has been denied explicitly. The most I have said is that 'religious understanding' is a term which has application (but to understand *that* is not to be a religious believer), that some things are likely to be understood

better by a worshipper or by a rebel against religion, and that in certain contexts philosophical and religious understanding may go hand in hand. There are no grounds here for the comprehensive thesis that only those who play the language-games involved in religious belief understand their character. Yet, this set response seems to be here to say and I am sceptical whether mere evidence will shift it.

37. L. Wittgenstein, *Lectures and Conversations on Aesthetics, Psychology and Religious Belief*, ed. Cyril Barrett (Oxford: Blackwell, 1966).

38. See Essay 7.

39. A. Kenny, *Wittgenstein* (London: Allen Lane The Penguin Press, 1973) pp. 229–30. Whether they are confused or not it is clear that those whom Kenny criticises indirectly in his review are reflecting Wittgenstein's style of thought more than he is doing himself in his review article. 'In Defence of God'. The charge that they are imposing alien features on Wittgenstein's philosophy becomes even more implausible.

    Cf. 'Some theologians regard religion as a way of life which can only be understood by participation and therefore cannot be justified to an outsider on neutral rational grounds. Such people must consider any attempt at a philosophical proof of God's existence to be wrong-headed, and must find it inconceivable that such matters as whether everything in motion has a mover could have any relevance to religion . . . To me it seems that if belief in the existence of God cannot be rationally justified, there can be no good grounds for adopting any of the traditional monotheistic religions', Anthony Kenny, *The Five Ways* (London: Routledge & Kegan Paul, 1969) p. 4.

40. O. K. Bouwsma, 'Notes on "The Monstrous Illusion"', *The Perkins School of Theology Journal*, xxiv (Spring 1971) p. 12.

41. I owe this observation to İlham Dilman. See Essay 13.

7

Primitive Reactions and the Reactions of Primitives: the 1983 Marett Lecture

I

In his 1950 Marett Lecture, Professor Evans-Pritchard gave an account of important methodological developments which had taken place in social anthropology.[1] I should like to use the occasion to concentrate on some of the deep contemporary divisions in another subject which interested R. R. Marett, namely, the philosophy of religion. I shall do so, however, by reference to some of the methodological issues which concerned Evans-Pritchard.

In many commemorative lectures, reference to the person commemorated ends after the opening acknowledgements. That this should be so is understandable, since his work has often been superceded by developments within the subject. Many would draw such a conclusion about Marett's anthropological writings. Evans-Pritchard extols Marett as a great teacher of social anthropology, but of his theory, together with the others he discusses in his excellent *Theories of Primitive Religion*, he says, 'For the most part the theories . . . are, for anthropologists at least, as dead as mutton, and today are chiefly of interest as specimens of the thought of their time'.[2] What, then, has been the value of such theories? Evans-Pritchard concludes his book with the words, 'The advance in this department of social anthropology in the last forty or so years may be measured by the fact that, in the light of the knowledge we now have, we can point to the inadequacies of theories which at one time carried conviction, but we might never have obtained this knowledge had it not been for the pioneers whose writings we have reviewed.'[3] There is a striking similarity between these remarks and the ways in which E. B. Tylor and James Frazer asked us to think of the thoughts and theories of primitives. First Tylor, 'To impress men's minds with a

doctrine of development will lead them in all honour to their ancestors to continue the progressive work of past ages, to continue it the
more vigorously because light has increased in the world.'[4] Second,
Frazer's well-known comment, 'We shall do well to look with leni-
ency upon their errors as inevitable slips made in the search for
truth.'[5] Evans-Pritchard was critical of the tendency to speak *in vacuo*
of man's development from a primitive to a civilised state, but
perhaps he was not averse to speaking of the primitive stages of
social anthropology.

No one would want to deny the developments and advances in
social anthropology to which Evans-Pritchard calls our attention. On
the other hand, I want this lecture to serve as a corrective to the view
that theories, such as Marett's, are of only antiquarian interest. It is
not surprising that such a corrective should come from philosophy,
a subject often accused of lack of progress. Philosophers keep return-
ing to the great philosophers; their puzzles become ours when we
reflect on the central questions which engage us. That anthropological theories should continue to be of interest to philosophers is not
surprising, since the history of anthropology is the history of changes
in its methodology. We continue to be puzzled about the character of
many human activities and about what is involved in investigating
them. It is not too much to say that where philosophers stand on the
kinds of issue raised by Tylor and Marett, determines their treatment of some of the deepest issues in contemporary philosophy of
religion. That this should be so is a happy intellectual fact on the
occasion of this lecture.

II

The anthropological theories Marett opposed are similar, in many
ways, to modes of philosophising which are still dominant *within* the
practice of the philosophy of religion.

What Marett opposed is captured in that sentence of his which
echoes in the memory more than any other he wrote: 'My own view
is that savage religion is something not so much thought out as
danced out.'[6] The 'thinking out' he opposed was Tylor's animism,
according to which, primitives react to the unknown in the world
which confronts them, by postulating the existence of beings higher
than themselves to explain otherwise inexplicable events. Thus, they
peopled the world with spirits.

Tylor believed he was giving an account of the origin of religion. Evans-Pritchard says,

> It was because explanations of religion were offered in terms of origins that these theoretical debates, once so full of life and fire, eventually subsided. To my mind, it is extraordinary that anyone could have thought it worth while to speculate about what might have been the origin of some custom or belief, when there is absolutely no means of discovering, in the absence of historical evidence, what was its origin.[7]

The debate does not subside so easily, however, once we recognise that Tylor was also interested in concept-formation in religion. In asking how religious concepts get a hold on human life, he was purely interested in the status of such concepts. As we have seen, Tylor thought magical and religious beliefs are explanatory hypotheses. As human knowledge increases, so the need for religious hypotheses declines. Tylor would have concurred with the description of the 'God' of religion as 'the God of the gaps'. He would have understood when theologians, such as Bonhoeffer, talk of man coming of age and putting aside his primitive ways. I have little doubt that the demise announced by the 'Death of God' theologians was of a kind of god Tylor would have found no difficulty in recognising.

It is extremely important to note that, for Tylor, religious belief is not irrational. Religious beliefs are *mistakes*, but they might have been true. Tylor would agree with Frazer when he said of the primitives, ' . . . their errors were not wilful extravagances or the ravings of insanity, but simply hypotheses, justifiable as such at the time they were propounded, but which a full experience has proved to be inadequate. It is only by the successive testing of hypotheses and the rejection of the false that truth is at last elicited.'[8]

Notice, 'the rejection of the false', not the rejection of the unintelligible. The reactions of many contemporary philosophers of religion has been simply to reaffirm that the hypothesis of God's existence *is* the best explanation of the world as we know it. They have had to come to terms with Hume's criticisms in his *Dialogues Concerning Natural Religion* which haunt all forms of argument from design or cosmological argument. Hume reminds us that we cannot infer more of God than the evidence allows, and that, with all the religious good will in the world, we would have to infer that he is, at best, capricious. Even this allows too much, for why should we think of design in the first place? Nature can be explained without recourse to religious hypotheses. If we say that God's existence is needed to explain why there is something rather than nothing, this seems to involve speaking of the world as though it were one big object, and speaking of 'nothing' in an absolute sense difficult to comprehend.

Philosophers have tried to meet these difficulties by arguing that the reasonableness of religious beliefs depends on the cumulative effect of considerations in themselves inconclusive.[9] In attempted restatements of the traditional arguments, some have argued that probabilities point in the direction of theism, but others respond by saying that probabilities point in the opposite direction.[10]

My aim is not to enter these disputes, but to bring their character to your attention. They are disputes between opposing hypotheses, so that believer and non-believer may be said to hold opposite beliefs from each other. This is still the dominant way of philosophising about religion among those who regularly engage with the subject. But this fits perfectly well with the views of Tylor and Frazer: 'It is only by the successive testing of hypotheses and rejection of the false that truth is at last elicited.' Whatever of anthropologists, animism is alive and well among contemporary philosophers of religion, their discipline being still, for the most part, at an animistic stage.

There are obvious difficulties in this mode of philosophising about religion. The god it argues over is a god of probabilities; the best available hypothesis. The God in whom believers put their trust does not seem to be a god who is merely probable. Further, belief and non-belief do not seem to be opposite opinions within a common system of belief. Coming to believe seems to be a change of direction, rather than a change of opinion. It is not a question of seeing that what one thought was false is in fact true, according to common criteria of truth and falsity, but of coming to see sense in what one thought was senseless, and embracing it. To accept such criticisms, however, would be to abandon an animistic philosophy of religion.[11]

III

Having said that the views Marett criticised are still with us in contemporary philosophy of religion, we shall see that the kind of view he held himself is even more in evidence in philosophy.

Marett held that Tylor had given too intellectual an account of primitive man, one which attributed to him a massive ignorance of causal connections. This never becomes plausible, since the primitives were skilled hunters, farmers, metal-workers. Had they been as ignorant of causal connections as some said they were, they could never have survived. On the other hand, alongside their ordinary purposive activities they perform rituals. How are the rituals related to the other activities? Marett's answer is that we have to appreciate what happens when purposive activities come up against the unknown and the unattainable. Emotional pressures build up in the individual and out of them comes the mimetic behaviour which eases his tensions. He convinces himself that he has attained what, in fact, he has not attained. The rituals and the beliefs associated with them are not the products of ignorance, as Tylor thought, but the products of confusion. They are not thought out, but danced out. This is the aspect of Marett's thought I want to concentrate on, rather than discuss the far-reaching criticisms which can be made of Marett's assumption that psychological states can be studied independently of the very contexts in which they have their sense.[12]

Like Tylor, Marett thought that as man matured the rituals would lose their hold on him, but what man is rescued from is not ignorance, but confusion. This is an important distinction and one echoed in contemporary philosophy. Religious beliefs, it is said, are not false, but meaningless.[13] It is easy to miss this possibility of the meaninglessness of religious beliefs. Because we see the primitives are not ignorant of causal connections, we may refuse to attribute confused causal expectations to them, preferring to say that rituals should be understood in expressive or symbolic terms. Some have attributed such views to Wittgenstein. No doubt they have remarks such as the following in mind: ' . . . Towards morning, when the sun is about to rise, people celebrate rites of the coming day, but not at night, for then they simply burn lamps.'[14] Again: 'The same savage who, apparently in order to kill his enemy, sticks his knife through a picture of him, really does build his hut of wood and cuts his arrow with skill and not in effigy.'[15] On the basis of remarks of this kind John Cook attributes to Wittgenstein an *a priori* so-called emotivist theory of magic. John Cook says,

Wittgenstein was going beyond the mere rejection of Frazer's theory. He was offering as theory of his own, a theory to the effect that the primitive magician in the performance of his rites no more intends to help his crops flourish or to harm his enemy than we intend to bring about some effect by kissing the picture of a loved one. But merely finding good reason for rejecting Frazer's theory does not give us a reason for embracing this new theory of Wittgenstein's unless, of course, we assume that these are the only possibilities from which to choose. Wittgenstein, perhaps, thought that they were the only alternatives and that his own positive theory could therefore be adequately supported by simply finding good reason to dismiss Frazer's.[16]

But does Wittgenstein embrace such a theory? On the contrary, he is opposed to *a priori* theorising and in fact recognises the very possibility Cook claims he has missed, namely, that the primitives may be guilty, not of mistakes about causality, but of deep conceptual confusions.[17] For example, Wittgenstein thought the ritual of the scapegoat in *Leviticus* a jarring symbolism. The scapegoat is said to carry the sins of the people with it into the wilderness. Here, as Rush Rhees says, ' . . . "carry" seems to mean what it does in "The goat carries on his back the basket in which we put our firewood"; and yet it *cannot* mean that.'[18] But we would not say a mistake is made in the ritual. We would say it is confused. Wittgenstein concludes, 'The scapegoat on which sins are laid and which goes out into the wilderness with them, is a false picture, like all the false pictures of philosophy. Philosophy might be said to purify thought from a misleading mythology.'[19]

The difference between mistakes and confusions in this context may be brought out by the following example. A person who wants to poison another mistakenly buys a harmless potion. His belief that the potion is harmful is false, but it might have been true. But can we say the same when I stick pins in a picture of someone, believing it will harm him? Can we say that sticking pins in the picture might have been effective, but in fact is not? Of course not. We have not the slightest idea of what it could mean to say that sticking pins in the picture could harm someone else. What we have is not a false, but a meaningless belief, and yet people believe it. None of this should surprise us, since we are by no means immune from these confusions ourselves. Although we are not ignorant of causal connections, nevertheless, our superstitions flourish alongside them.

Once we identify the confusion, the next step is to see how it came about. Here are some suggestions from John Beattie's influential book on social anthropology:

I am not saying that ritual and magical activities are not commonly thought to be causally efficacious; they certainly are. But they are expressive *as well* as being instrumental, and it is this that distinguishes them from strictly empirical, instrumental activity. Indeed often they are believed to be instrumental just because they are expressive, many people think that the word, the *logos*, has its own special power. Often it is believed that to say or even to think something solemnly and emphatically enough is somehow to make it more likely to happen. Even members of modern societies may be frightened or ashamed when they become conscious of hidden wishes for the death or injury of someone they dislike, and may feel guilty when the object of their antipathy is run over by a bus. Belief in the power of words, thoughts and symbols is by no means a monopoly of simpler peoples.[20]

The confusion involved here is not like a mistake *about* anything; about causal connections, for example. What we have is a confusion which springs from a misunderstanding of the logic of our language, a misunderstanding which has a deep hold on us. These misunderstandings give rise to metaphysics. Wittgenstein began an earlier version of his remarks on Frazer by saying, 'I think now that the right thing would be to start my book with remarks on metaphysics as a kind of magic.'[21]

The formality of rituals marks them off from the ordinary discourse of daily affairs. On the other hand, there is an affinity between the words and gestures used in ritual and those words and gestures used elsewhere. For example, I may expresses the wish that someone should come to me by beckoning or calling out to him. When he comes, I may feel this is due to some inherent power in the beckoning or calling; almost as if a power accompanies the gesture or words. When the beckoning by gesture or word expresses a wish in the ritual, we may then feel that since the power is in the beckoning, the condition of fulfilling the wish is given in the inherent power of the beckoning, although the persons or spirits beckoned are absent. In this context, the misunderstandings involved could be called a kind of magical treatment of words – belief in the power of words.[22]

So far from wanting to defend magical or religious rituals against all charges of confusion, as Cook thinks, Wittgenstein is recognising possibilities – and, I emphasise, *possibilities* – of confusion in the rituals, confusion which may still go deep with us.[23] The spirit in which these possibilities are noted by Wittgenstein is very different, however, from the attitude to religion we find among most contemporary philosophers. The *a priorism* is not his, but theirs, since they want to say that *all* forms of magic and religion are confused. Not content with saying that conceptual confusions *may* be present, they say that they are necessarily present. How does this come about?

Evans-Pritchard thought that Marett ducked the issue of the validity of religious belief: 'Maybe he found himself, as Fellow of an Oxford college at that time, in an equivocal position; and, being a philosopher, he was able to (appear to) get out of it by distinguishing between the task of social anthropology to determine the origin of religion – a mixture of history and causation – and the task of theology, which was concerned with its validity; a position we all to some extent take up.'[24] Evans-Pritchard did take up this position, and so can be said to duck the issue too. He says of the anthropologist:

> As I understand the matter, there is no possibility of his *knowing* whether the spiritual beings of primitive religions or of any others have any existence or not, and since this is the case he cannot take the question into consideration. The beliefs are for him sociological facts, not theological facts, and his sole concern is with their relation to each other and to other social facts . . . The validity of the belief lies in the domain of what may be broadly designated the philosophy of religion.[25]

For most contemporary philosophers, however, the reference to philosophy simply postpones the issue. Philosophy shows that religion necessarily involves metaphysics. But metaphysics, it is argued, is not a theory *about* anything. On the contrary, it is itself the product of deep confusions about the logic of our language. John Cook points out that Evans-Pritchard argues that because gods, ancestral spirits, etc., ' . . . if they exist, have a mode of being that is not open to empirical investigation . . . anthropologists must leave their existence an open question'. Cook replies:

> This seems like an eminently sensible view to take – so long as it is assumed that religious beliefs are either true or false, i.e. that either there are or there are not ancestral spirits who deserve human consideration, that either reincarnation occurs or it does not occur, etc. Yet this is not how philosophers generally see the

matter. Take the matter of disembodied existence after death. Philosophers nowadays do not regard this as an obviously possible state of affairs which may or may not occur. On the contrary, viewed philosophically the issue is whether this idea makes any sense at all, and at least most philosophers think it has been shown that the idea does not make sense. Extrapolating from this example, then, what I am suggesting is that if we think carefully about gods and spirits and so on, we may find that these ideas are in some way confused, unintelligible. If they are, then, of course there is no possibility that gods and spirits exist.[26]

Notice that Cook is able to speak confidently of 'how philosophers generally see the matter', 'philosophers nowadays', and of what 'at least most philosophers think'. I said that *within* the practice of the philosophy of religion, animistic modes of argument prevail; religious beliefs are true or false, reasonable or unreasonable hypotheses. What has to be said, however, is that the majority of philosophers pay little, if any, attention to religious beliefs, believing that the conceptual confusions they necessarily exhibit have been exposed long ago. The theories of Tylor and Marett, so far from being dead as mutton, reflect where most philosophers stand. On such a survey, the prospects for any insight into religious beliefs seem bleak.

IV

Having reached these rather daunting conclusions, it must be said that there have been other developments in the philosophy of religion in the last twenty years. These argue that we do not have to regard all religious beliefs as true or false hypotheses or as forms of conceptual confusion. There are other possibilities, but to draw attention to them it has been necessary to philosophise against the stream.

But what do these developments have to do with Marett? My suggestion is that the possibility of such developments was present in the reply Marett made to sociological criticisms of his views. This reply could have led to a more promising version of his view that primitive religion is not so much thought out as danced out.

Durkheim said that the psychological explanation of a social phenomenon is invariably the wrong one. Evans-Pritchard insisted, 'A rite is part of the culture an individual is born into, and it imposes itself on him from the outside like the rest of his culture. It is a creation of society, not of individual reasoning or emotion.'[27] He reminds us ' . . . that in an individual's experience the acquisition of rites and beliefs precedes the emotions which are said to accompany them in later life. He learns to participate in them before he experiences any emotion at all, so the emotional state, whatever it may be, and if there is one, can hardly be the genesis and explanation of them.'[28] Evans-Pritchard concludes, ' . . . if any emotional expression accompanies rites, it may well be that it is not the emotion which brings about the rites, but the rites which bring about the emotion'.[29]

Marett was aware of criticism of this kind. He countered some of it by saying that the fact that rites were performed in the absence of emotional stress shows that, with time, provision was made for such stress before it occurred. The rites have a preventive role and their regenerative effect is such that people return from them strengthened to meet the harsh realities of life.

More important, Marett was aware of the difficulties in seeking a priority, temporal or logical, for either 'dance' or 'thought'. He admitted to having used the term 'preanimistic' chronologically, but at other times he tried to avoid the 'chicken-or-the-egg' question which sought to give priority to 'dance' or 'thought'. He tried to suggest that they are bound up with one another in such a way that asking which came first is itself a confusion.

Marett's main emphasis is on the importance of the individual's active response in religious belief. Here, it is not at all obvious that Evans-Pritchard's objections have all their own way. After all, Marett recognises that an explanation of rituals in terms of an individualistic psychology is not feasible. On the other hand, he is right in insisting that the rituals would be a dead formality without the active response of the participants. When Evans-Pritchard says that people may acquire religious beliefs before they show such responses, what could 'acquiring belief' amount to? What would it mean to say that one believed in God without this involving any affective state in one's life? Even if sense could be made of these 'beliefs' divorced from active responses, what would be particularly religious about them?

I am not suggesting that we can overcome all difficulties in Marett's view of comparative religion as an empirical science the main method of which is social psychology allied to individual psychology and social morphology. I *am* suggesting that Marett was struggling towards a view, how distant a one I let others judge, that we should look at the formative responses of primitives as, in some sense, a fusion of 'dance' and 'thought': 'My theory is not concerned with the mere thought at work in religion, but with religion as a whole, the organic complex of thought, emotion and behaviour.'[30] Instead of saying that primitive religion is not so much thought out as danced out, Marett might have said that a kind of dance is the condition of thought, that what is primary is active response rather than reflection. Had he done so, such an account of the reactions of primitives would have been close to Wittgenstein's notion of primitive reactions.

Wittgenstein said, 'Language does not emerge from reasoning'.[31] We do not reason our way to our primitive reactions concerning pain, colours, sounds. At later, more refined stages, reasons and discriminations become appropriate. Such refinements, however, are dependent on the brute fact that we react as we do – jump with fright, call colours light or dark, call sounds loud or quiet, cry out in pain or express concern or shock at the pain of others. We do not agree to react in these ways. Rather, the fact that we agree shows itself *in* these reactions. The possibility of the development of the concepts concerned is rooted in such reactions. Primitive reactions play a central role too in enquiries where, we are inclined to think, the interest must emerge from intellectual reflection and experimentation. We think this must apply to our interest in causal connections. But Norman Malcolm asks us to consider the following example: 'Suppose that a child runs into another child, knocking him down . . . The child would not be doubting or wondering what made him fall. He would not want to observe what happens in other cases. Nor would he be said to *assume* that in similar cases the same thing occurs.'[32] Wittgenstein remarks, 'There is a reaction which can be called "reacting to the cause" – We also speak of "tracing the cause", a simple case would be, say, following a string to see who is pulling it. If I then find him – how did I know that he, his pulling, is the cause of the string's moving? Do I establish this by a series of experiments?'[33]

In calling our attention to primitive reactions, Wittgenstein is opposing the rationalistic view of language which suggests that language is the result of intellectual reflection. There is a striking similarity between what he has to say and remarks by Simone Weil on concept-formation. She says, 'The very nature of the relationship between ourselves and what is external to us, a relationship which consists in a reaction, a reflex, is our perception of the external world. Perception of nature, pure and simple, is a sort of dance, it is this dance that makes perception possible for us.'[34] Peter Winch comments:

> Simone Weil's account, like Wittgenstein's, achieves this by making the notion of *action* central. Action is conceived, in the first instance, as a series of bodily movements having a certain determinate temporal order. In its primitive form action is quite unreflective. Human beings, and other animate creatures, naturally react in characteristic ways to objects in their environments. They salivate in the presence of food and eat it; this already effects a rudimentary classification which doesn't have to be based on any reflection between 'food' and 'not food'. Our eyes scan objects and connect with other characteristic movements of our bodies, we sniff things (or sometimes hold our noses), we exhibit subtly different reactions to things we put into our mouths – corresponding to such tastes as 'sour', 'sweet', 'salty', etc. – and so on. The reactions are developed and refined as we mature; and some of these refinements and developments are responses to training by other human beings around us. A staircase is something to be climbed, a chair is something to be sat in: compare Wittgenstein's remark: 'It is part of the grammar of the word "chair" that this is what we call "to sit in a chair".'[35] As Simone Weil expresses it: 'everything that we see suggests some kind of movement'.[36, 37]

Speaking of these primitive reactions, Wittgenstein says,

> The origin and the primitive form of the language-game is a reaction; only from this can the more complicated forms grow.
>   Language – I want to say – is a refinement; 'in the beginning was the deed'.[38]

Wittgenstein and Simone Weil are saying – in the beginning was the dance. We can see how Marett's claim, that primitive religion is not so much thought out as danced out, could have been a far-reaching one if he had developed it in certain ways. Language concerning fear, pain, surprise, causation and perception develops from primitive reactions, the dance of the body; it is hardly surprising, then, that such reactions should be of central importance in magical and religious practices.

But what of the confusions in magical and religious practices? I emphasised when we noted them, that what we have here are possible confusions, not necessary confusions. The same is true of the other confusions about the logic of our language which may mislead us. Although the language of wishing or expectation may mislead us, so that we think that what is wished for is somehow in the wish and can make it come true, Wittgenstein did *not* conclude that the language in which wishes are expressed needs revising. Rush Rhees emphasises,

> Wittgenstein would not have said there need be anything mistaken in our using the different forms of expression: 'I am expecting him', 'I am expecting him to come', and 'I expect that he will come'. He would not have said that only the second of these expresses correctly what the fulfilment of my expectation would be. If you asked 'What are you waiting for?' and I answered 'I'm waiting for my brother', there would be nothing inaccurate or inadequate in this; and Wittgenstein would not have said, 'what you *really* mean is you are waiting for your brother to come'.[39]

We cannot say, simply by looking at a form of words, whether these words are going to be confused or not. What we need is not to look at the sentence, but at what we do with it. The same lesson must be applied to the language of magic and religion. We cannot say *a priori* simply by looking at the language of curses, prayers, and sacrifices, that it leads to confusion. Where rituals express a wish, then, to know in what sense the ritual acts out the wish, we would have to take account of the role played by the ritual in the details of the lives of the people who celebrate it. As elsewhere, to see whether the 'acting out' is confused or not, we must not think – impose our *a priori* assumptions – but look.

When we follow this good philosophical advice in relation to magic and religion, we see possibilities come to light which we are tempted to ignore. Let us think again of sticking pins in a picture as the expression of a wish. We have already seen the possibilities of confusion the 'acting out' of the wish may involve, but are these the only possibilities? Let us consider a version of sticking pins in an effigy put forward by my colleague, H. O. Mounce. He asks us to imagine someone who has drawn an excellent likeness of one's mother asking one to stick a pin in the picture, taking special care to aim at one of the eyes. Mounce comments, 'There is hardly anyone, I suppose, who would not find it very difficult to comply with this request. This reaction . . . so far as I can see, is neither rational nor irrational; it is just the way most people would happen to react.'[40] Mounce does not tell us what he thinks of this reaction. He does not consider the possibility of its being a primitive moral reaction. This is important, since it might be vital in determining how one reads the acting out of the fulfilment of the wish. This is how Mounce does in fact continue to unfold the example:

> Suppose, however, that one does comply with the request and then discovers, a short time later, that one's mother has developed an affliction in the eye and is in danger of going blind. I wonder how many people would resist the feeling, if only momentarily, that there was some connection between the two events. But this belief . . . is just as absurd as anything held by the Azande.[41]

By 'some connection' Mounce means some causal connection, but we cannot assume that the 'acting out' must take this form. Discussing Mounce's example with a class of forty students,[42] fifteen of them said that they would have no difficulty in sticking pins in the picture, and that if they did, they would feel no guilt if the mother were visited later with the affliction. 'It's only a picture,' they said, 'how can it have anything to do with it?' When asked to elaborate, they said that there was no causal connection between the two events. The others in the class said they could not stick pins in the picture, and that if they did, they would feel guilty if the affliction developed. For them there would be a connection between the two events. The fifteen were surprised to discover, however, that by some connection, the others did *not* mean some causal connection. In discussion it emerged that what they meant was something like this: they felt that sticking pins in the picture reduces serious possibilities to a game; it plays around with things. When the affliction occurs, an internal relation between the 'playing around' and the event makes the guilt understandable. What this elucidation shows, however, is not that people refused to stick in the pins as a *consequence* of such beliefs, but that primitive moral responses occur and that people, if asked to reflect on them, may reply in this way.

For the fifteen students, no causal connection meant no connection at all. For some of them, the reactions of the others served as reminders of possibilities they had not thought of. But others could still make nothing of those responses. Shall we say that they misunderstood? Not if this means misunderstanding the logic of the language. The language does not get off the ground with them. They fail to understand, but they do not misunderstand.[43] They cannot take the reactions in the right spirit. This is a constant problem for the philosopher of religion's task of providing reminders to achieve clarity.

Think again of Beattie's examples of contemporary beliefs in the power of words. He says that even we, let alone primitives, feel frightened or ashamed at hidden wishes for someone's injury or death, and feel guilty if the event wished for occurs. But need such reactions lead us into confusions? Only if the injury or death is seen as a *consequence* of the wish. Think again of what the wish is for – the injury or death of someone else. Here, what is longed for is expressed in the portrayal of it, as may be the case with sticking pins in an effigy, and the 'tendency to confuse what belongs to the symbolism with what is expressed in the symbolism', to which Beattie refers, need not be present. The wish shows something about me. In that sense, I have my wish in the expression of it. Think of Wittgenstein's remark, 'The description (Darstellung) of a wish is, eo ipso, the description of its fulfilment.'[44] Rhees comments, 'If I translate *"Darstellung"* roughly in the phrases: "portrayal of my wish . . . portrayal of that which would satisfy my wish", then this second phrase is not the same as, "portraying the *satisfaction* of my wish" or "portraying the arrival of what I wish for".'[45] When, however, what I have wished for is satisfied, does arrive, my guilt, if guilt there be, can be understood in terms of the internal relation between my wish, the wish which frightens me or makes me feel ashamed, and the actual occurrence of what I had wished for. Such reactions, free of the confusions Beattie refers to, are as common among ourselves as they are among primitives. *That* is the reminder we stand in need of. Again, however, some will fail to understand such reactions; fail to see any sense in them.

I shall not labour the point I have been making by applying it to religious practices such as the laying on of hands, baptism, cursing, blessing, crossing oneself, homage to religious shrines, etc. It ought to be clear by now that confusion may or may not be present in these practices. Looking at the gestures or expression used will not answer these questions for us. Everything depends, as we have seen, on what is involved in the acting out of these gestures and expressions, how they are interwoven with the other details of ordinary life.

It may be said, however, that such practices still presuppose the existence of God, just as magical practices presuppose the existence of unseen powers. We still have to people the world with spirits. Yet, once again, we have to remind ourselves of the importance of primitive reactions in concept-formation in religion, as elsewhere. To bring this out, Peter Winch asks us to think of mountain-dwellers, who, before specifically religious expressions develop in their language, contemplate the mountains, prostrate themselves before them, celebrate rites in relation to them, in such ways that we call them primitive religious responses. Later, they come to speak of gods in the mountains. Rituals and stories develop which are said to be *about* these gods. Must we then say that talk of the gods expresses the existential presuppositions of the primitive reactions? Winch replies, '"They look to the mountains in order to show reverence to their gods", is not to *explain* why they look to the mountains, but to point to a conceptual connection between what they understand by their gods and their ritualistic practice . . . We use the term "gods" here because of its connection with their rituals. The case is quite different with, "They look towards the mountain to seek animals to hunt." This is explanatory and can be so because the term "animals" can be given a sense quite independently of the habit of the tribesmen of looking towards the mountains.' [46] As Winch points out, a decline in the religious practices would be an aspect of loss of belief in the gods, not a consequence of it. If someone asks why the stories of the gods could not precede any primitive religious reactions, the difficulty once again, as Winch says, would be to show what would be religious about the stories.

V

In the course of this essay, I have tried to present certain possibilities which many philosophers and, perhaps, anthropologists, are tempted to ignore. Someone may want to say that these possibilities are ignored, not because philosophers and anthropologists are unaware of them, but simply because they do not believe they are an accurate account of magic and religion. Would that the survey of the relevant literature bore this out! It will not do either to suggest that the omissions from the literature are due to the fact that the authors take them for granted, but consider them irrelevant. When the authors in question consider religious practices with which we are familiar, they characterise them as *necessarily* confused. They do not *allow* for other possibilities. They are like some of those fifteen students who find no difficulty in sticking pins in pictures and for whom reminders did not work. They do not misunderstand, mistake the logic of the language, for the language of religion does not get off the ground for them; they do not take it in the right spirit. Evans-Pritchard said in 1965 of the theorists of primitive religion he had discussed, 'Religious belief was to those anthropologists absurd, and it is so to most anthropologists of yesterday and today.'[47] Neither is he slow to offer a reason: ' . . . they had no more than a superficial understanding of the historical religions and of what the ordinary worshipper in them believes . . .'[48] As for the philosophers, it would be hard to quarrel with Norman Malcolm's assessment: 'In our Western academic philosophy, religious belief is commonly regarded as unreasonable and is viewed with condescension or even contempt.' Malcolm's remarks would apply to what I have called 'animistic' philosophy of religion. The condescension or even contempt would be said to be deserved because we, unlike the primitives, have no excuse for still entertaining the hypotheses of divine realities. Malcolm continues, 'It is said that religion is a refuge for those who, because of weakness of intellect or character, are unable to confront the stern realities of the world.'[49] These remarks could refer to those who see religion as the product of confusion. These attitudes dominate contemporary philosophy.

We can only break the hold of these prevailing attitudes by paying due attention to concept-formation in religion. I have suggested that although Tylor and Marett tried to do so, the resolution of their dispute about the reaction of primitives has more to do with primitive reactions, in Wittgenstein's sense of the term, than either of them recognised. As we have seen, giving these primitive reactions their proper place in our reflections depends on more than not being misled by the logic of our language. It depends, more fundamentally, on the spirit in which we are able to respond to the language in question. This is an issue which philosophers and, dare I say, anthropologists, cannot afford to ignore.[50]

Notes

1. 'Social Anthropology: Past and Present', in *Essays in Social Anthropology* (Faber & Faber, 1962).
2. E. E. Evans-Pritchard, *Theories of Primitive Religion* (Oxford: Clarendon Press, 1965) p. 100.
3. Ibid., p. 122.
4. E. B. Tylor, *Primitive Culture* (London, 1920) p. 53.
5. James Frazer, *The Golden Bough*, abridged edn (Macmillan, 1924) p. 264.
6. R. R. Marett, *The Threshold of Religion*, 2nd edn. (Macmillan, 1914) p. xxxi.
7. *Theories of Primitive Religion*, p. 101.
8. Frazer, *The Golden Bough*.
9. See, for example, Basil Mitchell, *The Justification of Religious Belief* (Macmillan, 1973).
10. For those opposite tendencies see Richard Swinburne, *The Coherence of Theism* (OUP, 1977) and J. L. Mackie, *The Miracle of Theism* (Clarendon Press, Oxford, 1982).
11. Such criticisms have been frequent themes in much of my own work. See *The Concept of Prayer* (Routledge & Kegan Paul, 1965); paperback edn (Basil Blackwell, 1981) and *Faith and Philosophical Enquiry* (Routledge & Kegan Paul, 1970).
12. For my discussion of these criticisms: see *Religion Without Explanation* (Basil Blackwell, 1976), chapter 4: 'Private Stress and Public Ritual'.
13. For a collection of papers which reflects the transition in philosophy from asking whether religious beliefs are true or false to asking whether they are even meaningful, see the once influential collection, *New Essays in Philosophical Theology*, ed. A. G. N. Flew and A. MacIntyre (SCM Press, 1955).
14. Ludwig Wittgenstein, 'Remarks on Frazer's *The Golden Bough*', trans. A. C. Miles and Rush Rhees, *The Human World*, no. 3 (May 1971) p. 37.
15. Ibid., p. 31.
16. John W. Cook, 'Magic, Witchcraft and Science', *Philosophical Investigations*, VI, no. 1 (1983).
17. Rush Rhees had anticipated the kind of reaction we find in Cook: '"So Wittgenstein was coming forward in defence of the ancient rituals!" That remark could have sense only if Wittgenstein had recognised no other "co-ordinates", no other standards than that of knowledge, of what may be established in science, and error (and probably it would not have sense even then).' Rush Rhees, 'Wittgenstein on Language and Ritual', in *Wittgenstein and His Times*, ed. Brian McGuinness (Basil Blackwell, 1982) pp. 80–1.
18. Ibid., p. 82.
19. *MS* 109, 210 f.
20. John Beattie, *Other Cultures* (Cohen and West, 1964), p. 204. Cook quotes this passage in 'Magic, Witchcraft and Science', p. 6.
21. Ludwig Wittgenstein, 'Remarks on Frazer's *The Golden Bough*', p. 19.
22. Compare the following: 'The gestures made in these rituals had been learned in the daily life and language of those who made them – or

many, and probably most of them were. The gestures used *only* in the ceremony had their role as gestures – they were seen as gestures – through some affinity with the gestures made in daily life and practical affairs (in building, planting, hunting, fighting, and so on). And the same goes for words and sentences, which are as important in many ritual or magical practices as gestures are, in incantations, spells, curses, in prayers, vows, and so on. There may be words used only in ritual magic, but these are taken as *words* with the power that words have in speech – conversation, instructions, orders, quarrels, etc., outside ritual – a power which they bring with them into ritual.' Rhees, 'Wittgenstein on Language and Ritual', p. 72.

23. For further discussion of this issue see Essay 6.
24. E. E. Evans-Pritchard, *Theories of Primitive Religion*, p. 35.
25. Ibid., p. 17.
26. Cook, 'Magic, Witchcraft and Science', p. 35.
27. Evans-Pritchard, *Theories of Primitive Religion*, p. 46.
28. Ibid.
29. Ibid., p. 45.
30. Ibid., p. x.
31. Ludwig Wittgenstein, *On Certainty* (para. 475).
32. Norman Malcolm, 'The Relation of Language to Instinctive Behaviour', *Philosophical Investigations*, vol. v, no. 1 (Jan. 1982) pp. 5–6.
33. Ludwig Wittgenstein, 'Cause and Effect: Intuitive Awareness', *Philosophia*, vol. 6, nos 3–4, pp. 391–408, Sept., Dec., 1976. Selected and edited by Rush Rhees, English translation by Peter Winch, p. 416.
34. Simone Weil, *Lectures on Philosophy*, trans. H. S. Price (CUP, 1978) p. 51.
35. Ludwig Wittgenstein, *The Blue and Brown Books* (Basil Blackwell, 1978) p. 51.
36. Weil, *Lectures on Philosophy*, p. 31.
37. Ibid. Peter Winch, Introduction, p. 12.
38. Ludwig Wittgenstein, *Culture and Value*, trans. Peter Winch (Basil Blackwell, 1980) p. 31.
39. Rush Rhees, 'Wittgenstein on Language and Ritual', p. 88.
40. H. O. Mounce, 'Understanding a Primitive Society', *Philosophy*, xlviii, Oct. 1973, pp. 347–62.
41. Ibid., p. 353.
42. At the University of Carleton, Ottawa.
43. For a development of the important distinction between 'misunderstanding' and 'failing to understand', see Rush Rhees, 'Wittgenstein on Language and Ritual'.
44. Ludwig Wittgenstein, 'Remarks on Frazer's *The Golden Bough*', p. 31.
45. Rush Rhees, 'Wittgenstein on Language and Ritual', p. 90. The extent of my indebtedness to this outstanding essay should be obvious. This is not to say, of course, that Rhees would necessarily approve of the use I have made of it in the lecture.
46. Peter Winch, 'Meaning and Religious Language', in *Reason and Religion*, ed. Stuart Brown (Cornell University Press, 1977) p. 197.
47. *Theories of Primitive Religion*, p. 15.
48. Ibid., p. 17.

49. Norman Malcolm, 'The Groundlessness of Belief', in *Thought and Know-ledge* (Cornell University Press, 1977) p. 204.
50. The Marett Lecture was delivered at Exeter College, Oxford on 17 May 1983.

8

Belief and Loss of Belief
(A Discussion with
J. R. Jones[1])

D.Z.P.: Jargon is the enemy of philosophy. It creates a screen between the enquirer and the possibility of understanding. Furthermore, if a certain jargon has become a prevalent fashion in philosophical circles, using it, and hearing it used, may lead a person to think he has understood, when, in fact, he has not. There is a great need to cut through some prevalent jargon in contemporary philosophy of religion. We need to be forced to see that many religious beliefs cannot be understood in terms of the neat categories which, we are tempted to think, are the only categories which intelligible notions have. For example, in his lectures on religious belief,[2] Wittgenstein considers religious beliefs like belief in the Last Judgement, or that one's life is being lived under the eye of God. We cannot grasp the nature of these beliefs by forcing them into the alternatives: empirical propositions or human attitudes. And yet, again and again, philosophers of religion force our hands by saying, 'But come now, which is it? Is the Last Judgement a future event? Is it something which is going to happen at a certain time? Or is belief in the Last Judgement simply your own attitude, a value, a way of looking at things, which you confer on the world about you?' What Wittgenstein does is to free us from this jargon. It is as if he said to us, 'Don't say it *must* be one or the other. Look and see what kind of things these beliefs are. Don't let the jargon determine your thinking.' Or, as Wittgenstein used to say, 'Don't think, look.' Don't say that religious beliefs *must* be of this kind or that, but look to see what kind of beliefs they are. And when we do this, Wittgenstein suggests, we stop asking many questions of religious beliefs which we thought it quite reasonable to ask. For example, we stop thinking of religious beliefs as conjectures, hypotheses, for which the evidence is not particularly good. In the light of our reflections on religious beliefs, we may be led to revise our opinions about the distinction between the rational and the irrational, and to think again about what might be meant by saying that one does not have any religious beliefs. What does it mean to believe in the Last Judgement? What does it mean to say that one does not believe in it? Must we say one or the other, or is this a mistake we are led into because of the hold of a certain jargon on us? These are some of the questions Professor Jones and I are going to try to discuss. We do no more than touch lightly on them. At this stage, all we are attempting to do is to indicate a direction in which these questions can be pursued with profit.

J.R.J.: I should like to draw you out first, Mr Phillips, on the point that religious belief is nothing like the acceptance of a hypothesis or the holding of an opinion, however well- or ill-founded. I wonder whether this can be seen to be so by just looking at the role beliefs have in the believers' lives. We have been told, in this kind of context, not to think and allow ourselves to get into the grip of jargon, but to just look. Well, what is it that shows that, to take Wittgenstein's example, belief in the Last Judgement has obviously nothing in common with a hypothesis?

D.Z.P.: I think that if we do look at the role this belief plays in at least many believers' lives, we find that it is not a hypothesis, a conjecture, that some dreadful event is going to happen so many thousand years hence. We see this by recognising that a certain range of reactions is ruled out for the believer. What I mean is this: if it were a conjecture about a future event, he might say, 'I believe it is going to happen' or 'Possibly it might happen' or 'I'm not sure; it may happen', and so on. But that range of reactions plays no part in the believer's belief in the Last Judgement. It is not a conjecture about the future, but, as it were, the framework, the religious framework, within which he meets fortune, misfortune, and the evil that he finds in his own life and in life about him.

J.R.J.: It would seem, then, that you could say that a genuine religious belief has a certain firmness which is quite peculiar to itself. That indeed, in a sense, the expression of a genuine religious belief could be described as the firmest of all judgements. Well, I wonder what is the character of this firmness, because it doesn't seem to mean the same thing as, for example, firmly grounded; because, of course, the whole notion of grounding, of obtaining good evidence, of weighing evidence, is right out of place here. What, then, is the character of the firmness?

D.Z.P.: Well, certainly the firmness does not mean, as you say, what it means in 'firmly grounded prediction'. Wittgenstein considers the example of a man who said, 'I had a dream last night in which I dreamt of the Last Judgement, and now I know what it is.' Well, Wittgenstein says, if you compare that with a prediction of what weather we are going to get next week, it isn't any kind of prediction. 'I had a dream – therefore – Last Judgement.' We don't know what to make of that, if it is taken as an inference. So, in that sense, one might say the belief in the Last Judgement isn't firm at all, isn't well-established at all. So what could be meant, then, by firm belief here? Wittgenstein suggested that belief in religion has much more this role: I have this picture of the Last Judgement before my mind whenever, perhaps, I am tempted to perform a despicable deed. It regulates my thinking. It is firm in that it is to this picture that I appeal in such situations as these.

J.R.J.: If this, then, is the sort of firmness that a religious belief has, that is to say, not at all the firmness of a well-founded hypothesis or conjecture, what, then, is the non-believer doing when he rejects belief? You see, in not having a use for what you have called 'the picture', and in rejecting it because it has no force or significance in his life at all, is he then, or could he then be said to be, contradicting the believer?

D.Z.P.: In his lectures, Wittgenstein suggests that in certain cases, anyway, the non-believer would not be contradicting the believer. He takes the example of a man who, when he is ill, says, 'This is a punishment from God.' Wittgenstein asks, 'What am I saying if I say that this plays no part in my life? Am I contradicting the man who does believe this?'[3] Wittgenstein wants to deny this. What he would say is: 'It plays no part in my life at all; this collection of words means nothing to me, in the sense that it does not regulate my life; I do not adhere to it; I do not aspire to what it stands for. Therefore, I am not involved in the same form of life as the man who does regulate his life by this picture and aspires to it.' On the other hand, if I said, 'There is a German aeroplane overhead'[4] and you doubted this, we would both be participating in the same activity, namely, locating the German aeroplane; we would be appealing to the same criteria: I would be certain, you would be doubtful. But if I say that the idea of a Last Judgement plays no part in my life, then I am saying that in this respect you are on an entirely different plane from me; we are not participating in the same language-game, to use Wittgenstein's phrase, at all.

J.R.J.: It looks, then, that no evidence could count against or for; in that no evidence can count for, then, of course, it follows that no evidence can count against, what might naïvely be called the truth of these pictures. And yet, we know well, from experience and from the history of religions, that belief, religious belief, is something which can be undermined by scepticism; and scepticism would be in this case scepticism concerning what is thus naïvely called the truth of the picture. But, when this happens – and this is what interests me – when belief is thus undermined, or weakened, it then looks as though the picture itself begins to lose its hold on the life of the believer. And I wonder what this really signifies? Doesn't it suggest that there is some sort of internal relation between the weight or force of the picture – and I mean by that, it's having weight for me – and the state of my mind that is capable of being undermined by doubt? This seems to reintroduce the notion of a literal truth, as against a literal falsity, you see. It is in this kind of connection that doubt and scepticism work upon people's minds, and it looks as though it does do its job here. When there is this corrosion by doubt, the pictures are somehow corroded; they lose their hold.

D.Z.P.: I think this is an extremely important and difficult region to be reflecting about, and the best I can do, I think, is to make the following initial distinction. Let us distinguish between, on the one hand, someone, that is, a given believer, for whom the force of the Last Judgement no longer means anything. In his life, this picture of the Last Judgement means nothing at all, whereas it used to once. Now, what has happened here, I suggest, is that the *attention* of the individual has been won over either by a rival secular picture, or, of course, by worldliness, etc. Because his energies are now focused in another direction, this picture which was once powerful in his life, has lost its grip. Interestingly enough, when you say that the notion of literal truth is reintroduced, I suggest that it is reintroduced in this way: that when the old force of the picture is lost, the new force it has is that of a literal picture, which, as far as I can see, is simply a matter of superstition. But we might want to distinguish between the case of the picture losing its hold for a given individual, with religious pictures losing their hold anyway, not through the fault of any particular individual, but because of changes in the culture. Certain religious pictures decline, and yet you can't ask, 'But whose fault is it that they are declining?' You can't trace the decline to the bio-graphical details of the life of any single individual.

J.R.J.: This cannot be done because it is a decay of belief which is affecting a whole culture or a whole epoch. Couldn't we be said to be living in such a period today – a period of what you might call prevalent disbelief? And I would be interested to know what you would say to this: why doesn't it make sense, then, in a period such as this, of the decay of belief, to suppose a group of people – of well-minded people – trying to bring about a renewal of faith, possibly from within a religious context or even from entirely without it; people with a secular background, noting the effect of the decay of belief on the morals of the culture generally, trying to bring about a renewal of faith by devising new and more acceptable pictures, and then trying to induce belief in them? Why is this somehow non-sensical? Why couldn't such a thing work?

D.Z.P.: I think this is linked to a point that we have neglected. So far, we have been concerned to emphasise that these religious beliefs are not conjectures, or hypotheses, with insufficient evidence for them. The beliefs are not empirical propositions. Once this is said, many philosophers assume that the beliefs must be human attitudes, values conferred, as it were, by individuals on to the world about them. But this does not follow and is in fact untrue. It is important to recognise that these pictures have a life of their own, a possibility of sustaining those who adhere to them. Part of the answer, though I think not the complete answer, to the question why it would be nonsensical to imagine theologians, let us say, creating pictures – new pictures – to meet the crisis of the age, the declining faith that they perceive about them, is that whatever they created would pre-cisely be their creation, and you would have a curious reversal of the emphasis needed in religion, where the believer does not want to say that he measures these pictures and finds that they are all right or finds that they are wanting. On the contrary, the believers wish to claim that it isn't they who measure the pictures, since in a sense, the pictures measure them; they are the measure in terms of which they judge themselves. They do not judge the picture. Or again, to link with the earlier points we made, when people do judge the picture, that is the time when they are beginning either to rebel against it, or when the picture is beginning to lose its hold on their lives as individuals.

J.R.J.: Yes, I agree with this, but there seems to me to be another thing that could be added to that. Isn't it, or wouldn't it be, precisely the element of believing as part of a tradition of belief that would be wanting or lacking in this attempt on the part of a group of people to bring about a renewal of faith by devising new pictures? You see, this group of would-be reformers wouldn't be dealing with a faith nourished by time and handed down from the past within which certain pictures are to be found. They would, rather, be presenting their new-fangled pictures first, and then trying to get people to believe them. Well, now, in such a situation, it seems to me, pictures degenerate into mere pictures; but – and this is interesting – not because they would be in the nature of hypotheses or conjectures for which the evidence is found wanting. Not that at all, but because they would be, as it were, trying to become, or trying to be made to become, operative as beliefs outside the sphere of, or you might say, in the absence of the surroundings of, belief – all that goes with believing in a tradition of belief, I mean, in an historical faith. I can't see that anything could be a substitute for that.

D.Z.P.: I agree entirely. This makes it necessary to say something about our use of the term 'picture'. Sometimes, at a casual glance, it might look as if by 'pictures' we meant what you have now referred to as 'mere pictures'. Indeed, many philosophers of religion today have spoken of devising new pictures, finding new symbols, to communicate the essence of the divine to people. It's as if there were a deliberate *use* of the picture to communicate the essence of the divine. 'We now find that that picture isn't working, so let us revise what is called, naïvely, our image of God.' 'Our image of God must go', we are told. As if, independently of the picture, we have a notion of divinity. You then compare the picture with this notion and you say, 'Oh, well, it's not doing its job properly', and we have another picture. Wittgenstein stressed in his lectures that the whole weight may be in the picture. The picture is not a picturesque way of saying something else. It says what it says, and when the picture dies, something dies with it, and there can be no substitute for that which dies with the picture.

J.R.J.: Well, could this, then, have the implications that when the picture, which is a picture of the divine, as it were, which is God, having a role through faith in the whole life of a believer, is corroded by doubts and scepticism, the picture can be said to have died; but that when the picture dies or decays or is phased out in a whole culture, that in a sense, on your own presuppositions, God could be said to have died?

D.Z.P.: Yes, this is a difficulty that some people have felt about this way of talking. For instance, if you said that certain modes of moral conduct were to pass away, some people might say that there would be no goodness in the world any more. So why do we not want to say that if these pictures were to die, God dies, as it were, with the pictures? I think the answer to that, though I don't see this very clearly, is that the desire to say that God dies is literal-mindedness attempting to reassert itself. The point is that from within the picture something can be said now about such a time, that is, a time when people might turn their backs on it altogether. What can be said is that in such a time, people will have turned their backs on God. In other words, if people believe, there is nothing within belief which allows them to say that God can die. What they say is that there may come a time when people will turn their backs on God.

J.R.J.: It is as though you were saying that although the picture has, in one sense, died, not only in the lives of particular individuals, but even prevalently through the whole of a culture, it is still possible to speak from within the picture.

D.Z.P.: I am saying that it is possible for believers to say something now about such a time. You may find, of course – perhaps we do find – that only a handful of people do derive sustenance from this picture. But a picture may die in a culture because believing in it is not an isolated activity. To call the belief a language-game can be misleading if it does suggest an isolated activity. Other cultural changes can affect people's worship. For example, in *Brave New World* there is a decline in the notion of moral responsibility. In such a society one can see, without too much difficulty, how the notion of God as a Judge might also be in decline.

J.R.J.: So that, in that kind of society, the picture 'Last Judgement' would have no power over people's lives. But the interesting thing is that it wouldn't be this because it was a hypothesis for which people found that there wasn't sufficient evidence. It is not as a weak hypothesis that it declines, but because everything else surrounding it has declined out of that particular society.

D.Z.P.: As I said at the outset, we aimed to do no more in this discussion than to point out a direction in which the hold of a certain jargon could be avoided, a jargon which forces us to think of religious beliefs either as hypotheses about some future events or as human attitudes in which values are conferred on the world by the believers. In trying to elucidate what such a direction involves we have discussed what kind of beliefs religious beliefs are; the kind of firmness they have; in what sense they are unshakeable for the believer; on the other hand, what can happen to a believer when an unshakeable belief begins to lose its hold on him, and he becomes an unbeliever – what happens to him then; and also what is happening despite all his efforts to believe; what is happening in the culture in which he does believe, where, as it were, the surroundings from which the religious picture is nourished are changing, so bringing about changes in the nature of that religious picture itself.

Notes

1.   This discussion first took place on BBC Radio.
2.   Ludwig Wittgenstein, *Lectures and Conversations on Aesthetics, Psychology and Religious Belief*, ed. Cyril Barrett (Blackwell, 1966). The lectures on religious belief belong to a course of lectures on belief given by Wittgenstein some time during the summer of 1938.
3.   These are not quotations. See also Essay 5.
4.   Wittgenstein's example.

9

From Coffee to Carmelites

In his paper, 'The Aroma of Coffee',[1] H. O. Mounce wants to expose what he takes to be a deep prejudice in philosophy, one which is at work in our culture more generally. Philosophers are reluctant to admit that there is anything which *passes beyond* human understanding. Of course, they are quite ready to admit that there are plenty of things that they *fail* to understand but this they would say simply happens to be the case. It does not mean that what they fail to understand is something which is beyond human understanding. Thus even when they fail to understand something, that 'something' remains, in principle, within the reach of their understanding. For Mounce this prejudice flies in the face of what is platitudinously obvious: that there is much that passes beyond human understanding.

Mounce argues for his conclusion by considering a number of very diverse examples, ranging from the aroma of coffee to the contemplative practices and mystical experiences of that great Carmelite, St John of the Cross. I shall argue that the examples do not always show what Mounce thinks they show. Moreover, I think his purpose in referring to such examples is a confused one. It is often said that religion has to do with things which pass beyond human understanding. Many philosophers resist this notion. Mounce wants to show them, I suspect, that in doing so they are not resisting something esoteric, something confined to religion. Rather, they are resisting the commonplace. Mounce's examples are meant to show that in perfectly ordinary contexts there is a great deal which passes beyond human understanding.

But is the sense in which religion has to do with things which pass beyond human understanding the familiar one Mounce reminds us of in his examples? If not, the examples will throw little light on it. That will be my final conclusion, but before reaching it, we must explore what Mounce's distinction between 'failing to understand' and 'passing beyond one's understanding' amounts to. There is one

131

conception of the latter notion which he thinks, rightly, is confused, although he is not always free of it himself.

One way in which it might be thought that something is beyond human understanding is to say that it is inherently inexpressible, that words cannot capture it. This might be said of something extremely ordinary such as the aroma of coffee. Someone might say that the aroma cannot be captured in words. But then someone may convey its character to someone who has not experienced it by comparing and contrasting it with other aromas. Mounce says that this will not impress the person who says that the aroma cannot be captured in words. Such a person will point out that those comparisons and contrasts can only be made because of non-verbal acquaintance with aromas the person possesses. This complaint, Mounce argues, amounts to saying 'that words are inadequate so far as they derive their meanings simply from the ways in which they enter into people's lives, into their experiences' (p. 160). The objector wants words to fit the phenomenon, the aroma of coffee, for example, 'independently, as it were, of human interference' (p. 160). In criticising such a view, Wittgenstein, in his *Philosophical Investigations*, gets us to see that descriptions do enter human life in a variety of ways, and that this is not a matter of 'human interference'. Consider, for example, the way in which we wrinkle up our noses, grimace, turn away, etc., in the circumstances in which we talk of unpleasant smells. Such reactions are not 'human interference' with the phenomenon of an unpleasant smell. On the contrary, without this agreement in human reactions there would be no notion of an unpleasant smell. Similarly our descriptions of the aroma of coffee depend on such an agreement in human reactions for their sense.

This conclusion, however, may make us prematurely confident that all our experiences are common ones, and that every experience is inherently describable, available to all language-users. But, Mounce argues, if language gets its sense from the ways it enters human life, then, if people's lives differ radically, they can be radically alien to each other. It will not do to say that language will bridge the gulf between them, since, Mounce says, 'there will be as many differences in their languages as there are in their lives' (p. 161). Societies may be as alien to each other as individuals. Mounce claims that it is futile to say, as some philosophers have done, that we would not call them societies if we could not understand them. Of course, there will be overlaps between them, but, Mounce says, the differences between them may be far more important.

Mounce contrasts the example of alien societies with that of the aroma of coffee. In the case of the aroma, 'one can imagine, easily enough, how a person who lacks the experience may acquire it, or something like it' (p. 162). In the case of societies remote from our own, it is idle, Mounce argues, to say that they 'may be understood in principle when, in innumerable cases, one has no idea even in principle, how that understanding might be acquired' (pp. 162–3).

What does Mounce mean by calling a society alien to us? He cannot simply mean that it is remote in time; a society of which we have no detailed records. True, we would not know how to go about understanding such a society, but the question whether we could remains an open one. It is simply that in our ignorance, the issue cannot be resolved. But Mounce has more than this in mind.

For Mounce, an alien society is one which we cannot understand from within the mode of understanding we possess. We do not simply fail to understand it; it passes beyond human understanding. There is a radical *incommensurability* between the two societies. It is often important, in philosophy, to emphasise this incommensurability which can separate people. One does so to combat the tendency to think that all differences in perspective can be cashed in terms of a common rationality by which they can be assessed. Recently, I emphasised the point as follows: 'When Socrates says that the just man is happier than the unjust man, it may seem that he is advocating a naturalism by means of which the superiority of justice over injustice can be demonstrated. The use of the comparative "happier" may mislead us. When Socrates says that the just man is *more* happy than the unjust man, we may be misled in the same way. But Socrates is saying: "Let justice be your conception of happiness" or "Happy is the man who is just". A neutral conception of happiness is not being used to judge between justice and injustice. Rather, moral conceptions determine what is meant by happiness.'[2]

When these observations are made to some philosophers, they make nothing of them.

> Shall we say that they misunderstand? Not if this means misunderstanding the logic of the language. The language does not get off the ground with them.[3]

Mounce and I made the same distinction in *Moral Practices*[4] as a corrective to naturalism. We resisted attempts to show why one ought to be good in terms of what is in every person's interest.

No doubt Mounce takes himself to be repeating this distinction in his emphasis on the difference between failing to understand and that which passes beyond human understanding. But there is an essential addition. He now insists that when something passes beyond human understanding, we do not know, even in principle, how an understanding of it can be acquired. If a society came to understand one which was remote from it, I suspect Mounce would say that the society was not remote or alien after all. The first society had simply failed to understand the second; the second does not pass beyond the understanding of the first. Please note, however, that this new distinction does not correspond to the previous distinction between misunderstanding and lack of understanding.

Mounce wants to emphasise that not every lack of understanding is simply a matter of failing to understand. What Mounce does not recognise is that not every acquiring of understanding is a matter of succeeding within the same mode of understanding within which one had previously failed. One's understanding may be extended or transformed. For example, someone may think that he understands an alien society when he does not. Or someone, while admitting that he does not understand thinks of it as a failure which can be rectified within his present mode of understanding. But supposing that they come to see that they are guilty of a condescending misunderstanding. They come to see that their understanding has to be extended to come to grips with the alien society. It does not follow that before this extension the alien society did not pass beyond their understanding. Neither is their new understanding a correction within their old mode of understanding. An extended understanding is not simply the old understanding corrected. Or again, a person's old understanding may not be extended, but transformed. It is commonplace to speak of religious conversion as a change of direction, and not as succeeding where previously one had failed in the same old direction.

Here in examples of transformed or extended understandings we have cases of people coming to know what once passed beyond their understanding. But according to Mounce there is no way by which such lack of understanding can be removed. Clearly he is wrong if he is presenting this as a general thesis. Sometimes what he seems to be saying is not that the lack of understanding cannot even in principle be removed, but that there is no principle or method by which it can be removed. This latter observation is correct. But then why should the way extensions or transformations come about be reducible to a principle or method?

Mounce may insist that anything we come to understand he is going to refuse to call 'that which passes beyond human understanding'. So if we come to understand an alien society through an extension or transformation of our understanding, Mounce will conclude that the society in question was not really alien, and that it did not pass beyond our understanding after all. But in that case all Mounce presents us with is a rather unilluminating tautology: if X passes beyond understanding Y, and Y does not change, there is no way even in principle by which X can be understood in terms of Y. Since some people do not change, those things which are beyond their understanding if they do not change will remain beyond their understanding. For reasons which will emerge later, Mounce states his conclusion by saying that he has shown that some things pass beyond human understanding, whereas what he has shown is that there are things that pass beyond the understanding of some human beings; other human beings understand them perfectly well.

But there are further complications. Mounce says that two sets of people may be enigmatic to each other because their lives differ radically. This is undeniably true. They may not simply fail to understand each other. They pass beyond each other's understanding. But once again Mounce insists, in general, that there is no way of removing this enigma. But is he going to say that if the enigma is removed the two sets of people did not differ radically after all? If he is he is on the way to another unilluminating tautology. But he is also led to deny familiar possibilities, possibilities by which we understand radical differences between us and others. As we shall see, Mounce wants to equate 'understanding a life' with 'living that life'. Thus if two sets of people have radically different lives, on this view, they cannot understand each other. Of course, they *may* not. But, on the other hand, they may, and that does not make their differences any less radical. So one cannot equate 'something being radically different from one's views' with 'that which passes beyond one's understanding'. Mounce argues as follows: since language gets its sense from the way it enters human life, human lives which differ radically cannot be bridged by language, since 'there will be as many differences in their languages as there are in their lives' (p. 161). What this argument takes no account of is that language sometimes enters human life in the form of an understanding of radical differences. One form a growth in understanding takes is to see that what one took to be the same is, in fact, radically different. In *Moral Practices*, Mounce and I had that aim in combating the tendency in some philosophers to deny the radical diversity of moral perspectives. Consider the following comments by Paul Holmer:

> Nietzsche's aversion to Christianity was so profound and so detailed that his pages outline a faith in Jesus that is worthy of offense. For this reason, his work helps us to see how blessed someone is who is not offended by Jesus. Nietzsche understood but was antipathetic. Voltaire's conception that Pascal's account of Christianity is misanthropic suggests that both Voltaire and Pascal had seen the logic of faith correctly. In one sense, both had the grammar straight – one so that he could accept it, the other so that he could at least reject the right thing.[5]

So far, then, the most Mounce has shown is that, sometimes, some human beings pass beyond the understanding of some other human beings. But as I have said what Mounce really wants to show, for reasons which will emerge later, is that there are things which pass beyond the understanding of all human beings; things which human beings can never come to understand.

Mounce thinks he has found an example of one such thing in the condition of his family dog, who came home one day whimpering and trembling, with blood in his fur. His mother said that the dog was in pain, but his father said that it was in a state of shock. Mounce says that the dog's behaviour was consistent with either supposition. He is interested in the radical indeterminacy in his parents' judgements. The fact that Mounce may be factually wrong about this example, may obscure from us the philosophical issue at stake. When dogs are in pain, they attempt to lick the painful region, as if in an effort to get at the pain.[6] The philosophical issue is whether it makes sense to speak of the dog's condition as something which cannot be determined by any human being. What kind of dispute is the difference between the parents' judgements? What does the indeterminacy in their judgements consist in?

Before answering this question, let us ask another one: Do fish feel pain? Some people say they do, while others say they do not. Mounce takes this to be a factual dispute. He would say that the indeterminacy is not a verbal one, as in a disagreement over what is to be called a heap. In the case of the fish, the indeterminacy, Mounce would say, is in the phenomenon itself. But Mounce is wrong in thinking that conceptual indeterminacy is a verbal matter. In his example of the heap, how is 'the precise understanding of the phenomenon' determined? Surely, in terms of the agreed reactions in terms of which talk of the phenomenon has its sense. The only dispute is over what label to give it. That, indeed, is a verbal dispute. But in relation to the fish there are no agreed reactions with respect to it. Some react to fish in such a way that they think it obvious that fish feel pain. Others do not react in this way at all. This is a difference in what they think it *makes sense* to say about fish. It is in this context that we speak of a *conceptual* indeterminacy. But this is no verbal matter, since with the indeterminacy goes the difference in reactions to the fish, a difference which will be reflected in what people say and are prepared to do with respect to fish.

Let us now return to the example of the family dog. It is important to note that, on given occasions, we are in no doubt that a dog is in pain or in a state of shock. Mounce, as we have seen, emphasised the fact that language gets its sense from the way it enters human life. But gestures, reactions, expressions, also get their sense from the life that surrounds them. For example, we react to dogs in ways which make us talk unhesitatingly about them as sexually aroused, frightened, angry, playful, hopeful, etc. As I rummage around in a bag, a dog may act in a way to which I react by calling the dog hopefully expectant. But we do not speak of a dog hoping I will bring something in the bag the week after next. There is nothing in the life of a dog which leads me to react in such a way that I would say this.

On given occasions in relation to the family dog there may be an indeterminacy of judgement, as there is in the report Mounce gives us. Mounce misunderstands the character of the indeterminacy. He turns his parents' judgements into hypotheses, and claims that the behaviour of the dog is consistent with both. But whose reaction to the dog is *that*? Not one shared by either of Mounce's parents. They are not in any doubt about the dog's condition. One said that the dog was in pain. The other said the dog was in a state of shock. For Mounce, such judgements fail to get at 'the condition of the dog'. But the indeterminacy in judgements, rather than recording a failure, marks the context in which different convictions concerning the dog's condition are expressed. When Mounce says that the indeterminacy is *in the phenomenon*, he has not specified what phenomenon he has in mind. By placing 'the phenomenon' beyond all reactions to the dog, Mounce seems to be in the grip of the very conception of a pure phenomenon he wants to avoid; a phenomenon which would have a sense independent of any position it occupies in the life that surrounds it, including the ways we react to it.

The point is even more obvious when we turn to indeterminacy of judgements concerning human beings. Wittgenstein warns us *not* to draw the conclusions from this feature of our lives that Mounce is tempted to draw:

> If it is said, 'Evidence can only make it probable that expressions of emotion are genuine', this does *not* mean that instead of complete certainty we have just a more or less confident conjecture. 'Only probable' cannot refer to the degree of our confidence, but only to the nature of its justification, to the character of the language-game. Surely this must help determine the nature of our concepts: that there is no agreement among men as to the certainty of their convictions. (Compare the remark about agreement in colour-judgments and agreement in mathematics.)
>
> Given the same evidence one person can be completely convinced and another not be. We don't on that account exclude either one from society as being unaccountable and incapable of judgment.[7]

I suspect that Mounce thinks that such conclusions lead to scepticism, that we can no longer take seriously the question of what condition the dog is in, or what the character of the emotion is. Perhaps he thinks we are only taking up different attitudes towards them. This is an impoverished 'emotivist' conception of an 'attitude', but let that pass. 'But what *is* the condition of the dog?', 'What *is* the character of the emotion?', Mounce and others want to ask. Of course, these questions are as much reactions as those they find problematic. For Mounce, eliminating the indeterminacy in our judgements, were it possible, would be a gain in clarity. For Wittgenstein, such a loss would mark a change in our concepts; our relations to animals and human beings would not remain as they are now. We would not be clearer about *the same* relations. We would have different relations. Wittgenstein makes the point succinctly:

> A sharper concept would not be the same concept. That is: the sharper concept wouldn't have the value for us that the blurred one does. Precisely because we would not understand people who act with total certainty when we are in doubt and uncertainty.[8]

But if Mounce is looking for something which is beyond *all* human understanding, the example of the family dog does not quite serve his purpose. He and his family stood in familiar relations to the family pet. If we want to look for creatures which pass beyond all human understanding, the place to find them, perhaps, is among those creatures with whom we have few dealings, bats, for instance. Like Thomas Nagel, Mounce claims that we have no idea of what it is like to be a bat. The reason, we are told, is that such 'knowing' 'is subjective in its very essence' (p. 163). Mounce takes this to be so platitudinous that there would have been no point in Nagel's making the observation were it not for the obtuseness of other philosophers. So we human beings can never know 'from the inside', as it were, what it is like to be a bat. In fact Mounce thinks that Nagel has understated his case. He says: 'His use of the phrase 'what it is like to be' is not entirely happy, because it is so often associated with differences of degree rather than of kind . . . The bat is a creature radically alien, which in many respects passes *beyond* our understanding, so that in these respects it would make little sense even to try to understand it' (p. 164). This alien character of the bat, according to Mounce, is one which evokes awe and reverence towards such creatures.

I find Mounce's discussion of this example baffling. Why does he say that we can never understand what it is like to be a bat? At first, his reason seems to be that our knowledge about bats is impersonal. A bat is a living creature; 'it is not like a leaf blown in the wind or a pebble bouncing on a fountain' (p. 164). It is true that we can have a pretty impersonal, biological account of the bat. An anatomy lesson could be presented in this way – full of facts, dissections and diagrams, but not capturing the life of the bat. A student who had come to the subject because of his fascination with bats might express disappointment with how impersonal it all is. But, as we know, that complaint can be met. There are imaginative studies of bats, studies which absorb and satisfy the fascination of the bat lover. But what might be learned through such study is not what Mounce means by knowing what it is like to be a bat.

Mounce argues: 'Thus unless we happen to be specialists in bat behaviour, there will be much about the bat we would fail to understand. But also there will be much that passes beyond our understanding. Moreover, with regard to what passes beyond our understanding, the specialist is no better off than we are: the only difference is that he is more likely to be aware of the fact' (pp. 166–7). So, for Mounce, no amount of attention to bats can change the situation. Why should this be so? There are two answers which may be given to this question, both of which are confused.

First, it appears that for Mounce, to understand what it is like to be a bat one would have to be a bat. The suggestion may be that in addition to, or maybe accompanying, everything a bat does there is a special awareness describable as 'the experience or awareness of what it is to be a bat'. If so, Mounce is employing a notion of 'experience' or 'awareness' which does not get its sense from any position it occupies in the behaviour of the bat – a 'pure phenomenon' in fact. He would then be saying that we cannot find the language to fit the phenomenon. But this is a view Mounce thought he had disowned at the outset of his paper.

Although I do not think Mounce is free from the above confusion, a second suggestion is one more likely to appeal to him in this context. Presumably, if Mounce thinks that in order to know what it is to be a bat one would have to be a bat, he must also think that in order to know what it is to be a human being, one must be a human being. Well, what *is* it like to be a human being?

In answering this question, Mounce need not commit himself to saying that 'being human' is a simple experience or process which can be identified, or which accompanies everything human beings do. Rather, he might argue that 'being a human being', like sight, is not a single process. One can only understand what sight is by grasping the innumerable ways it enters into human life. But 'being a human being' cannot be compared with sight. 'Seeing' is an activity I engage in in the innumerable ways referred to. But 'being a human being' is not an activity, and neither is 'being a bat'. I have not the slightest idea of what it is to be a human being, not because I cannot identify 'the experience' in question, or because I confusedly look for one when I should be noticing the innumerable ways in which 'being a human being' enters human life, but because the whole notion of 'knowing what it is like to be a human being' is a confused one. Mounce makes a distinction between *much* that we simply fail to understand about the bat, and *much* that passes beyond our understanding. This distinction seems to refer to *specific* aspects of the bat's life. But what aspects are these? We react to bats in various ways. We see bats get hungry. If a fire breaks out in a belfry, the bats are startled and agitated. They will burn and feel pain if the flames get to them. Characteristic reactions, ours as well as the bats', give us confidence in such talk. But being startled, agitated, burned and pained are not ways of being a bat, any more than they are ways of being a human being, although, of course, bats and human beings have these experiences.

The notion of 'being an x' is important to Mounce, since he wants to equate it with an exactitude of understanding which those outside this mode of being cannot attain; it passes beyond their understanding. 'For example', Mounce argues, 'the rich do not know what it is like to be on the dole. But then one can imagine how they might find out. Very occasionally, one of them has' (p. 164). Mounce holds that to understand what it is to be poor, you have to be poor. This thesis turns out to be either a tautology, or false.

First, let us consider the context in which Mounce's thesis is false. On his view, it should be a contradiction to say that a poor person does not understand poverty, or that a rich man does. But consider the following case. It is well known that reactions to poverty vary enormously. Poverty can create self-centredness. A person may become absorbed by his own plight and become immune to the plight of others, even when they are poorer than he is. He may be prepared to take advantage of them in any way he can to improve his own miserable lot. Contrast such a man with a rich person who hears that a former employee of his has fallen on hard times. He seeks him out, gives him money, helps him to find another job, etc. In this context many would say that the rich man possessed more understanding of poverty than the poor man.

Mounce would respond to this by saying that no matter how much understanding of the poor the rich have, they do not know *exactly* what it is like to be poor. What standard of exactitude does Mounce have in mind? It is one, apparently, which is conferred automatically by the state of poverty. What does saying this amount to? Imagine a rich man, who, in a moment of romantic indulgence, gives away his fortune to 'identify' himself with the poor. The results, one would have to allow, could be disastrous. He might live the rest of his life absorbed in his condition in the most self-destructive way. 'Well', someone might say, 'at least he knows now what it's like to be poor.' This is a perfectly natural use of the expression. 'You don't know what it's like to be poor', in this context does amount to saying, 'You've never been poor'. But 'being poor' would be consistent with a whole range of different reactions to poverty. What poverty means would vary enormously from person to person. So Mounce's notion of exactitude, in this context, turns out to be a tautology. Knowing what it is like to be poor is having to live with poverty. Since the rich do not have to live with poverty, they do not know what it is like to be poor.

This does not mean that there is nothing additional attained by those who, with a compassionate understanding of poverty, give up their riches to become poor. On the contrary, the understanding they possessed is now applied in the context of living a life of poverty. But the state of poverty, as such, does not confer this understanding. Indeed, one could say, with some confidence, that many poor people would not dream of giving up riches to become poor. They may well spend a good deal of time dreaming of acquiring such riches.

The time has come to ask why Mounce is interested in these very diverse examples: the aroma of coffee, alien societies, the condition of a dog, what it is like to be a bat, and what it is like to be poor. They are all meant to illustrate the difference between that which we fail to understand and that which passes beyond human understanding. Mounce's longest discussion of the distinction is in terms of a religious example for which the others have been meant to be a preparation. As we have seen, Mounce's examples do not always show what he thinks they do. We shall see that the same is true of his treatment of mysticism.

The example Mounce considers is that of the remarkable experiences of St John of the Cross. Mounce tells us that the greater part of his waking life was spent in prayer. 'Sometimes there was urgent business which required that he be disturbed: on those occasions, he would beat his head against a wall in order to regain ordinary consciousness' (p. 166). He wrote about his experiences and spiritual exercises. In his instructions for young Carmelites, 'He assumes that they have reached a certain level of religious dedication' (p. 168). He urged them to practise a radical dying to the self. But for him even such detachment was but a stage on the path to the dark night of the spirit. Mounce says, 'This is a condition of the most intense suffering . . . occasioned, at least in part, by one's being so close to deliverance, to union with God' (p. 169). Such suffering may seem paradoxical to some. How can a saintly soul, nearer to God than the vast majority of mankind, feel intense pain at the thought of separation from God? Surely, it might be thought, it is those who are far away from God who should experience the suffering. But the paradox is only apparent. In a helpful analogy, Mounce reminds us that 'a short delay very near home is less bearable than a long one further away' (p. 169). We might also remind ourselves that the intensity of pain at hurting a loved one increases, not diminishes, in proportion to the quality of the love.

This, then, is the case Mounce considers. He asks whether we understand it, and his reply is that we do not. But we do not simply fail to understand the mystical experiences and contemplative practices of St John of the Cross. Rather, they pass beyond our understanding. The moves in his argument have become familiar in his treatment of the other examples. Some of the moves are unobjectionable. Mounce rightly wants to resist the view that there is some one thing called 'reason' which yields criteria by which the tenability of mysticism can be assessed. So anyone trying to understand mysticism while ignoring its distinctiveness would not simply fail to understand it. It would pass beyond his understanding. This has happened, according to Mounce, in the case of Anthony Kenny,[9] who treats St John's writings as though they were philosophical essays. Kenny assumes that mystical experience is vacuous unless it can be explained in terms available to everyone. But this ignores what is distinctive in the language of the mystic.

Yet, as in the other examples, Mounce goes on to make a further claim which I find problematic. Given that for a certain person mystical experience passes beyond his understanding, there is no way, Mounce claims, even in principle, by which this situation can be remedied. Again, at one level, this becomes an unilluminating tautology: If a person in state S cannot understand M, and that person remains in state S, M will always pass beyond his understanding. But must every person remain in state S? Obviously not, since mystics were not born mystics. So in the case of some people, they came to experience something which, at one time, was beyond their understanding. In their writings they tell us how this came about. Mounce would reply by saying that what they came to experience came about as a transformation, not an extension of their prior understanding. He then makes the claim that it is only through such a transformation that mystical experience can be understood. In short, to understand a mystic is to be a mystic. As far as the rest of us are concerned, the mystic's words are 'like reports from an unknown country' (p. 168). The reports are given by 'not even a person whom we fail to understand but one who passes beyond our understanding' (p. 166). Can this view be maintained?

Can one come to understand the language of the mystic without becoming a mystic? After all, the language of the mystics is in our midst. We can read them for ourselves. This does not impress Mounce. For him, we are related to St John's reports as the blind are related to the sighted. Mounce asks, 'But in what sense do the blind have any concept at all of colour? Presumably only in the sense that they are aware of it as something that enters into the lives of the sighted' (p. 171). The saint's words from unknown realms have significance for us as something that has purchase in those realms, realms from which we are excluded.

This analogy is misleading in many ways. In *Zettel* (para. 267), Wittgenstein asks how one knows that a blind man cannot imagine colours. He replies: ' . . . he cannot play a certain language game (cannot learn it). But is this empirical or is it the case *eo ipso*? The latter.' One can see why the analogy of blindness is applied to aspect-blindness in human life. When a person comes to embrace a radically new perspective on his life, he may say that whereas he was blind, now he sees. He has not simply acquired new facts, corrected a mistake or modified an opinion within a mode of understanding he already possesses. Rather, his life is transformed in certain fundamental respects. He comes to a new mode of understanding for the first time. What was afar off has been brought near. The trouble is that Mounce overstates his case by dwelling on this one example. But that which was afar off can be brought near in more ways than one. When I cease to be blind to some aspect of human life, it does not follow that I must embrace it. As we have seen, Mounce gives no account of understanding radically different aspects of human life. I may respect some which I do not embrace, or I may positively oppose them. Yet these different aspects cannot be cashed into a common terminology. The possibility of these different reactions is an embarrassment for the view which tempts Mounce, namely, that one has to embrace a perspective in order to understand it.

The language of mutual exclusion is essential for Mounce's all-or-nothing style of argument. He has such exclusion in mind when he distinguishes between ordinary language and the extraordinary experiences of the mystic. Mounce refers to St John's commentary on one of his poems '*En una noche oscura*' (On a dark night). On one level the poem is an account of an erotic encounter, but, on another, it is an account of an encounter with God. Mounce says, 'St John is attempting to express in the language of common experience something that falls outside that experience' (p. 167). St John is certainly using analogies with the ordinary to convey what is not ordinary, but he does not do so in the language of common experience. This is because the language itself is extended and even transformed in his hands. The use of sexual imagery in religion is, of course, well known. If the language were not extended, however, the vulgar account of religion as sexual sublimation would be correct. Mounce himself says, 'The levels are not arbitrarily connected, but inter-fused' (p. 167), but he does not build on this insight. Sublimated sexuality is not sexual sublimation. Because Mounce emphasises discontinuities to the exclusion of continuities, he misrepresents possible relations to mysticism in two contexts, the relation between unbelievers and mysticism, and the relation between believers and mysticism.

Mounce says, 'It is clear that St John's accomplishments were not extensions of ordinary abilities; in many respects they ran *counter* to ordinary human nature; they worked against its grain' (p. 167). He has in mind what St John has to say about detachment. Mounce says, 'I believe I have some inkling of what this means, not because I am acquainted in any detail with the state itself but because I am famil-iar with its opposite, namely, attachment. To be attached is to feel one *must* have certain things, whether it be a visit to the theatre or another glass of beer. Without them, life would darken and one would be a misery to oneself and to others' (p. 168). As for detach-ment, Mounce does not think it 'prevents one quite literally from taking pleasure in things . . . The point rather is that one does not need them. A pleasure which comes may be accepted as a gift; but if it does not come, one is just as happy. Perhaps it would be tedious to emphasise that this is a condition unknown, except in fleeting mo-ments, to almost all human beings' (p. 168).

I find Mounce's account of detachment rather bleak. It almost merges into indifference and its practitioner would certainly be a cold fish. But pointing this out is not my main purpose now. Rather, I want to note possibilities of detachment of a kind among non-believers. Someone may learn to exercise detachment with respect to some of his most fundamental desires, for example, to achieve a certain excellence in music, or to have his love for a person recipro-cated. He comes to terms with the fact that he is never going to achieve that excellence, or to receive that love. I do not mean that he simply becomes resigned to the fact. He learns from what cannot be, perhaps by coming to speak of excellence and love as gifts, which may be withheld and cannot be taken by storm. But it would be odd to describe such a person as being just as happy whether this excellence or love is given to him or not. This would be a distortion of his detachment.

Of course, I am not saying that such a person is a mystic. But I suspect that someone incapable of such detachment would not progress very far on the contemplative path. Further, someone capable of it may see sense in the mystic's talk of becoming nothing so that God may be everything, although he is not a believer. That is why some believers find themselves closer in spirit to some unbelievers than to some of their fellow believers. It was a recognition of such continuities that led St Thomas Aquinas, partly, to speak of grace as the perfection of nature. It is certainly odd to say, as Mounce does, that we simply have an inkling of what detachment is from our acquaintance with its opposite. Absorption in attachment blinds one to the possibility of detachment.

But Mounce is talking, primarily, about the relation between believers and mystics. Here, his thesis is even more difficult to sustain. The blind, in Mounce's analogy, are not unbelievers, but believers. For example, whereas most believers find it difficult to pray for five minutes, St John could pray for hours, feeling more at home in prayer than in the conduct of everyday affairs. But, again, Mounce overstates his case. Mounce himself says that St John is trying to express something which 'can be fully understood only by those who have been specially prepared to receive it' (p. 167). But what does 'specially prepared' refer to? Surely to spiritual training of the kind St John wanted young Carmelites to undergo. This is a matter of building on, extending, ordinary religious practices. This is not to deny that a qualitative transformation takes place in mystical experience, but the transformation is not unconnected with what precedes it. In fact, those connections are not optional. One of the familiar misconceptions spiritual teachers have to combat is the conviction in the immature, that mystical experiences can be attained by some kind of unmediated initiation; in short, a magical view of mysticism.

Now Mounce does not want to say that mystical experiences are inherently inexpressible. If he did, he would be in the grip of the confusion he talked of at the outset of his paper. I do not think Mounce is altogether clear of this confusion at all times, but at this point his claim is simply that the language of the mystic means little to the ordinary believer. The language would mean something to a fellow mystic like Teresa of Avila. This is because the language enters her life in a way it does not enter the lives of ordinary believers. According to Mounce, when St John is faced with those who are not mystics, 'There is little he can say to those who have not gone through it, however intelligent they may be' (pp. 172–3). Little he can say! St John wrote voluminously about mystical experience. He was not writing simply for fellow mystics. Yet, according to Mounce's thesis, his language should pass beyond the understanding of all but them.

Mounce ignores the diverse ways in which the language of the mystics *does* enter the lives of believers. Let us simply note a few of them. Mounce does not comment on the striking similarity of the language of the mystics, or the fact that it comes to us within a wider religious tradition. Yet, without such a context, the language would be quite meaningless. The claims made in the name of mysticism are not self-authenticating. In this context it is necessary, as St Paul said, to test the spirits to see whether they are of God. Young Carmelites found food for their souls in St John's writings. Contemplating them helped them to develop spiritually. How is this possible on Mounce's view? Further, believers who are not on the contemplative path may also be informed by the writings of the mystics. The language of the mystics, like great love poetry, has had an enormous influence on ordinary belief. Ordinary love is different from what it might have been otherwise due to the existence of that poetry. That does not mean that those who are influenced need have loved as the particular poets have loved, or that they have read the poetry. Mounce reminds us that St John wrote great poetry, but he makes little of the fact. But ordinary faith is different from what it might have been otherwise because of this poetry and the language of the mystics. This does not mean that those influenced need have had mystical experiences, or even read the work of the mystics. But ordinary believers who do read the works may wonder at them. On Mounce's view, how do I appreciate the wonderful? Unless I do appreciate it, how am I able to be struck by the little I achieve by comparison? Christians are called on to be crucified by Christ. On Mounce's view, either they do not know what they are called to, or, if they do understand it, they must have already achieved it. Neither alternative, I suspect, would be accepted by the majority of those who call themselves Christians.

Of course, to respond to St John's mystical experience in the ways I have mentioned is not to have had that experience. The responders have not worked their way through to the experience as St John has done. Some may be on the road to it, but, as Mounce says, the vast majority are not. What they have is the life and language of the mystics. It is something which arrests their attention and evokes wonder. They are shown possibilities in man's relationship to God, possibilities they will not attain.

As we have seen, most of Mounce's examples show that some experiences people have pass beyond the understanding of some other people. He has let the reader extrapolate for himself the possibility of something which necessarily passes beyond the understanding of all human beings. In the case of the bat, he attempted to give an example which falls into this category. But, for Mounce, the obvious example would be the divine itself, for is not God said to be beyond human understanding? How then could even a mystic tell of him? Mounce makes this stronger claim at the end of his paper. Having compared coming to have a mystical experience with the blind coming to see, Mounce says that this is why 'no very lucid description can be given to the person of what will happen to him before it occurs' (p. 172). But, then, Mounce says, 'But, what is more important, a person thus transformed can give no very lucid account of his condition, even *after* it has occurred' (p. 172). What does this claim amount to? I do not think Mounce is clear about what he wants to say with respect to it.

First he seems to say that the mystic can give no lucid account of his experience, because it is a phenomenon which falls under no definite description. But Mounce does not want to say that mystical experience is inherently inexpressible, otherwise St John would have no intelligible view of what is happening to him, and would not be able to talk about it to fellow mystics. Is the language of that conversation, then, different from the language of the mystics we have? There is no reason to think so. But if *that* language lacks lucidity, we do seem to think of the mystical experience as inherently inexpressible. The trouble is in the conception of the mystic's language as a flawed report. It is no such thing. It is an expression of what mystical experience is.

Second, Mounce gives a different reason for saying that the mystic can give no lucid account of his experience. He says it is because mysticism, like love, cannot be captured in a set of definite descriptions. Mounce says, 'One can mention any number of things . . . But any one feature is no more essential than any number of others, and, in different cases of love, may not even occur' (p. 172). All that follows from this is that it is foolish to expect a certain *kind* of account of love or mysticism, one that consists of a set of definite descriptions. But that is not what we have in the language of the mystics. What they give are not reports or descriptions which fall short of the mark, but expressions of their encounter with God.

But what kind of encounter is this? If it is an encounter with God, it must be an experience of something which passed beyond all human understanding. This thought is at work, it seems to me, when Mounce says that what St John experienced is something which falls under no definite description, something of which no lucid account can be given. The way the language of the mystic enters human life would then be in the form of a confession that he has encountered something he does not understand, something no human being understands. This is not to say that the divine is inherently inexpressible, since, given certain conditions after death, it will be made plain. Within human life, however, the divine enters as something which passes beyond human understanding.

These attempts at coming to grips with the religious sense of that which passes beyond human understanding, it is evident, have us going in circles. This is because the religious sense has been misunderstood. For Mounce 'understanding' is paramount. Where God is concerned he thinks there is something to understand, but it is something which passes beyond our understanding while we are on earth. Religious reactions, it seems to me, are very different. When they speak of that which passes beyond understanding, they invite us to consider the possibility of reacting to human life in a way other than by the understanding.

There are moments in Mounce's paper where he might have moved towards an appreciation of such reactions, but the priority he gives to the understanding gets in the way. For example, he says: 'There are some things I have come to understand, such as a second language, because I wanted to do so, knew how to acquire the understanding and made the necessary effort. But there are others I have come to understand, such as my first language, not as the product of my own effort, but because they have been given to me in the manner of a gift' (p. 165). Mounce does not develop the example, and even in terms of it, it is coming to *understand* which remains central. But there are other possible responses to the gift of language. To appreciate them we must come to the limit, and not simply to the limitations of the understanding. The limit I refer to is a grammatical limit, and the responses I have in mind lie on the other side of it. Wonder and gratitude would be two examples.

Speaking of the agreements in reactions shown in our language I said, elsewhere, that

> the agreement that we show in our ways of acting is a brute fact. *That* we do agree in the way we do is given. That this is so may well be the object of wonder: wonder at the agreement which makes possible our talk of colours; wonder at our agreement in our reactions to sounds without which what we call music would be impossible; and so on and so on. I do not say that any of this need be the cause of wonder, only that it *may* be . . . If this wonder takes a religious form it is not difficult to see how these gifts of nature can be seen as gifts of grace – a grace of nature, one might say. But, someone might object, aren't religious possibilities *given* too; doesn't it follow from what has been said that the existence of religious modes of thought too is not guaranteed by any kind of necessity? That is correct. But, then, why should we assume that there is any necessity in our coming to God? Is not that possibility, too, a gift of grace?[10]

The contemplative path cannot by-pass ordinary things and there are spiritual exercises. But this does not turn mystical experiences into the predictable product of method. If and when mystical experiences come, they, too, are accepted by the mystic as a gift of grace.

That which is given to us in ordinary things will seem, to a religious believer, to pass all understanding, just as the peace of God does. But it is hard to hold on to this reaction in the press of everyday affairs. Yet, it is this reaction, above all, which is developed in mysticism. This is missed entirely if we characterise religion as discontent with the ordinary; a discontent which sets off a search for the extraordinary, a 'something' behind it all which passes beyond all human understanding. This indulgence misses the mystery in ordinary things which is developed and extended in mysticism.

In Mounce's hands, to say that God passes beyond human understanding is to report a failure in religious language. He tends to speak of the language of the mystic in the same way. As we have seen, he talks of it as an attempt to capture, within the ordinary, that which is not ordinary. He chides Kenny for talking of the life of the saint as 'mere effects' which do not warrant any inference as to their cause, but he is tempted to speak in the same way. For example, when Mounce considers the claim that St John might have been deluded, he replies, 'But the effect of such an absorption seems not to have been harmful. St John was remarkable not simply for his virtue but also for his shrewdness and good sense . . . If we had known nothing about his life, we should still remember him for his poetry, which is amongst the greatest in Spanish literature. I do not know whether he had an artistic training, but he left a drawing of Christ on the cross, which is of remarkable power' (p. 166). If, as Mounce has argued, language gets its sense from the way it enters human life, then the language of walking with God, meeting God, gets its sense, if it does anywhere, from the way this language entered the life of St John of the Cross. But that is not the conclusion Mounce comes to. Instead he says: 'Evidently we have some reason to suppose that he was not deluded at all. Naturally, we have no proof: all things are possible and St John may be a unique case of compartmentalised delusion or of delusion uniquely compartmentalised' (p. 166). What notion of 'proof' is Mounce operating with here? Further, if language gets its sense from the way it enters human life, then one cannot say, as Mounce does, that 'all things are possible' with respect to what we can say of that sense. It isn't always possible to make accusations of delusion. What *is* true, as Mounce at other times agrees, is that the sense the language of the mystic has, is not open to any person. In some cases, it may pass beyond a person's understanding. But, then, that would not lead us to expect to hear Mounce saying, 'Surely there is enough here to convince any reasonable person that something remarkable is going on' (p. 172), a remark which seems to run counter to the main thrust of his paper.

In that remark, however, the language of the mystic is no more than a hint to the reasonable man that something remarkable is going on. It can hardly be more to an ordinary religious believer, on Mounce's view, since what is going on passes beyond his understanding. For Mounce, since the mystic is trying to report his experiences to those who have not had them, his language is a necessary failure in that respect. But this is Mounce's basic confusion. The language of mysticism for us, is not a flawed report. If the human body is the best picture of the human soul, the language of mysticism is the best expression of mystical experience. The philosopher endeavours to become clear about this language. No doubt he will have to get rid of many prejudices to achieve the clarity he seeks, and he may fail to do so. But the language which puzzles him is open to view. Few may understand it. Certainly, fewer use it in the first person. But the language, like all other language, is in our midst.

Notes

1. H. O. Mounce, 'The Aroma of Coffee', *Philosophy*, vol. 64, no. 248, pp. 159–73.
2. D. Z. Phillips, *Faith After Foundationalism* (London: Routledge, 1988) p. 242.
3. Ibid., p. 329. For a development of the distinction between 'misunderstanding' and 'language not getting off the ground' with someone, see Rush Rhees, 'Wittgenstein on Language and Ritual', in *Wittgenstein and his Times*, Brian McGuinness (ed.) (Oxford: Basil Blackwell, 1982). See also the concluding sections of Essays 6 and 7.
4. D. Z. Phillips and H. O. Mounce, *Moral Practices* (London and New York: Routledge & Kegan Paul and Schocken Books, 1969).
5. Paul Holmer, *The Grammar of Faith* (New York: Harper and Row, 1978) p. 194.
6. This was pointed out to me by R. W. Beardsmore.
7. Ludwig Wittgenstein, *Remarks on the Philosophy of Psychology* (Oxford: Basil Blackwell, 1980), vol. II, paras. 684–5.
8. Ludwig Wittgenstein, *Last Writings on the Philosophy of Psychology* (Oxford: Basil Blackwell, 1982), vol. I, para. 267.
9. Anthony Kenny, *Reason and Religion* (Oxford: Blackwell, 1987).
10. See *Faith After Foundationalism* (London: Routledge, 1988) pt I, ch. 9, p. 127.

10

On Not Understanding God

Theodicies are an extreme example of the philosophical reluctance to accept that there may be something beyond human understanding; not something accidentally or temporarily beyond it, but something necessarily beyond human understanding. Secular explanations, offered as alternatives to theodicies, exemplify the same reluctance. That something could be necessarily beyond human understanding seems to be an intolerable thought, the denial of a philosophical vocation. Surely, it is said, the philosopher must seek to understand anything. But, then, might not a philosopher come to understand that there is something beyond human understanding? My aim in this essay is to show that the great divide in contemporary philosophy of religion, is not between those who offer religious explanations, and those who offer non-religious explanations, of the limits of human existence, but between those who recognise and those who do not recognise, that the limits of human existence are beyond human understanding.

I

Theodicies testify to the philosopher's confidence that not even God is beyond human understanding. His ways, it is thought, can be explained and justified to men, and theodicies are attempts at doing so. The natural desire for these explanations and justifications arises because of the various evils which are so evident in human existence. On the theodicist's view, such evils must be shown to be a means to a higher good in the economy of the divine plan. But the plan must be one that we understand, otherwise, on this view, how can its existence silence our questions?

It is gratifying to find, in theology at least, contemporary attitudes to theodicies beginning to change. For far too long theodicists have appealed to orthodoxy and tradition, taking it for granted that they are the philosophical reflections of the primary language of faith,

making explicit the theoretical underpinnings the faith is thought
to depend on. Philosophical analyses which have disputed this,
have been represented as marginal exceptions, deviations from the
norm. But the only norm which has been deviated from is the practice of theodicists. Of this practice, Kenneth Surin notes: 'It is certainly no exaggeration to say that virtually every contemporary
discussion of the theodicy-question is premised, implicitly or explicitly, on an understanding of God overwhelmingly constrained by
the principles of *seventeenth and eighteenth century* philosophical theism'.[1] This theism has three characteristics to which Surin draws our
attention. First, God is conceived of in deistic fashion, externally
related to the world. The problem of evil thus becomes one of re-
conciling the evils in the world with this abstract notion of God.
Second, evil, like God, is treated as an abstraction, and the problem
of evil is treated as an intellectual one. Unsurprisingly, these speculations are easily embarrassed when confronted by examples of real
evils and afflictions. Third, the ways of God are discussed by analogy with the ways of men. Theism systematically neglects the grammar of religious concepts in their natural contexts. As a result, the
God of philosophical theism has been rightly called the God of the
philosophers.

It is the third characteristic of contemporary theodicies which is of
special concern to me, the relocating of God in man's image. God is
regarded as an agent whose activities, like that of any other agent,
are capable of being understood, assessed and judged. This assumption is shared by advocates and many opponents of theodicies. The
advocates think that religious belief can only be justified by some
form of philosophical theism. The opponents agree, except that they
do not think the justifications work. On the contrary, they argue,
they reveal the true nature of religious belief as a monstrous creation. Religion falls with its attempted metaphysical defence. So advocates, along with these opponents of theodicies, insist that God
must be understood by man. Neither camp seriously considers the
possibility that what we need is to put theodicies aside, and thereby
come to see the sense in which God is said to be beyond human
understanding.

Few would deny that the Biblical paradigm for the questions
theodicies are designed to answer is found in the Book of Job. In Job,
as Herman Tennessen has rightly said, we meet 'a man with profoundly personal knowledge of pain, of violent passions and with a
lucid power of reason . . . a man with a fanatic will to intellectual

honesty and a poet'.[2] Urged on by those who seek to comfort him in his affliction, Job tries to reason with God. Almost from the outset, however, he realises the difficulties this involves: 'For he is not a man as I am, that I should answer him, and we should come together in judgement' (9 : 32). How different that response is from that of those who debate over latter-day theodicies, who seem to be arguing over the kind of end-of-term report which should be given to the deity. Those who want to construct theodicies look on the world and ask briskly: 'Isn't this what you would expect from a being of high moral excellence?'. After a few detours to explain away apparent blemishes in the workmanship, they conclude, with breathtaking confidence, that it is. The workman is conceived by analogy with human workmanship. The motto of such an enterprise seems to be that of Hume's Cleanthes: 'the liker the better'. One feature of such theodicies is the absence of any grammatical exploration of our use of the word 'God'. As a result, there is not the slightest indication in such quarters that their efforts at theodicising might be greeted with the words of God's response at the end of the Book of Job: 'Who is this that darkeneth counsel by words without knowledge?' (38 : 2). Job is silent when asked: 'Where wast thou when I laid the foundations of the earth? declare, if thou hast understanding' (38 : 4). Not so our present-day theodicists. In effect, their books and articles reply: 'It is true that we were not there, but we know exactly what it must have been like!'. I confess to finding this one of the most comic spectacles in contemporary philosophy.

To call the spectacle comic is not, of course, to deny its terribleness. It amounts to no less than a denial of humanity and a denial of divinity. At its best, it portrays God as acting as a less than averagely decent father. At its worst, given the extent of the divine experiment with human suffering, it portrays a monster. The essential argument against theodicies is this: If we judge man and God by common standards of justice, we are brought to the following choice: either we justify God and abandon common decencies, or we observe common decencies and condemn God. Alternatively, if we judge man and God by different standards, and pass different sentences on them, God still does not escape human judgement. In such a procedure, man remains subject to the demands of common decency. God, however, falling outside these parameters, becomes unworthy of worship, a crude joke, a creature beyond the reach of spiritual sensibilities. In either event, there is no escape from human standards. What other standards do we have by which to understand

God? Tennessen gives insistent expression to this conceptual challenge:

> And neither shall we tolerate that swindle which the believers are guilty of when they call an act 'a most shameful crime', 'a most irreparable infamy', as long as it is done by a man, but an 'act of inscrutable love' if God is its author. Either one or the other: the same law and the same sentence for both, or separate laws and different sentences, but not the same law and different sentences. If we are to accept the direction of the universe as something just, claims Job . . . then this must mean: just by human standards. Otherwise God may be as 'just' as he pleases, in his own language. (p. 5)

It is extremely difficult to get theodicists to appreciate the radical character of this conceptual challenge. The first aspect of the challenge is that if God is weighed in the scales of human justice, by analogy with a human agent, he is found wanting. In his essay on the Book of Job, Herman Tennessen explores the consequences of this verdict:

> The human demand for order and reason is leaping towards the heavens like a flame; Job is hammering away at the ear of his God, hoping to strike a cord of human fibre. If you are inquiring about my sins and misdeeds, there exists comprehensible contact on at least one single point, then a common principle must sustain your evaluations as well as mine. Then there must be something commensurable in our apprehensions and judgements; and this similarity must also include my sense of justice, a sense you have created along with all other things. (p. 5)

Within the context of this commensurability of judgement, I summarised the conclusions of one contemporary theodicist, Richard Swinburne, with respect to it:

> There are good reasons for saying that the various ills in the world are compatible with the existence of an omnipotent, omniscient, all-good God. Such evils as we bring on others give us the opportunity of feeling or being responsible, and that is a good thing. After all, such evils are not unlimited, since there is a limit to what anyone can stand. Evils give us the opportunity to be seen at our

best in reacting to them. God does not intervene to prevent evil when any decent man would, because he has a wider knowledge of the situations in which evils occur. In order to prompt us in the right direction without imposing characters on us, God has seen to it that physical and mental evils are linked to things going wrong. According to Swinburne, this is how we *must* think if we are to answer the problem of evil.[3]

The trouble, obvious to critics like Tennessen and myself, is with *the character* of Swinburne's arguments. Summarising my own response to them I said:

> Looking back at the details of his case, Swinburne says that 'a morally sensitive anti-theodicist might well in principle accept some of the above arguments'.[4] This conclusion is a somewhat embarrassing one since it is clear from my comments that one of the strongest criticisms available to the anti-theodicist would be the moral insensitivity of the theodicist's case.[5]

The theodicist finds it difficult to accept that his critics are not disagreeing with him within an agreed form of moral reasoning, but are criticising *the form* of reasoning the theodicist wants to call 'moral'. Similarly, Job cannot make *sense* of his afflictions in terms of the arguments of his would-be comforters. They suggest that his predicament must be due to sins he is unaware of or has forgotten. Alternatively, it is suggested that it is due to the sins of his ancestors, his family or his people. But when Job compares his situation with others, no sense can be made of it in terms of desert, proportion or correlation. It follows that no *sense* can be made of it in terms of justice. Job combines passion with this demand for conceptual and moral clarity. As Tennessen says, 'It is in the interest of elucidation, for the sake of the problem *per se*, that he scrutinises his conduct. He wants to know what they *mean* by sin when they build their entire argument on the premise that the wicked will perish and the righteous will triumph' (p. 3). What *kind* of understanding can be achieved on this basis? Similarly, Swinburne believes a theodicy makes God's ways understandable to us. But what the understanding reveals is the destruction and distortion of moral response to suffering. That suffering becomes a divine experiment meant as a means to a higher good. Swinburne seems to think that my objections could be met, and my fears put to rest, if only I did not jump to hasty conclusions.

After all, how can I know what future benefits might accrue from this suffering? All future benefits must be taken into account, and I cannot possibly know, within my finite span, what all those benefits are going to be, etc. Swinburne did not appreciate that I am objecting to this *whole way of talking* about human suffering. Swinburne spoke as though I am too hasty in my calculation, whereas I am objecting to his *starting* such calculations. I object to the *concept* of calculation in this context, because it excludes *moral* concepts. Yet this very exclusion is presented by Swinburne as a picture of the highest moral rectitude to be an inspiration to man! Such is the result if we judge God by analogy with human agents according to common standards of justice.

What of the second aspect of the conceptual challenge to theodicies which depends on *not* judging God and man by common standards? After all, it may be said, critics, like Tennessen, are looking in God for that which cannot be found there, 'a cord of human fibre', a commensurability between human and divine judgements. They have forgotten Job's early admission, which we have already noted: 'For he is not a man as I am, that I should answer him, and we should come together in judgement' (9 : 32). But this response would not deter Tennessen at all. He is quite prepared to admit that the creature beyond human justice is not a man. But that creature, called God, occupies the place reserved for the monstrous. God is characterised, not by justice, but by sheer power. Tennessen comments:

> We can easily imagine Job's boundless astonishment at this tangible appearance by Jehovah. Here Job has been sitting, attaching the most profound and central importance to the problem, in the belief that he was dealing with an opponent who would convince him at the point of mortal embarrassment as soon as his tongue touched the burning issue – a god of such holiness and purity that even his indictment would release exultation! Only to find himself confronted by a ruler of grotesque primitivity, a cosmic cave dweller, a braggart and a rumble-dumble, almost congenial in his complete ignorance about spiritual refinement. (p. 8)

What does Tennessen make of Job's famous repentance in dust and ashes? To Tennessen,

> Job is now speaking to the Lord in the placative manner one would employ were one to address a mentally deranged person.

He has fought against the Lord on completely erroneous premises
. . . The new thing for Job is not God's quantitative greatness; he
had realised this in advance . . . his discovery lies in God's qualitative smallness . . . By capitulating in this manner he inflicts the
worst conceivable of indignities on the tyrant, Jehovah: that his
opponent is not even worthy of a battle! (pp. 8–9)

Little wonder, given his analysis, that Tennessen cannot read the
Book of Job as anything but a masterpiece of blasphemy, and in the
subsequent fate of this story there is found a painful and mellow
irony: 'Through the interpolations of believers, this book of frenzied
execrations has been included among those rocks of faith on which
men, even men of today, build their metaphysical consolation!'
(p. 2). The result of understanding God within the parameters of
theodicies such as Swinburne's, is God's conceptual fate in the
monstrous.

II

So far, we have discussed problems which arise from thinking that
the ways of God can be understood. But what if the ways of God are
beyond human understanding? What are the characteristic facts of
human existence which might lead someone to say this? Surprisingly enough, we do not have to look beyond Tennessen's article to
find mention of them. After all his criticisms, Tennessen suddenly
asks in the final paragraph of his paper: 'But this god in the Book of
Job, does *he* concern us? Is the whole of it any more than a poetic
game with an alien and out-dated concept of the divine? Do we *know*
this god?' (p. 10) He replies: 'Yes, we know him from the history of
religion; he is the god of the Old Testament, "the Lord of Hosts" or,
as we might put it, the Lord of Armies: the jealous Jehovah' (p. 10).
Yet, for Tennessen, our knowledge is not simply historical, hence he
pursues his questions further:

But does he live only in the history of religion? No, he also lords
it over our own experience, today as many millenniae ago. He
represents a familiar biological and social milieu: the blind forces
of nature, completely indifferent to the human need for order and
meaning and justice . . . the unpredictable visitations by disease
and death, the transitoriness of fame, the treason by friends and

kin. He is the god of machines and power, of despotism and conquest, of pieces of brass and armoured plates. There are other men than Job who counter him with weapons of the spirit. Some of them are being trampled down in heroic martyrdom. Others recognise the limitations of martyrdom, then yield on the surface, but hide the despair in their hearts. (p. 10)

So here, at the end of his paper, we find Tennessen recognising the vicissitudes of human life. He is too much of a humanist and poet himself to gloss over them or attempt to tidy them up. More importantly, Tennessen is admitting that these vicissitudes are beyond human understanding. Up to this point, Tennessen has criticised theodicies because they violate the claims of justice. He had said: 'The human demand for order and reason is leaping towards the heavens like a flame'. But now, it seems, that same flame is leaping towards the limits of human existence itself, limits which are 'completely indifferent to the human need for order and meaning and justice'. *The important conclusion which follows is that whether one is reacting to the vicissitudes of human life religiously or non-religiously, one is reacting to something which is beyond human understanding.*

I said at the outset that the great divide in contemporary philosophy of religion is between those who accept and those who reject this conclusion. It has certainly been rejected by religious and secular apologists alike. When a sense of the limits of human existence has led to bewilderment and the natural cry: 'Why is this happening to us?', 'Why are things like this?', it is essential to note that these questions are asked, not for want of explanations, but *after* explanations have provided all that they can offer. The questions seem to seek for something which explanations cannot give. This is what theodicies and secular attempts at explanation fail to realise.

Theodicies make the mistake of thinking that, faced with the limits of human existence, what is needed is some kind of super-explanation of *them*. When such explanations have been provided they have run into familiar difficulties. If the transcendental divine plan refers to a future state of affairs after death which, continuous in some sense with this life, is supposed to justify its tribulations, it is difficult to see why this future life should not be as puzzling as our present one. If, on the other hand, the future existence is discontinuous with the present one, how can it have anything to say to the bewilderment we may feel faced with life's limits? There are logical difficulties, however, prior to these. They concern the conception of the super-explanations theodicies claim to provide. Having sought explanations for particular states of affairs, we confusedly go on to ask for an explanation of the universe as such. Having asked for the purpose of particular things, we think it makes sense to ask for the purpose of something called 'everything'. The remedy for this confusion, it is said, is to come to see what led us to ask such questions in the first place. We must work through our confusions, and free ourselves from these questions, which are unnecessary obstacles to human understanding. The presence of such confusions in philosophical arguments cannot be denied,[6] but they do not touch the questions which cry out through the Book of Job. These latter questions are *not* the product of conceptual confusion. They are cries in face of the vicissitudes of human existence.

There have been plenty of movements of secular enlightenment which have sought to provide explanatory categories designed to transcend the limits of human existence. As Flannery O'Connor pointed out, 'Since the eighteenth century, the popular spirit of each succeeding age has tended more and more to the view that the ills and mysteries of life will eventually fall before the scientific advances of man'.[7] But, as Rush Rhees notes, 'When we speak of a progressive enlightenment, we take for granted a common measure where we cannot even imagine one. Suppose it were said that science has freed us from subjection to fate. And suppose we asked *how* science has done this. As though men had spoken of fate because they knew no better. As though the reasoned beliefs of science could *replace* any thought of fate.'[8]

Tennessen, however, does not think that the limits of human existence can be explained away by theodicies or systems of secular enlightenment. He sees that they are facts which have to be faced rather than data awaiting further explanation. By these limits, as we have seen, Tennessen means the blind forces of nature, the unpredictable visitations of disease and death, the transitoriness of fame, and treason by friends and kin. He might also have mentioned the limitations of time and place to which we are subject. Flaws and imperfections loom large: 'I thought I had the strength to see that through, but . . .'; 'I thought I could rely on that relationship and then . . .'; 'We had worked hard, the worst seemed to be over, and then look what happened'; 'He had everything to live for, and yet'; etc. There seems to be no rhyme nor reason to these contingencies. They certainly do not reflect a systematic order and meaning born of justice. In reflecting on these limitations of time and place, the thought, 'If only . . .' keeps recurring; 'If only it hadn't happened just then at the time when I was ready to . . . wanted to . . . seemed able to . . .'; 'If only I'd been born twenty years earlier when there was an opportunity to . . .'. Limitations of place are also evident: 'Why was I born into the family just when those problems occurred?'; 'Why are conditions such that my energies are expended simply in avoiding friction?'.

Recognising the limits of human existence, however, need not lead to a sense of the strangeness of human life. Instead, someone may say: 'Strange? No, that's exactly how life is, full of ups and downs'. Others may say: 'Get on with what you can do something about, and come to terms with what cannot be changed'. Reactions such as these are certainly not to be despised. They put aside romantic indulgence in *angst*.

But Tennessen's reaction is different. For him, human life is strange, baffling, bewildering. Theodicies have the immoral audacity to try to impose a false order on life's contingencies. This does not mean, however, that a god cannot be believed in in these circumstances. Of course, this is not the god of theodicies. For Tennessen, *nothing* could be that. The god we can believe in, the god who still lords it over our experience, is a god of blind caprice. Further, for Tennessen, the only decent response to such a god is in terms of what he calls 'weapons of the spirit': heroic martyrdom or hidden despair in the heart. He would agree with Camus, who asks: ' . . . since the order of the world is shaped by death, mightn't it be better for God if we refuse to believe in Him, and struggle with all our might against death, without raising our eyes to the heaven where He sits in silence?'.[9] For Camus and Tennessen, better silence than theodicies. Tennessen never considers whether the contingencies of life he mentions, without being compromised or falsified, could play a part in forming a belief, not in a god of caprice, but in a God of grace.

III

Tennessen does not simply reveal the character of belief in a god of caprice. Implicitly, he also denies that concept-formation could take any other course in religious belief. How does this come about? Job, as we have seen, admits that God cannot be addressed as though he were a man. But Tennessen will not allow any other mode of address. He thinks this is determined by 'the human demand for order and reason', a demand which operates within the imperatives of justice. The appropriateness, or otherwise, of any concept of God, is to be assessed in these terms alone:

> The concept of the deity is not to be derived from 'the given God'. But that God which we can accept must flow from the norms of the deity, with our image of God as an optimum. . . . We also demand that the God shall represent the highest wisdom, shall inspire creation with order and meaning. (p. 7)

Here, 'God' is conceived of as the highest case in a continuum of moral excellences; he is required to be the best of a kind. God must be judged by human standards, otherwise, as we have seen, Tennessen argues: 'God may be as "just" as he pleases, in his own language' (p. 5).

That we have to appeal to our language in order to understand what might be meant by 'the ways of God' is not in dispute. What can be disputed is Tennessen's further claim that *human language only speaks of human standards.* Evidently, that is not so, since *in our language* there *is* talk of the ways of God, ways said to be beyond human understanding. Nothing Tennessen has said shows why the philosopher cannot explore the grammar of this talk. The exploration will not be successful, however, if *prior* to looking at the use of language in question, we come to it with our minds already made up about what it *must* mean. Tennessen comes to that language armed with conceptions of 'the norms of the deity' and an 'image of God as an optimum'. God is located on a human continuum of wisdom and hence is answerable to it. Inevitably, he fails the test of answerability. God fails, however, given Tennessen's preconceptions about what religious language must mean. To free himself from these preconceptions, Tennessen must be prepared to do something he explicitly warns us against, namely, derive the concept of the deity from 'the given God'. What this amounts to, philosophically, is a readiness to explore the grammar of talk about the ways of God *given* in our language, instead of assuming *ab initio* standards by which such talk *must* be assessed.

Were Tennessen ready to do this, he would discover that many who speak of the inscrutable ways of God *agree* with his criticisms of theodicies. Theodicies, and the apologetics of Job's comforters, falsify human realities. But many who insist on distinguishing God's ways from man's ways, also insist that the former should not falsify what we know of the latter. For example, Flannery O'Connor insists that we must not 'reflect God with what amounts to a practical untruth'.[10] She also insists that if someone wants to show how 'the natural world contains the supernatural . . . this doesn't mean that his obligation to portray the natural is less; it means it is greater'.[11] O'Connor is speaking of Catholic novelists, but the same can be said of a philosopher who wants to elucidate concept-formation where belief in the supernatural is concerned:

> if he is going to show the supernatural taking place he has no-where to do it except on the literal level of natural events, and . . . if he doesn't make these natural things believable in themselves, he can't make them believable in any of their spiritual extensions.[12]

In the task of giving perspicuous representations of these spiritual extensions, O'Connor refers to Conrad's conviction that he had to do the highest possible justice to the visible world because it suggested an invisible one,[13] and to Baron von Hugel's insistence that the apologist for religion should not try 'to tidy up reality'.[14] This last remark reminds one of Wittgenstein's insistence to philosophers that 'what's ragged should be left ragged'.[15]

The point of enumerating these remarks is simply to illustrate how perfectly in accord they are with the respect for the human which Tennessen rightly wants to insist on. Once again, his complaint is that theodicies do not make the natural believable, or do justice to the visible world; they do try to tidy up reality and refuse to leave the ragged ragged. While agreeing that the natural and the visible should not be falsified, O'Connor also quotes with approval St Gregory who wrote that 'every time the sacred text describes a fact, it reveals a mystery'.[16] What this means for the philosopher concerned to clarify the place in human life occupied by talk of the inscrutable ways of God, is that he must show the relation between such talk and facts concerning the limits of human existence, ragged facts, which must not be tidied up. No spiritual extension from the facts Tennessen mentions can be believable, unless the believability of the facts themselves is retained.

Among the limits of human existence Tennessen refers to, as we have seen, are 'the blind forces of nature' and 'the transitoriness of fame'. Although Tennessen does not think that enlightened thought can dispense with these conceptions, there are religious extensions of them which he simply does not consider. For example, consider the belief that we are subject to the inscrutable will of the gods. Lucretius thought that invoking the gods to explain natural events and human destinies demeaned them. In turning to natural explanation as an alternative, Lucretius makes reference to the gods, at best, irrelevant. Given the direction of his questions, however, it is clear that the fate of reference to the will of the gods, is to be replaced by natural explanation:

> But if Jupiter and other gods shake the shining regions of heaven with appalling din, if they cast fire whither it may be the pleasure of each one, why do they not see to it that those who have not refrained from some abominable crime, shall be struck and breathe out sulphurous flames from breast pierced through, a sharp lesson to mankind? Why rather does one with no base guilt on his conscience roll in flames all innocent, suddenly involved in a tornado from heaven and taken off by fire? Why again do they aim at deserts and waste their labour? Or are they then practising their hands and strengthening their muscles? And why do they suffer the Father's bolt to be blunted against the earth? Why does he himself allow this, instead of saving it for his enemies? Why again does Jupiter never cast a bolt on the earth and send his thunder when the heaven is clear on all sides? Does he wait until clouds have come up, to descend into them himself, that he may be nearby to direct hence the blow of his bolt?[17]

Horace points out, however, that such questions miss possibilities of meaning given in religious responses to such phenomena. Lucretius asks, sceptically, why Jupiter never thunders from a clear sky. Horace confesses to having thought this way himself, but that he has had to revise his opinion:

> I, a chary and infrequent worshipper of the gods, what time I wandered, the votary of a foolish wisdom, am now compelled to spread my sails for the voyage back, and to retrace the course I had abandoned. For though it is the clouds that Jove is wont to cleave with his flashings bolts, this time he drove his thundering steeds and flying car through a sky serene – his steeds and car, whereby the lifeless earth and wandering streams were shaken
> . . .

What has led Horace to change his mind?

Power the god does have. He can interchange the lowest and the
highest: the mighty he abases and exalts the lowly. From one man
Fortune with shrill whirring of her wings swiftly snatches away
the crown; on another she delights to place it.[18]

Here we have an instance of 'the transitoriness of fate'. In such
circumstances, Horace is suggesting, it makes sense to say that Jupiter thundered from a clear sky.[19] This is always a possibility. Our
lives are in the hands of the gods, and it is hubris to deny this: the
kind of hubris that led Oedipus to deny that he *could* ever be the
cursed among men.[20]

There are religious reactions to the unpredictable visitations by
disease and death, and it is difficult to see how these could be
supplanted by natural explanations. Rhees gives the following
example:

Suppose there has been an earthquake, and geologists now give
an explanation of it. This will not be an answer to the woman who
has lost her home and her child and asks 'Why?'. It does not make
it easier to understand 'what has befallen us'. And the woman's
question, though it may drive her mad, does not seek an answer.
'It was fate' may some day come to take the place of asking. A man
whose son is in danger of death may say: 'The outcome will be
whatever is fated to be.' And he is not predicting anything. Or if
he says: 'Whatever happens will be the will of God' – this cannot
mislead us about what is going to happen.[21]

The question 'Why?' in these circumstances does not seek an
answer. It does seek reactions or responses to replace the question.
Religious responses to the vicissitudes of life are among these. If we
begin with the terrible openness of human life, and *then* ask how the
events which characterise it are compatible with a divine plan, we
have already committed ourselves to a hopeless misunderstanding.
The notion of the divine plan is unmediated. It is introduced as a
philosophical abstraction, rather than as a religious concept. The
contingencies of life which befall an individual, are not seen as part
of a plan which has singled him out for this treatment. On the
contrary, in the religious responses I have in mind, the very notion
of God's will arises from and is internally related to these very
contingencies: things come from God's hands, the God who sends
rain on the just and the unjust. We are not sufficient unto ourselves.

Everything is ours by the grace of God, something we can be re-minded of by both trials and blessings. Nothing is ours by right. When he sees those who are the perpetrators of 'treason by friends and kin' the believer says: 'But for the grace of God, there go I'. And when he is guilty of such treason himself, he knows that grace is the vehicle by which he can come to the knowledge and significance of what he has done. The natural world, and other people, are seen as God's gifts, not to be appropriated through domination by us. To think otherwise is to fail to die to the self, to play at being God. Where the believer speaks of God's gifts, and the need for divine grace, others may speak of luck and the need for charity. Those who speak in these different ways are closer to each other than they are to the authors of theodicies and rational secular systems which seek to explain human existence.

Because Tennessen does not consider the possibility of these spir-itual extensions from the limits of human existence, he misses the irony in the reference to the hippopotamus in the Book of Job. Tennessen takes the reference to be a divine denigration of man: *'Do you know what is my most outstanding work? No, it is not the human spirit with its sickly sense of justice, as you believe, you fool. No, my dear boy, it's the hippopotamus!* (p. 8). The point of the reference is very different. It is meant to be a comic, ironic, denigration of that form of rationalism which emanates in an argument to or from design. If we think we can understand God's creation in this way, bring it within the confines of human explanation, the challenging question is: What about the hippopotamus? What is its rationale in the scheme of things? Job is invited to put aside such questions, and to let wonder take the place of explanation. It is in this spirit that he is asked whether the rain has a father, whether he knows the treasures of the snow, and to reflect on the laying of the foundations of the earth, 'When the morning stars sang together, and all the sons of God shouted for joy' (38 : 7). This wonder at creation is also Job's redemp-tion. It is what enables him to say: 'The Lord gave, and the Lord hath taken away; blessed be the name of the Lord' (1 : 21).

What we have seen is that Tennessen's attack on theodicies is shared by many who speak of the inscrutable ways of God. Theodicies are all too scrutable and we have seen the results of scrutinising them. They refuse to admit, along with certain secular explanatory systems, that there is anything beyond human understanding. Tennessen, on the other hand, is prepared to admit this. He recog-nises that the limits of human existence are not manifestations of order, meaning and justice. He notes that people react to these limits with protest or despair. What he does not recognise is that there are religious reactions, too, to these limits, which do not falsify them. These reactions see all things in God's hands and confess that his ways are beyond understanding.[22] Here, then, are two reactions to that which is beyond human understanding: protest and praise.

It has not been my aim in this paper to give anything approaching a full account of religious reactions to the vicissitudes of life, or of the further difficulties they may occasion.[23] My main concern has been to insist on the philosophical division between those who assert, and those who deny, that there is something necessarily beyond human understanding. Within the group who are prepared to admit this, there are those, as we have seen, who react in anti-religious and religious ways. What is essential to both is *that what they recognise are the limits, not the limitations, of human understanding.* This distinction is essential if we are to appreciate what is meant by 'dying to the understanding' in these contexts.

If we speak of the limitations of understanding, in a secular context, it would make sense to hope that some succeeding generation may transcend these limitations. On this view, there is something to understand. It is simply a contingent matter that it is not understood at any given time. But when there is a secular recognition of *the limits* of human understanding, matters are very different. Here, it is accepted, that although there is something to accept or respond to, *there is nothing to understand; nothing to be put right by understanding.* Beckett has his character Hamm say: ' . . . You're on earth: there's no cure for that!'.[24] Prometheus does not solve, he protests.

If we speak of the *limitations* of human understanding in a religious context, even if theodicies are rejected, we still believe that there is something to understand. This is so, even when people speak of the *necessary* limitations of human understanding. They may say that there is no hope of understanding the ways of God in this life, but that these ways will be clarified after death. Here, there is no dying to the understanding. The explanation of all things is simply postponed. It may be said that human hubris is carried to the heavens. But when believers come to the limits of human understanding, they, too, confess that there is nothing to understand. Understanding is not the appropriate response.

A philosopher tries to understand what is meant by saying that God's ways are beyond human understanding. If he succeeds in doing so, this does not mean that he understands God. What he understands is the place the belief that God's ways are beyond understanding has in the lives of believers. He tries to understand the kind of belief, it is, to clarify its grammar. Of course, if a philosopher thinks that nothing is beyond human understanding, he is hardly likely to succeed.

Notes

1. K. Surin, *Theology and the Problem of Evil* (Blackwell, 1986) p. 4. Surin gives evidence of growing concern on this issue by contemporary theologians. He also shows how misleading it is to read back into the work of Augustine, Irenaeus and Aquinas, the preoccupations of philosophical theism.
2. H. Tennessen, 'A Masterpiece of Existential Blasphemy: the Book of Job', *The Human World*, no. 13, Nov. 1973. All quotations from Tennessen are from this essay.
3. D. Z. Phillips, *Belief, Change and Forms of Life* (Macmillan and Humanities Press, 1986) pp. 70–71. See Chapter Four for details of my criticisms. These are taken from a symposium with Richard Swinburne on 'The Problem of Evil', in *Reason and Religion*, ed. S. Brown (Cornell University Press, 1977). For related criticisms see my *The Concept of Prayer* (1965) (Blackwell, 1981), Chapter Five and *Death and Immortality* (Macmillan, 1970) Chapter Two.
4. R. Swinburne, 'The Problem of Evil', in *Reason and Religion*, p. 100.
5. *Belief, Change and Forms of Life*, p. 71.
6. See D. Z. Phillips, 'From World to God?', in *Faith and Philosophical Enquiry* (Routledge & Kegan Paul, 1970).
7. F. O'Connor, 'Some Aspects of the Grotesque in Southern Fiction', in *Mystery and Manners*, selected and ed. by Sally and Robert Fitzgerald (Farrar, Strauss and Giroux, New York, 1974).
8. R. Rhees, 'Science and Questioning', in *Without Answers* (Routledge & Kegan Paul, 1969) p. 16.
9. A. Camus, *The Plague*, trans. S. Gilbert (Penguin, 1960) pp. 107–8.
10. F. O'Connor, 'Catholic Novelists and Their Readers', in *Mystery and Manners*.
11. Ibid., p. 175.
12. Ibid., p. 176.
13. Ibid., p. 80.
14. O'Connor, 'Catholic Novelists and Their Readers', p. 177.
15. L. Wittgenstein, *Culture and Value*, trans. Peter Winch (Basil Blackwell, Oxford, 1980), p. 45.
16. O'Connor, 'Catholic Novelists and Their Readers', p. 184.
17. Lucretius, *De Rerum Natura*, Bk. vi, trans. W.H.D. Rouse (The Loeb Classical Library, London and Cambridge Mass., 1943) pp. 472–3.

18. Horace, *Odes*, Bk. I, Ode XXXIV, 'The Poet's Conversion', in *The Odes and Epodes*, trans. C. E. Bennett (The Loeb Classical Library, London and New York, 1919) p. 91.
19. I am indebted to David Sims for suggesting the reference to Lucretius and Horace.
20. See D. Z. Phillips, 'What the Complex Did to Oedipus', in *Through A Darkening Glass* (University of Notre Dame Press and Basil Blackwell, 1982).
21. R. Rhees, 'Science and Questioning', pp. 16–17.
22. See D. Z. Phillips, *The Concept of Prayer* (1965) (Blackwell, 1981), Chapter Four: 'Prayer As Talking To Someone One Does Not Understand'.
23. My most recent detailed elucidations of these religious responses can be found in a literary context, in *R. S. Thomas: Poet of the Hidden God* (Macmillan and Pickwick Books 1986); and in an epistemological context in *Faith After Foundationalism* (Routledge, 1988) Part Four: 'Religion and Concept Formation'.
24. S. Beckett, *Endgame* (Faber and Faber, 1976), p. 37.

11

Waiting for the
Vanishing Shed

I want to explore a tendency, found in some people, to think that the possibility of religious belief is related to the possibility of *lusus naturae*, in the philosophers' sense of of that term. That use is not its primary use. Its primary use is found in the following examples by R. F. Holland: 'In the pleasure gardens at Blackpool before the war, you could pay sixpence to see a five-legged calf, a two-headed hen, midgets . . . in cages.' As he says, 'these exhibits are exactly the sort of thing it would be appropriate to cite if one were seeking to explain the meaning of the expression *lusus naturae* (sport of nature) by examples'[4] (p. 45).* Examples of what philosophers have in mind by the term are very different. They include: a lump of phosphorous turning into a little bird or a piece of bread[1]; pencils turning into lizards[19]; exploding goldfish[2] (p. 56); water turning into wine; a horse existing without nourishment[5]; sheds and people simply vanishing[20]; houses gradually turning into steam without any obvious cause; trees gradually changing into men and men into trees, cattle in the fields standing on their heads, laughing and talking[22] (para. 513). (The first three of the above examples were cited by Holland.[4])

The examples of the primary use of *lusus naturae* are of empirical occurrences for which there are explanations. Holland notes that the nineteenth century saw the development of teratology, the study of the abnormal descendants of normal animals. A taxonomy of fetal abnormalities was established and later, pioneering work on embryos 'showed how environmental vicissitudes affect the division of cells and the development of cellular structures'[4] (p. 46). The philosophers' examples, on the other hand, are supposed to be occurrences which are beyond the bounds of explanation (not necessarily to the philosophers whose examples they are, but to those who want

---

* All numbers in the references refer to the numbers of works in the Notes at the end of the chapter.

to use them in the way I am discussing). They could not be studied and given a systematic basis. In the hands of some, they are meant to illustrate a mysterious universe beyond our comprehension.

To a certain kind of religious mentality, the appeal of such examples is obvious: Is there not a supernatural realm beyond the natural one? For the most part, it is said, we know little of it but, now and again, it breaks in on our familiar surroundings, disturbing and disrupting our normal descriptions and expectations. We call these intrusions 'strange,' 'bizarre,' 'occult,' but, it is argued, their credibility must not be denied prematurely. By keeping the door open to such possibilities, at the same time, it is thought, we keep the door open to the stranger realities religion may have in store for us.

But what does accepting the philosophers' examples as real possibilities involve? What would be the implications of such an acceptance for what we normally regard as limits of intelligibility? These issues are explored in Peter Winch's British Academy lecture 'Ceasing to Exist' and in philosophical reactions to it by R. F. Holland, Norman Malcolm and H. O. Mounce. I shall enter the philosophical fray in this context and, like the others, concentrate on the example over which controversy has raged. The example is taken from a short story by Isaac Bashevis Singer. Zalman the glazier tells of the following incident:

> Near Blonia there lived a man, Reb Zelig, the bailiff. He had a store and a shed where he kept kindling wood, flax, potatoes, old ropes. He had a sleigh there too. He got up one morning and the shed was gone. He could not believe his eyes. If during the night there had been a wind, a storm, a flood! But it happened after Pentecost – calm days, quiet nights. At first he thought he had lost his mind. He called his wife, his children. They ran out. 'Where is the shed?' There was no shed. Where it had been, everything was smooth – high grass, no beams, shingles, no sign of a foundation. Nothing. Everyone in the small town of Blonia knew Zelig the bailiff. When they went for a walk they usually passed the shed, and if it was raining they took shelter inside it. As the news passed around the whole town came running. 'People pinched their cheeks to make sure they were not dreaming. They walked around the field and even dug in the earth where the shed had been, but found nothing. Two men drove for miles trying to locate the lost shed. They asked the peasants, but no one had heard or seen anything.' Zalman the glazier sums up the incident in these words: 'A heavy shed built of logs had burst like a bubble.'[16]

It is extremely important to be clear, at the outset, about what exactly Winch is asserting and denying in relation to this story. He understands it as a story, but what if someone asked him to entertain, as an actual possibility, that sheds and people sometimes simply vanish? At first, it may seem that we are being offered a possible description of what has happened to the shed, especially if we are impressed by the compatibility of the two propositions, 'The shed was there on Monday night' and 'The shed was not there on Tuesday morning.' Of course, there are any number of ways in which the disappearance of the shed could be accounted for. None of these are necessary explanations of the shed's ceasing to exist. It does not follow, however, that the shed could disappear without *any* cause of this kind. Further, if we say the shed *simply* disappeared, it is important to note, as Norman Malcolm points out, that we are not using the word 'disappear' as we normally do:

> A ship disappears over the horizon. A squirrel disappears in the tree top, a mouse disappears in its hole: but to say this does not imply that ship, squirrel, or mouse ceased to exist. Sometimes we do use the word 'disappeared' with that implication, as when we say that in two minutes after the ice cream was given to the children it had disappeared, or that the water in the saucer on the window sill disappeared. But here explanations are ready to hand: the ice cream was eaten up, the water evaporated. In Zalman's tale there is no explanation of what happened to the shed. If we speak of its 'disappearance' . . . this will mean no more and no less than its 'ceasing to exist'.[9] (p. 3)

But what does it mean to say that the shed has simply disappeared. In being puzzled as to what these words mean, Winch does not want to deny 'that we may be confronted with circumstances which defeat our attempts to describe them coherently'[20] (p. 95). In such circumstances, we may say that the shed has simply vanished. In *those* circumstances, Winch knows what the use of the words amounts to. The expression 'is something we're driven back on: to say when we despair of finding any other explanation. But I should not say, as I just did, "any *other* explanation," since . . . "It has vanished" is not an explanation at all. It is just an expression of despair at the prospect of finding an explanation.' But 'It has vanished' not only does not function as an explanation; it does not function either as a description of an occurrence awaiting explanation. For example, Winch says, 'People vanish' 'would be a resigned admission that there are

occurrences of a sort for which we cannot hope to find an explanation. But occurrences of *what* sort? Not occurrences of the sort:
people vanish! For to say that would precisely presuppose that we
had fixed a use for this expression other than as an expression of
resignation about the finding of explanations.'[20] (p. 86). These are
Winch's conclusions about the meaning this expression has *for us*.

   This conclusion is important in the light of some of the ways in
which he has been criticised. It has been thought that Winch's arguments are based on a prior philosophical thesis he is supposed to
hold. The thesis is said to concern the status of our practices. It
claims that since the distinction between what is reasonable and
unreasonable is determined *within* practices, we cannot ask whether
practices themselves are reasonable or unreasonable. This becomes a
matter about which philosophers can have differing opinions. They
will discuss the concept of a practice. Further, they will raise the
question whether, given a certain practice, other possibilities *could*
be allowed to overthrow it or co-exist with it. In the present case, the
question will be whether our normal practices involving causal explanations and the empirical certainties we express in the course of
them, *could* allow the possibility of emphasising or describing what
happens to a shed by saying, 'It simply vanished.' Philosophers will
dispute whether or not the concept of a practice rules out such a
possibility. In doing so, they look in entirely the wrong direction and
miss the philosophical issue Winch is posing.

   There are times when H. O. Mounce's criticisms of Winch force
the issue in this wrong direction. He agrees with Winch that 'it is
certainly true that in our normal procedures we do not consider the
possibility of an object's simply vanishing.' He adds: 'Moreover this
is not an oversight. One might say that our not considering such a
possibility is part of the *character* of our normal investigations. In
other words it indicates, at least in part, what *counts* with us as a real
issue, what a serious investigation amounts to'.[10] What if someone
advances the possibility of the shed vanishing in a normal context?
Mounce gives the following example. 'Zalman and I are discussing
the best way to dismantle a shed in my backyard. We take various
considerations into account. Then suddenly he says "On the other
hand, why bother? Perhaps it will simply vanish." I assume he is
joking. But the joke has no point. I suspect he is serious. I feel a slight
shiver. "What makes you say that?" I ask. "Some remarkable experience?" "Oh no" he says, "I just thought we ought to cover all the
possibilities." Now that certainly is weird. In that context, I should

certainly be baffled. By "that context" I mean one that counts as run of the mill or ordinary. What is weird is that he makes such a remark as if it were itself run of the mill or ordinary'.[11] Mounce argues, however, that Winch is making a much stronger claim, namely, that Zalman's proposed explanation of what happened to the shed is unintelligible in itself. All Winch has shown, Mounce argues, is that this explanation is unintelligible relative to our normal practices of investigation. What is unintelligible in one practice may be quite intelligible in another. On this view, Winch is guilty of sliding from a relative to an absolute use of unintelligibility. This leads to an abstract debate on whether a specified use of language *could* rule out the proposition 'The shed has simply vanished' as an explanation in *any* use of language, one which again leads us away from the real philosophical issue.

The issues which seem to arise out of Mounce's objections are non-issues for Winch, as they are for Wittgenstein. The so-called 'absolute' sense of unintelligibility does not mean anything to either of them. Are we to wrack our brains over the question whether people who do contemplate the possibility of vanishing sheds could have the same causal concepts as we have? What we need to concentrate on is the actual differences the possibility they contemplate make in their lives. It is these differences which will show us what the possibility amounts to, if anything. Adapting remarks by Cora Diamond (to whom I am indebted for my criticisms of Mounce at this stage) we can conclude: 'Something that other people do, may, despite certain resemblances, have a very different position in their life and different connections. And if we are able to note that fact and give it its weight, we do not have an . . . *answer* [to our abstract questions] but will be able to stop asking [them]'[3] (p. 19).

It is Mounce, not Winch, who indulges in abstract possibilities. Thinking that Winch is advancing an absolutist thesis about the unintelligibility of saying that the shed has simply vanished, he responds: Winch 'infers . . . that if someone in ordinary life did raise the possibility of an object's simply vanishing, his remarks would be unintelligible. Now that is simply fallacious. All that follows is that we should not be conducting a normal investigation, that an investigation would cease to be normal the moment someone seriously raised such a possibility'[10] (p. 239). Mounce's argument is far too abstract to have any weight. It begs the question as to what is to count as seriously raising a possibility. Is the normality of our circumstances threatened by merely uttering the words, 'Perhaps the shed has vanished'? Mounce cannot want to say that. As we have seen, Mounce has already admitted that he would be as baffled as the rest of us if the possibility were offered as an ordinary, run of the mill explanation. But the words may be offered as some strange sort of suggestion. Those who put forward such suggestions seriously may become long-term patients in our mental hospitals. Their words did not mean that the circumstances in which they were said ceased to be normal as soon as they were uttered. On the contrary, our normality determined the speakers' fate. It is not the claim that the shed has simply vanished, considered in philosophical abstraction, which will determine what kind of claim is being made, or whether these words constitute any kind of claim at all.

It is simply the actual utterance and the position it occupies in people's lives, Winch argues, which should command our attention. He says,

> I have not wanted to say in any absolute sense that purported reports of some physical thing's ceasing to exist can only have a sense when it is presupposed that we could, with sufficient knowledge, give some naturalistic account of what has happened. I have concentrated on the bewilderment that we – that is, you and I – are liable to feel at a claim about the bare cessation of existence of some physical thing where any sort of naturalistic explanation is ruled out. I have done so simply because the expectation of such explanations plays such a dominant role within the mode in which we are brought up to make sense of things. That is the prevailing direction in which the stream of our life goes.[20] (p. 104)

But this is not an absolute thesis about the direction in which the stream of *any* human life *must* go. Winch says, clearly, 'I should not want to deny that people in whose lives thoughts about the Powers of Darkness played a central role could make a sort of sense of accounts of happenings which remained opaque to us. The same goes for miracles'[20] (p. 105).

The mention of miracles brings about an important change of scene. We are not talking, now, of an imaginary people who *might* find employment for such notions as the Powers of Darkness. Rather, we are considering what it means in *our* culture, if someone says that a shed has simply vanished. What does saying this involve and what bearing does it have on our normal methods of investigation? Winch's claim is that, in this context, 'It has simply vanished' neither constitutes an explanation nor a description of what has happened to the shed.

Further philosophical issues are raised when we consider the reactions of Holland, Malcolm and Mounce to this claim. These centre on what has emerged as the crucial issue: the determination of the position occupied in human life and the difference made to it by the uttering of the words 'The shed has simply vanished,' for this determination is the determination of the sense or lack of it the words have. If someone wanted to speak of a miracle in this context, then, to clarify the grammar of such talk, 'Our first task,' as Winch says, 'in trying to understand what a miracle might be would be the imaginative reconstruction of a mode of life in which there could be such untroubled talk'[20] (p. 105). He believes, rightly or wrongly, that in our culture the attempt to talk of miracles is not untroubled. I agree with him. In fact, the tendency I mentioned at the outset of the essay might well be one of the troubles he has in mind. I should like to try to elucidate its character.

What are the surroundings in which the expression, 'The shed has simply vanished' is supposed to have its sense? Malcolm asks us to concentrate on the bewilderment of the Zelig family when they find the shed has gone. They could not possibly deny all their past associations with the shed.

> If all of this shed-related activity could be rejected as delusion, then Reb Zelig might ask himself, 'Who is this woman? Is she my wife? And who am I?' To believe that there had never been a shed would, for the Zeligs, mean the destruction of the sense of their individual and collective lives. To avoid being plunged into chaos, to hold on to the framework within which they think and act, they would have to accept it as a fact that their shed had inexplicably ceased to exist.[9] (pp. 5–6)

Malcolm poses the vital question when he asks, 'What is the logical force of that bewilderment?'[9] (p. 6). He says, 'The intention of Zalman's story is to deprive us of any description of what happened to the shed'[9] (p. 3), but he is mistaken. The comic intention of Zalman's tale is precisely to convince us that, sometimes, people and sheds simply vanish. But Malcolm agrees with Winch that 'To say "It ceased to exist" is not to give a description of *what happened* to it. If someone who was fully aware of what did *not* happen to the shed were to say "It simply ceased to exist," he would be using those words to imply that there is *no* description of what happened to it'[9] (p. 3). But, as Malcolm admits, neither is the concept of a happening secure in this context. He says, 'Now it is true that the Reb Zelig family cannot describe coherently *what happened* to the shed. They cannot, therefore, intelligibly claim to be *certain* that such-and-such *happened* to it. Winch is entirely right on that point'[9] (p. 8). Again, Malcolm says that since 'there is no possible description of what happened to it; one cannot, therefore, rightly speak of *anything* as having happened to it'[9] (p. 11).

Malcolm concludes with an account of what the Zelig family could be certain of: 'I think they could be certain that the shed had been there for a long time, that suddenly it was no longer there, *and* that there was no intelligible explanation of the change from its being there to its not being there.' When he refers to this 'change', however, he is still not describing a change in the shed or to the shed. Simply to say that the shed is there on Monday and gone on Tuesday is not to give an account of 'what happened to the shed.'

Malcolm says that what the Zelig family come to accept is the 'fact that their shed had inexplicably ceased to exist'[9] (p. 6). But we must remember that this, too, is neither a description nor an explanation of a happening, a change from one state to another. Earlier, as we have seen, Malcolm mentions normal uses of 'disappearing' or, one might say, 'vanishing', where ready explanations are available. But there are not two ways of vanishing, explicable ways and inexplicable ways. An inexplicable vanishing is not a way of vanishing. To say that the shed has inexplicably ceased to exist is to say that there is no explanation for the disappearance of the shed.

What, then, is the difference between Malcolm and Winch? Very little, it seems, Malcolm claims, 'Winch seems to think that the Zelig family and their neighbours could not be certain of anything concerning the shed'[9] (p. 6), but I do not see how he can maintain this. Winch says everything of the Zelig family that Malcolm wants to say. Malcolm wants to say that in saying that the shed has simply vanished, the family would be protecting their sanity and their memories of their past life. Malcolm says that on discovering the shed had gone, 'They would be bewildered, but this bewilderment would not necessarily undermine that certainty. Indeed, *that* bewilderment would arise from *that* certainty'[9] (p. 6). Winch, it seems to Malcolm, holds that 'It simply vanished' would *only* function as an expression of bewilderment. But bewilderment about *what*? It would be impossible to elucidate the character of their bewilderment without invoking the kind of background Malcolm refers to. So I do not see that Malcolm is adding anything to what Winch has already admitted. What does remain an open question is what *further* role, if any, the family's bewilderment plays in their lives. If, as Malcolm says, its role is to help them hold on to what they had *prior* to the occurrence of the inexplicable event, then, so far, no grounds have been addressed for concluding that their way of life was not what it seemed or that they had been wrong to be certain of the existence of their shed. Indeed, nothing has been said to show that, if they built another one, they should be any less certain about its existence.

In his well-known paper, 'The Miraculous',[5] R. F. Holland speaks of this bewilderment as having been prompted by a contradiction in experience. The contradiction is supposed to consist of our being empirically certain of something which, according to the dominant concepts in that context, is supposed to be impossible. For example, he claims that we may become empirically certain that water has turned into wine, that a preternatural change has taken place. On the other hand, we have no concepts which enable us to explain such a change.

> This idea of a pure turning, if there can properly be said to be any idea of it, would leave no room for there to be any way in which the turning takes place; and for that reason, if for no other, I doubt if it can intelligibly signify the turning of one material thing into another. It is as if someone were to propose that, while the (non-transparent) solid objects we have encountered up to now have been of one colour or another through being of some hue or combination of hues, it is also possible logically for there to be, and for us actually to meet, things that have a colour without being of any hue of colour and without being of any amalgam, pattern or product of hues.[4] (p. 49)

This is how he argues in 'Lusus Naturae.' But the crucial issue, in his dispute with Winch, concerns what we can be empirically certain of, despite its lack of backing by such theoretical considerations. In the case of the example of the shed, Winch argues that the analogous considerations take the following form: 'our understanding of the conjunction: "The shed existed on Monday and did not exist on Tuesday" is such as to presuppose that the shed was destroyed between Monday and Tuesday in some intelligible way. And what is an intelligible way is limited by our understanding of what a shed is'[20] (p. 88). This is a prevailing understanding in our stream of life. Winch argues that to accept 'that something like a human being or like a shed, could just cease to exist from one moment to the next, is to remove both the object in question and oneself contemplating it from that "stream"'[4] (p. 58). Holland wants to say that there is a tension between this background, evoked by Winch, and the following possibility: 'If someone were to say for example, on the basis of judgements not far removed from the instinctual, "This much I know – that a minute ago there was a shed in this field, but now there is no trace of one," the relation between the two judgements in that statement would be non-logical. There would be no theoretical way of linking them; but that would not necessarily prevent them from being true as far as they go'[6] (p. 37). If someone believed, by faith, that a preternatural change had taken place, Holland sees no philosophical objection to prevent him from doing so.

In the context which Holland calls 'a contradiction in our experience,' he wants to claim that there can be reactions which go beyond 'cognitive paralysis'[6] (p. 35), beyond the bewilderment Winch speaks of. A person in such a situation may be convinced that a shed has simply vanished, describe his situation in this way, despite the 'sense-gap'[6] (p. 36) between this conviction and the weight of normal procedures which tell him that no sense can be given to 'sheds simply vanishing'. Holland thinks this view can be sustained because the conviction that the shed has simply vanished is rooted in two primitive reactions which do not depend on the normal procedures: the conviction that at one moment the shed is there, and the conviction that at the next moment it has gone. These primitive reactions, Holland argues, are pre-conceptual and are shared by all living higher animals. He gives the following examples:

> When something bulky comes speedily towards us, we dodge out of the way; or we may catch it – we react to what it is, and training can make a difference. There are also what might be called primitive expressions of a sense of absence, associated usually with deprivation, but sometimes with relief. This pre-conceptual understanding of existence is a phenomenon of perception and memory combined. At the human level, only *some* judgements of perception and memory are expressed in animal reactions. Nevertheless it makes good sense to regard all such judgements as *extensions* of animal awareness.[6] (pp. 34–5)

Without disputing these remarks, I shall argue that they count decisively against, not for, Holland's contention that Zelig's description that the shed has simply vanished is based on two primitive reactions, awareness of the shed's being there one moment and gone the next. Holland is right in emphasising that primitive reactions are *pre-conceptual*, but wrong in trying to make them *pre-contextual*. The primitive reactions of which judgements of perception and memory are extensions, exhibit an *agreement* in reactions. We do not agree to react in the way we do, *but we agree in our reactions*. It is in the context of such agreement that concept-formation can take place. Consider the primitive reaction of reaching out for an object. The reaction is connected with what Wittgenstein calls general facts of nature, for example, the fact that physical objects persist over time and do not have an intermittent existence in which they are constantly disintegrating and reassembling from one moment to the next. In such a context we reach out to touch an object. We locate it in this familiar, primitive way. The notion of the presence of an object is inextricable from this agreement in primitive reactions. One test of serious disability in a child, at a pre-conceptual stage, is seeing whether it does in fact reach out successfully for, say, a coloured block. If the child's hand regularly fails to locate the block, going to one side or the other of it all the time, this is an indication that something is seriously amiss. The child's reaction is certainly an instinctive, animal reaction, but it is *not* the kind of primitive reaction Holland needs for his case. The kind he needs is part of the agreement in reactions we exhibit in reaching out for an object. The child's instinctive reaction is not such a primitive reaction. It is not part of an agreement in reactions. On the contrary, it is *that* agreement which marks the child's instinctive, animal reaction as abnormal.

Let us now apply this lesson to the example Holland asks us to imagine, an object's being there one moment and gone the next without any conceivable explanation. The kind of thing involved would be my reaching out for an object, the coloured block say, only to find my hand passing through the space it appeared to occupy. My reaching out is certainly a primitive reaction, but the subsequent experience certainly is not. On the contrary, it is entirely baffling. Surely, the same has to be said of the experience of the Zelig family. Let us call seeing the shed at one moment a primitive reaction. Finding it gone the next moment is certainly not a second one. What is it then? The reaction of the Zelig family, as we have seen, is one of sheer bafflement, bewilderment. 'The shed has vanished!' is an expression of that bewilderment. But that is something Winch has not denied. His claim is precisely that this is what the employment of the expression amounts to. Nothing Holland has said shows that it is otherwise. His argument does not succeed in showing that the judgement 'A preternatural change has taken place' is an extension of two primitive reactions by the Zelig family. He does succeed in showing that the Zelig family have an experience which is opaque to them. Again, however, this is something Winch has never denied.

Whereas Holland turns to the notion of a primitive reaction, in an attempt to establish that 'It has simply vanished' is a description or explanation of what has happened to the shed, Mounce turns to the notion of a primitive experience in an attempt to establish the same conclusion. He considers the example of a child telling his mother that his ball has disappeared or vanished in the garden. Naturally, the mother will help the child to look for it. 'But,' Mounce argues,

> the looking presupposes the experience of loss; it is not involved in the experience of loss itself. It is true that the mother might say 'Now Johnny don't fuss. It *must* be somewhere. We only have to look.' But then again she might not; and, even if she does, these once again presuppose the experience of loss and are not involved in it. Consider now a phrase such as '3 o'clock'. Could a child *first* experience its being 3 o'clock and *then* learn some method for telling the time of day? What could that mean? It is evident that time of day is internally related to a method of measurement. But then it is equally evident that in this way it may be *contrasted* with 'It's disappeared' or 'It's vanished.' Indeed is it too much to suggest that the primitive experience is precisely the one that is captured by the words 'It's simply vanished'? Speaking strictly for myself, as I recall my mother's words 'It *must* be somewhere,' I recall also a distinct feeling of scepticism. Even at the time, the words smacked of propaganda, seemed too consciously designed to keep up the spirits. 'What makes her so certain?' whispered within one an insidious voice.[11]

The 'even at the time' rules out the view that Mounce is referring to a childish reaction which he has put aside now that he has become a man. For those interested in philosophy in children his reaction will be unsurprising. What is more surprising is that the voice within has now developed into a public, philosophical one holding the same opinion. Mounce's attempt to sever 'the experience of loss' from its familiar surroundings cannot be sustained. The surroundings are not the same in all cases, of course, since there are different kinds of loss. The father who keeps looking for years for his son, reported missing in military action, cannot accept the loss of his son. Here, to accept the loss would involve ceasing to look or expecting to find. The experience of loss, the terribleness of it, would be unintelligible without that lack of expectation of finding ever again one cut off from the land of the living. But with the example Mounce has in mind, the surroundings and one's expectations are different. As with Holland's example, these surroundings are connected with very general facts of nature, such as the fact that physical objects do not have an intermittent existence, there one moment, disappearing or disintegrating, only to reappear or reassemble a moment later. If a physical object, a pen, let us say, did behave in this way, I would not be said to lose it. When the pen disappeared I might say, 'There it goes again. How inconvenient!' but I should not have lost it. With an actual pen things are different. If I put my pen down and later fail to find it, it is important that I take for granted that someone must have moved it, that I might have made a mistake, that it might have been destroyed, or some such related explanation. If the pen has not been destroyed, it *must* be somewhere. Further, if I am looking for my pen a moment after I have put it down, 'somewhere' cannot be anywhere. I do not consider the possibility of the pen being in Australia, any more than I consider the possibility of it simply vanishing. But there is a difference. In certain circumstances, I may wonder whether my pen is in Australia, whether my friend who flew there picked up my pen by mistake. But in no circumstances can I wonder whether the proper description or explanation of what has happened to my pen is that it has simply vanished. If we divorce our sense of loss from our normal expectations surrounding the behaviour of pens, that 'loss' cannot retain its sense.

In arguing to the contrary, Mounce is led into inconsistencies, and has to strain the cases he considers. For example, as we have seen, Mounce admits that he would be baffled if, in the ordinary circumstances of dismantling a shed, someone were to suggest that they should not bother since the shed might simply vanish[10] (pp. 238–9). Why is he not equally baffled by someone suggesting in equally ordinary circumstances, that we need not look for a lost ball since it might have simply vanished? So far from being baffled, Mounce suggests that Zalman's explanation 'It has simply vanished,' would be a better explanation, in this context, of a familiar contradiction in our experience, than the explanations which are ordinarily available. The lost ball in the example Mounce considers is a lost golf ball which he drove into a clump of grass. What is the familiar contradiction in our experience supposed to consist in? Mounce replies:

> I checked and double checked that clump of grass, my checking being itself checked by my partner. That would pass, according to ordinary methods, as an adequate verification. By that I mean, an adequate verification that the ball is not in the clump of grass. But I also saw the ball enter the clump of grass and that observation was confirmed by my partner. Now that, by ordinary methods, would also count as an adequate verification, this time that the ball is in the clump of grass. So now our ordinary methods have pushed us into what looks like a contradiction. We have proved that the ball is and is not in the clump of grass.[11]

Of course, Mounce has proved no such thing. To do so, he would have to establish a truth in this context against which thousands of golfers will testify: Given that the ball has not been removed or destroyed, seek and ye shall find. Mounce equates failure to locate the ball, with the belief that it is not there to be located. This is not an equation which anyone makes in normal circumstances.

Mounce also claims that this alleged contradiction is resolved by Zalman's explanation. It 'would perfectly explain,' Mounce claims, 'first, why we saw the ball enter the clump of grass, and, second, why, when we searched the clump of grass, we could not find the ball. Zalman's claim, so far from being unintelligible, will in fact explain some of our experiences far better than will our ordinary methods'.[11] Apart from the fact that Mounce has given the explanation no content, since it is offered in ordinary circumstances, why is he not baffled by it as he claims he is in other similar circumstances? Speaking of the report that water was turned into wine at the wedding at Cana, Mounce says, 'The reports may be dismissed if it was a normal party. But, then again, the party may not have been normal and water may have been turned into wine.' But if reports are dismissed from a normal party, why are they not also dismissed from a normal golf course?

So far, I have argued that Malcolm, Holland and Mounce have not succeeded in showing that the expression 'It has simply vanished' has any employment in the contexts we have considered, other than as an expression of bewilderment at an inexplicable occurrence. Malcolm's question 'What is the logical force of that bewilderment?', how the experience of an inexplicable occurrence is related to the rest of a person's life, remains an open issue.

It does not seem to me that Winch is committed to saying that any interest we show in inexplicable events *must* be an interest in causally investigating them. Malcolm has no difficulty in showing that every event in human life does not have to be explicable in causal terms. He mentions the confused attempts by philosophers and psychologists to give an account of memory in terms of physiological memory traces: confused, partly because the relation between an occurrence and the ability to remember it is not a causal one. But, as Malcolm says, he has no reason to think that Winch would disagree with him on this matter. Neither does he think Winch would disagree with him when he says that, causal investigation having failed to come up with an answer, interest in the inexplicable event concerned may cease to be a causal one. Malcolm gives two examples, one real and one imaginary. The real one concerns the remarkable ability of two quite helpless retarded brothers, backward in elementary arithmetical operations, to determine quickly whether a large number is a *prime* number; an ability for which there is no known explanation, causal or otherwise. Oliver Sacks, who recorded and witnessed the case, found it uncanny.[15] The imaginary example is from Wittgenstein, who asks us to think of two different kinds of plant, A and B. The seeds of an A-plant always produce more A plants, and the seeds of a B-plant always produce more B-plants. The bafflement comes from the fact that no difference can be found between the seeds. Wittgenstein says: 'And to protest: "There must be a difference in the seeds, even if we don't discover it," doesn't alter the facts, it only shows what a powerful urge we have to see everything in terms of cause and effect'[21] (p. 410).

Faced with inexplicable occurrences of the kind we have been discussing, someone may say that there must be a causal explanation of them. What this amounts to is that he will keep looking for one, or believe that others, at other times, will succeed where he has failed. A person may take such a view of the reports of what happened at the wedding at Cana. Mounce responds: 'This is not a view that seems to me congenial or even sensible; it smacks of a mind dangerously closed to certain areas of experience. Nevertheless it is sustainable. I have no objection to it on purely philosophical grounds'.[11] What Mounce objects to, rightly, is a Humean philo-

Wittgenstein and Religion

sophical thesis which suggests that pure reason dictates that our interest in the inexplicable must be a causal interest. Of course, this leaves us once again with the question of the relation between these other interests and causal interests. The difference in the answers Holland and Mounce give to this question is highly instructive. Even though, as we have seen, Holland wants to speak of preternatural change as a possible description or explanation of what has happened to Zelig's shed, he says he prefers 'not to speak of preternatural change as something that it makes sense to contemplate as a worldly possibility, because I want to avoid the implication that there would also be sense, e.g., in our taking insurance against it. There can be no sense in entertaining expectations, positive or negative, in regard to preternatural change. It follows that the idea cannot be put to any ordinary practical use. Nevertheless, the person for whom it is a nullity thinks differently from the person who does not. He takes a different view of the world'[6] (p. 36). Holland does not elaborate on what this different view might amount to, but he does not think it has any bearing on the workings of our normal procedures of causal investigation. The stream of life, in that respect, flows on unaffected. Speaking of Zelig's shed, Holland says, 'Something might have happened to the stream of the world: but only in that field, while everything else remained normal. The flow of a stream is not impeded by a stone's dropping in it'[4] (p. 59).

Mounce's reactions are very different. He does not like Holland's talk of a contradiction in our experience. The proposal that the shed has simply vanished is only contradictory within our normal procedures. But, Mounce argues, the proposal comes from different procedures. '"People do vanish" says Zalman and it is evident that this is not to be construed as a move within the normal game. His aim is to startle, not to inform, to raise possibilities hitherto excluded. He wishes his fellows to admit that there are more things in heaven and earth than they are prepared to contemplate in their normal practices'[10] (p. 239). He accuses Holland of moving from the normal to the new practices in his argument, so creating the illusion of a contradiction in our experience. But does not Mounce move between the two contexts in an illegitimate way too? Having claimed that Zalman's proposal belongs to practices which have *different* interests from our normal causal investigations, he wants to speak of the proposal at the same time as a corrective to and extension of these investigations. The possibility of sheds and people simply vanishing revises our normal expectations; it changes their status; we become less than certain about them.

Holland disagrees strongly with this conclusion. He does not think everyday empirical certainties are impaired even by the countless scientific discoveries which remain to be made, let alone by the occurrence of preternatural changes. He says that it is a confusion to think it follows from the fact that boundless scope remains for further scientific discoveries 'that we are less than well enough acquainted with, and might have serious misconceptions about, what is and what is not possible in the behaviour under familiar conditions of common objects with which we have a long history of practical dealings'[5] (p. 182). Although Mounce, too, wants to say that acceptance of Zalman's proposals does not mean that we are credulous in taking our normal procedures for granted, he can do so only because, unlike Holland, he changes the status of these procedures: 'Our normal methods are simply working procedures; they are not supposed to embody the final truth about the universe'.[11] But if ordinary reactions to the existence of physical objects can be taken for granted, this is precisely because we do not regard them as 'working procedures'. If I build a shed, work in it, store things in it, etc., I should not speak of reaching the final truth about the universe. Neither would I deny that I had reached it. I should not indulge in such talk. But I would be certain that I had built, worked in and stored things in the shed, and would be baffled if anyone suggested I was not or should not be certain.

As we have seen, Mounce discusses Zalman's proposal as though it were meant to challenge our normal causal investigatory procedures. But is he saying that the proposal that the shed has simply vanished represents a different kind of interest from a causal interest in the situation? The ironical fact is that when Mounce comes to characterise this interest, our normal causal procedures continue to exert an enormous influence on him. This influence is shown in the language he uses. To refuse to consider proposals such as Zalman's, Mounce says, is to be 'dangerously closed to certain areas of experience.' To accept the proposal is 'to admit that there are more things in heaven and earth than [we] are prepared to contemplate in [our] normal practices.' This makes it sound as though these other things, these different areas of experience, *can* be explained, but not by our normal procedures. On the contrary, these procedures are challenged radically. So corresponding to normal experiences, the new contexts offer extraordinary experiences. Instead of ordinary explanations, we have super-explanations. Ordinary persons are the authors of ordinary explanations, but a super-explanation calls for a super-person as its author; in fact, a super-person no less than God himself. That our understanding of these explanations is limited is hardly surprising, since finite minds can hardly hope to comprehend the infinite mind of God, the final truth about the universe. Now and again, however, when sheds simply vanish, or water is simply turned into wine, glimmers of this final truth penetrate our limited domain.

We are acquainted, even within science, with radical challenges to normal procedures. So why should there not be the kind of challenge to scientific procedures which Mounce finds in Zalman's proposals? Mounce's scientific example is the challenge to the Ptolemaic system posed by the Copernican revolution. The analogy does not hold. However much one stresses the lack of comprehension between warring scientists in such contexts, the dispute and the challenge get their sense from the state of the subject, the respective explanatory powers of the rival systems, the kinds of considerations which made scientists go in different directions, the fruitfulness of data and explanations which prevailed, and the fact that the dispute can be written of by a historian of the subject. Without these surroundings, the dispute would have no sense. The whole point of Winch's arguments is that no surroundings have been provided in which Zalman's proposal has sense, either as a description, or an explanation, of whatever happened to Zelig's shed. My argument has been that the surroundings to which Malcolm, Holland and Mounce appeal give us no reason to revise Winch's conclusions.

A certain kind of religious mentality will not see the force of the request for elucidatory surroundings when it is said that profound experiences have occurred. Those possessing such a mentality think that the meaning of expressions such as 'It simply vanished' is conveyed immediately, independent of any mediation. They think that if we peer close enough at what is called an inexplicable occurrence, it will, as it were, take us by the throat, and force its profundity upon us. An inexplicable occurrence is treated as a kind of occurring. 'It only goes to show,' we are told. Show *what*? Until the 'experiences' are placed in the context of some story or other, some surroundings, testimonies by raconteurs of the ineffable remain staggeringly banal. That intellectuals are often taken with such testimonies should not impress us. After all, it is part of Singer's comic intention when he tells us that the enlightened, on hearing of the inexplicable disappearance of Zelig's shed, gave up playing cards and began discussing the existence of God. Their discussion is no more than transferred play.

This observation about Singer's intellectuals is connected with Winch's claim that talk of the miraculous in our culture is not untroubled. What does the trouble consist in? Lessing, speaking for his time, expressed it as follows in what is an overstatement: 'The proof of the spirit and of power is missing'.[8] He meant that there had been a severe erosion of those religious surroundings which might have bestowed an inexplicable occurrence with a certain significance, perhaps calling it a miracle. It might be said that an individual need not be religious first, before he can witness miracles. Thousands have come to religion through first witnessing a miracle. But this misses the point at issue. What must be available is a religious surrounding which makes available for an individual *the possibility* of coming to religion for the first time through witnessing a miracle. In the Bible, there is no question as to whether there are miracles. The reality of miracles is taken for granted. By the eighteenth century, the prevailing talk is of reported miracles, as though one were trying to establish something. There have been enormous shifts in the culture. In the Bible, the natural world is seen *ab initio* as God's world. By the eighteenth century, arguments to and from design have become attempts to establish the possibility and credibility of divine creation. In such a radically different context, talk of miracles is not unaffected. Lessing says, 'The problem is that this proof of the spirit and of power no longer has any spirit or power, but has sunk to the level of human testimonies of spirit and power. The problem is that reports of fulfilled prophecies are not fulfilled prophecies, that reports of miracles are not miracles'[8] (p. 52). When a religious sense of the miraculous is strong, it is that sense which may envelop an inexplicable occurrence. Now, inexplicable occurrences are appealed to in order to establish the credibility of miracles! We wait for the vanishing shed. But we do not wait in a vacuum. We wait in a cultural context in which the prestige of science is enormous. Thus, when we do try to speak of miracles, we do so in a way that turns religion into a kind of super-science and, as the examples we have considered show, we see 'religion, its hand in the machine's trying to smile as the grip tightened'[17] (p. 51). It is difficulties and developments such as these that Winch has in mind when he says that the *Weltanschauung* dominating our culture makes the attempt to bring the concept of a miracle into a usable relation with the habits of naturalistic explanation, a necessary and not an accidental failure[20] (p. 105).

In such a context, the conception of philosophy of religion and its tasks does not emerge unscathed. Torn from any religious associations, inexplicable occurrences, reports of the strange, the bizarre, the occult, become the minimal data from which a philosopher will either assert or deny that there is a God behind it all. Such procedures reflect a minimalist religion, the only kind they can capture. Speaking of the believer in such a religion, the poet R. S. Thomas writes:

How often I have heard him say, looking around him with his worried eyes at the emptiness: There must be something.[18] (p. 112)

The philosopher of religion who argues about whether there is a 'something' or a 'someone' behind inexplicable occurrences, is the counterpart, in his field, of those other philosophers who have searched for the soul behind the body, the emotion behind the smile, the meaning behind the use. He misses the significance of what is open to view. The philosopher of religion misconceives his task as that of establishing mysteries by invoking examples of inexplicable occurrences, whereas the religious use of 'mystery', assailed on all sides though it may be, is open to view. (I have tried to show this in relation to R. S. Thomas' hard won poetic celebration of belief in a *Deus Absconditus*.[14]) The philosopher is not faced with the task of establishing the credibility of 'an eternal order' on the basis of the minimal data of inexplicable occurrences. Peering at such data will not reveal eternity, as though by a magical operation. To simply say 'They must show *something*' is an exercise in vacuity. The significance of an inexplicable experience cannot be determined without considering what surrounds the citations of such experiences in human life. Kierkegaard accuses unmediated claims of depth and mystery as having 'a spurious eternal well-roundedness'[7] (p. 114). Such claims, *to be claims*, must be mediated. Kierkegaard says, 'What was there, in air-tight fashion pressed together in the completeness of contemplation, shall not be stretched out at its full length. It is now no longer rounded off but is in motion. For life is like a poet, and on that account is different from the observer who always seeks to bring things to a conclusion. The poet pulls us into the very complex centre of life'[7] (pp. 114–15). It is when claims are stretched, put in context, that what is genuine, bogus, romantic, superstitious and indulgent is revealed.

It may be thought that philosophy's task of clarification is necessarily thwarted where religion is concerned, since God's ways are said to be beyond human understanding. Job seeks a God who 'doeth great things and unsearchable' (5 : 9); the Psalmist testifies, 'Great is the Lord; and greatly to be praised: and his greatness is unsearchable' (145 : 3); St Paul exclaims as he wonders at the knowledge and wisdom of God, 'how unsearchable are his judgements, and his ways past finding out' (Rom. 11 : 33). All agree with the Psalmist's view of God's knowledge: 'Such knowledge is too wonderful for me; it is high I cannot attain unto it' (139 : 6). But, as I have said elsewhere:

> The first thing it is essential to note is that Job, the Psalmist and St Paul are not making statements *about* human language. Their expressions of religious mystery are expressions *in* language. They are not telling us that, because of the inadequacy of language, they cannot praise God. Praising God is precisely what they are doing! . . . [they] are not telling us that God is hidden from them because of the inadequacy of their language. Rather, they are showing us that the notion of God, *in* their language, is that of a hidden God: 'Verily thou art a God that hidest thyself, O God of Israel, the Saviour' (Isaiah 45 : 15)[12] (pp. 278–9).

Only when this is grasped will the philosopher, in his analysis, let mystery come in at the right place. This does not mean that through conceptual analysis the philosopher comes to understand the ways of God. What he comes to understand is the place the expression 'God's ways are beyond human understanding' has in human life.[13]

Winch does not say that all talk of miracles in our culture is nonsense. He does say that when attempts are made to bring such talk into a usable relation with naturalistic modes of explanation, 'mystery' is unlikely to come in at the right place. Even though the reality of miracles is taken for granted in the Bible, this does not mean that reactions to inexplicable occurrences were not mixed. Jesus, knowing the thoughts associated with prevailing reactions in his day, came to despise them. He said, 'This is an evil generation: they seek a sign' (Luke 11 : 29). Perhaps such signs were thought of as a kind of magic. Today, many who wait for news of vanishing sheds see it as signs of a religious super-science. As R. S. Thomas might say, that's what comes of experimenting with an Amen.

Notes

1. G. E. M. Anscombe, 'Times, Beginnings and Causes', in her *Collected Papers*, vol. II (Oxford: Basil Blackwell, 1981).
2. J. L. Austin, 'Other Minds', in his *Philosophical Papers* (Oxford: The Clarendon Press, 1961).
3. Cora Diamond, 'Rules: Looking in the Right Place', in *Wittgenstein: Attention to Particulars; Essays in Honour of Rush Rhees* (London: Macmillan, 1989).
4. R. F. Holland, 'Lusus Naturae', in *Wittgenstein: Attention to Particulars*.
5. R. F. Holland, 'The Miraculous', in *Against Empiricism* (Oxford: Basil Blackwell, 1980).
6. R. F. Holland, 'Naturalism and Preternatural Change', in *Value and Understanding: Essays in Honour of Peter Winch*, ed. Raimond Gaita (London: Routledge, 1990).
7. S. Kierkegaard, *Purity of Heart*, trans. Douglas Steere (New York: Harper Torchbooks, 1956).
8. *Lessing's Theological Writings*, ed. Henry Chadwick (London: Library of Modern Religious Thought, 1956).
9. N. Malcolm, 'On "Ceasing to Exist",' in *Value and Understanding*.
10. H. O. Mounce, Critical notice of Peter Winch's *Trying to Make Sense*, *Philosophical Investigations*, vol. 11 (1988), 238–9.
11. H. O. Mounce, 'On Simply Vanishing'. Unpublished discussion paper, quoted with the author's permission.
12. D. Z. Phillips, *Faith After Foundationalism* (London: Routledge, 1989).
13. See 'On Not Understanding God', Essay 10.
14. D. Z. Phillips, *R. S. Thomas: Poet of the Hidden God* (London: Macmillan, 1986).
15. O. Sacks, 'The Twins', in *The Man Who Mistook His Wife for a Hat* (London: Duckworth, 1985).
16. I. B. Singer, 'Stories from Behind the Stove', in *A Friend of Kafka* (London: Penguin Books, 1975).
17. R. S. Thomas, 'Asking', in *Experimenting with the Amen* (London: Macmillan, 1986).
18. R. S. Thomas, 'The Possession', in *Later Poems: 1972–1982* (London: Macmillan, 1983).
19. J. C. Thompson, 'Miracles and God's Existence', *Philosophy* (1954).
20. P. Winch, 'Ceasing to Exist', in his *Trying to Make Sense* (Oxford: Basil Blackwell, 1988).
21. Ludwig Wittgenstein, 'Cause and Effect: Intuitive Awareness', ed. Rush Rhees, trans. Peter Winch, *Philosophia* 6(1976).
22. Ludwig Wittgenstein, *On Certainty* (Oxford: Basil Blackwell, 1969).

12

On Wanting to Compare Wittgenstein and Zen

In his paper on 'Wittgenstein and Zen',[1] Professor Canfield argues that 'For both Wittgenstein and Zen, language and understanding do not require thought. For Wittgenstein, rather, language and understanding are grounded in what he calls "practice". Wittgenstein's idea of a practice overlaps with the Zen idea of what shall be called here "just doing" something; that is doing something with a mind free of ideas or concepts' (p. 383). In discussing the sense in which language does not require thought, Canfield wishes to combat the compelling picture that language conveys thoughts which are logically and temporally prior to it; thoughts without which there could be no such thing as language. In opposition to such a picture Canfield expounds Wittgenstein's view thus:

> To understand a concept is to be able to use the corresponding word or words in their language game, or to be able to play the language game (or one of the language games) in which a word expressing the concept has a home. Thus, mastery of a concept consists not in having some idea or other, but in having a certain skill: namely being able to participate, by means of 'just doing' in a certain pattern of interaction. This just doing will consist in using the word in the language game to do a certain job, namely that job which it is the word's role in the language game to do. In this sense of 'concept', the word is robbed of any mental attributes; in this sense to have a concept is not to have some particular idea' (p. 401).

Canfield argues that such a view of what mastery of a concept amounts to need not lead to behaviourism, to a view of human beings as automata, or to a mechanistic view of human action. My aim is not to argue over the exposition of Wittgenstein, but to question the character of the overlap which Canfield claims exists between Wittgenstein's work and Zen.

At times, Canfield's claims regarding the overlap are relatively modest, which is not to say that they are unimportant. These claims consist in seeing that 'The *Investigations* does generate a view of language consistent with the Buddhist doctrine of the relationship of thought and understanding. This view of language enables us to see that the picture which constitutes a barrier to the acceptance of Buddhism, the picture which presents thought as essential to understanding, may be rejected' (p. 406). In other words, philosophical confusions of a general kind concerning the priority of thought over language may be *one* reason why a person may not even begin to take Zen Buddhism seriously. Holding the view that thought is essentially prior to language, and that some form of mentalism is essential to explain the very possibility of language, he will not be disposed initially to any serious consideration of a body of teaching which stresses the importance of acting free of all thoughts. Coming to see the philosophical untenability of mentalism would remove this initial intellectual prejudice against a serious consideration of Buddhism. So far, so good. But Canfield goes on immediately to say: 'More than that, the phenomenon of language can be viewed, in the light of the *Investigations*, as based on the same activity-without-thought that is the manifestation, in Zen, of the Buddhist Nature' (p. 406). It is this far stronger claim of an identification between what Wittgenstein has shown and what is exhorted in Zen that I find difficult to understand. The difficulty is already present in the admission of the generality of the confusion which Wittgenstein exposes. Although examples of confusions emanating from mentalistic presuppositions may be importantly different, they may also share certain general confusions about language such as those which Canfield summarises. But is not this very generality a reason for resisting any close comparison of what Wittgenstein has achieved with the notion of action without thought in Zen? For if the confusions emanating from mentalism are widespread they will be as much a feature of what we mean by acting with thought, as they are of what we mean by acting without thought, in the Zen sense of these terms. What I mean can be illustrated by the example of a contemporary Zen practitioner which Canfield quotes from *The Three Pillars of Zen*. A Japanese-style fencing champion lost to three inferior opponents through preoccupation with tactics. He put all such thoughts aside in the fourth contest, simply giving himself to the task in hand. He returned to his place not knowing whether he had lost or won. Later, he was told he had achieved a splendid victory.

He claimed to have experienced, during the fourth contest, 'the naked expression of enlightenment'.[2]

There may be difficulties here about generalising from what constitutes acting without thought in this game to other games, say, chess, where one would have to give an account of what is going on when the players are thinking about the state of the game, neither making any move at the time, but I do not want to pursue such questions here. One may agree that such examples as thoughtful play in chess do not count against Wittgenstein's attack on mentalism. As Canfield says, 'one would have to show that it is not part of our concept of foresight (not part of the language game involving "foresight") that we apply the concept on the basis of having ascertained that the person in question has had thoughts of some kind in his mind. A Zen Master, his mind empty of thoughts, can also be said correctly and truly to have exercised foresight' (p. 393). What Canfield does not take account of is the fact that a fencer may be said *not* to have exercised foresight without this implying that his head was full of thoughts. The example of the fencer obscures this from us. Let us consider it in greater detail.

The fencer won when he ceased to deliberate about tactics, when he simply gave himself to the matter in hand. He did not think (in the bad sense) about what he was doing. Similarly we say of a soccer player who has only the goalkeeper to beat but who muffs his shot, or of a cricketer who drops a towering catch on the boundary, 'He thought about it, that was the trouble'. Here, a certain kind of reflection on what is taking place proves to be a hindrance to the task in hand. 'It would be better if he hadn't thought about it' we say, and the Japanese fencing-champion said this of himself. Yet, after his fourth game his victory is described as splendid. It might have been described as thoughtful, full of foresight. Clearly, whatever is meant by these compliments it cannot be the kind of preoccupation which proved disastrous in his previous encounters. So we seem to have the following contrast: (a) thoughtful play means play without thought in the sense of harmful preoccupation. The thoughtfulness of the play would be something which showed itself in the pattern of play, the strategy, the thrust and counter-thrust, without implying any thoughts prior to these activities. So in ordinary use we can call play thoughtful when it exhibits action without thought, 'just doing', in the Zen sense. (b) Thoughtless play means, in our example, play with thought in the Zen sense. But what we need to consider is thoughtless play which is *not* due to preoccupation or to thinking about the game in the bad sense already outlined. By choosing a one-sided diet of examples Canfield has ignored the fact that if mentalism can lead us to misconstrue what is meant by thoughtful play in certain instances, it can *also* lead us to misconstrue what is meant by thoughtless play. If calling play thoughtful need not entail thoughts occurring prior to the play, but is a way of referring to the character of the play, so calling play thoughtless need not entail the presence of thoughts either, but can equally be a comment on the character of the play. Thus, if the confusions connected with mentalism lead us to misconstrue, on occasion, what is meant by *both* thoughtful and thoughtless play, the realisation of these confusions, by the player who is also interested in philosophy, cannot be identified with the ideal of thoughtful play or with action without thought in the Zen sense, since, as far as ridding ourselves of the confusions of mentalism is concerned, thoughtful and thoughtless play are left precisely where they are. One needs something other than freedom from philosophical confusions *about* the game to attain the transition from thoughtless to thoughtful play. Similarly, to take an example from Christianity, the exhortation, 'Take no thought for the morrow' cannot be equated with the insight that reflective activity does not entail prior thoughts in the mentalistic sense, since this would be as true of an analysis of 'Take thought for the morrow', the 'Provide, Provide' of Robert Frost. Both the man who took no thought for the morrow, and the man who did, would be seen to be people who lived certain kinds of lives rather than as curious examples concerning a thesis that mental acts precede all actions. By choosing the example of the preoccupied fencer Canfield provided an example in which thoughts needed to be stripped away in order to achieve free unhampered play. He can then say, 'What is left if we strip away thoughts, and what exists anyway when superfluous thoughts are, even though superfluous, present, is the flow of life, patterned forms of just doing something, practice, the Buddha nature manifesting itself, the Tao' (p. 405). But what thoughts are there, in the philosophically pejorative sense, which need to be stripped away, when thoughtless play does not involve the presence of superfluous thought, or the confusions of mentalism? None at all. As O. K. Bouwsma has pointed out, the fool who says in his heart 'There is no God' is not to be construed as someone who says anything to himself, or as someone who could tell you, if asked, what is in his heart. The heart's saying 'There is no God' is a way of describing the fruits of his labours, the character of his life, the state of his soul. As Bouwsma says, unlike Anselm's fool, the fool of the psalm is not a literate fool. If his soul is in a confused state, it is not philosophical confusion.[3]

Canfield might reply to these criticisms by saying that they depend on stressing certain aspects of Wittgenstein's work and Zen while he is more concerned with other aspects. The analogy between Wittgenstein's notion of a practice and the Zen ideal of 'just doing' is greater, it might be said, than any such comparison which depends on the confusions of mentalism. It is true that mentalism may lead us to give as misleading an account of what is involved in thoughtless play as of what is involved in thoughtful play, but it might still be argued that bad play, in the sense of play preoccupied with tactics, etc., cannot be equated with 'just doing'. Thus it could be argued that a game could not be taught by teaching what preoccupied play means. This latter notion presupposes the notion of just playing, 'just doing', in order to have any substance. So Canfield might still say that although the differences between play and preoccupied play cannot always be brought out in terms of the philosophical confusions involved in mentalism, nevertheless the Japanese fencer's 'just playing', the Zen ideal in this case, can be equated with Wittgenstein's 'just doing'.

Yet there are further difficulties which meet any such argument. They have to do with the generality of Wittgenstein's notion and the relatively restricted application of the Zen ideal. In other words, much of what is covered by Wittgenstein's notion would not be acceptable as an instance of the Zen ideal. This can be illustrated in terms of another example Canfield quotes. He says that Buddhism and Taoism have obvious affinities and asks us to consider a well-known passage from Chuang Tzu:

> If a man, having lashed two hulls together, is crossing a river, and an empty boat happens along and bumps into him, no matter how hot-tempered the man may be, he will not get angry. But if there should be someone in the other boat, then he will shout out to haul this way or veer that. If his first shout is unheeded, he will shout again, and if that is not heard, he will shout a third time, this time with a torrent of curses following. In the first instance, he was not angry; now in the second he is. Earlier he faced emptiness, now he faces occupancy. If a man could succeed in making empty, and in that way wander through the world, then who could do him harm?[4]

Here we have an illustration of the distinction which has to be drawn between 'just doing' in Zen and 'just doing' in Wittgenstein, since, clearly, 'just being angry' or 'just cursing' could not be instances of 'just doing' in Zen, whereas that is precisely what they are in Wittgenstein. 'Cursing' appears in Wittgenstein's list of language-games (*Investigations*, I, para. 23). A confused language-game, given Wittgenstein's use of the term, is a self-contradiction. Yet the cursing boatman is said to face an occupancy which must be emptied, a confusion of soul which he is exhorted to rid himself of. Zen would say the same of anger. Yet, in Wittgenstein, anger is an instance of 'just doing' (see 'Remarks on Frazer's *The Golden Bough*', *The Human World*, no. 3, 1971). The lover does not smash the portrait of his beloved in order to express his anger. This is the form his anger takes. It is an instance of 'just doing', but not one which Zen would recognise as 'just doing'. Again, as in our consideration of Canfield's previous example, an essential distinction must be drawn between philosophical and spiritual confusion.

To some extent, Canfield recognises that there is such a distinction to be drawn towards the end of his paper, although he does not see that it has the implications I have been concerned with. Still, to the extent that he does recognise the need for such a distinction, it makes it difficult to know how much weight should be put on the stronger claims made earlier:

> Wittgenstein provides a 'theoretical' framework in which Zen theory (the doctrines of Mahayana Buddhism) can be embedded, at least in so far as the topics touched on in the present paper are concerned. 'Theoretical' here is in quotes because Wittgenstein does not have a theory but a certain way of looking at language, a way consistent with the Zen view. Wittgenstein's concerns are everywhere intellectual: he attacked the *Luftgebäude* constructed by the intellect. The aim of Zen, of course, is, to the contrary, not intellectual. Zen is in no way theoretical, nor even 'theoretical'. One can read Wittgenstein and come to acknowledge, or even, in Wittgenstein's terms, 'see' that understanding does not require thought. From the Zen point of view, this, in itself, would be an accomplishment of infinitesimal significance. For Zen, what is important, rather, is actually to strip away thought and see one's true nature face to face. (p. 407)

Yet Canfield thinks the comparison is somewhat unfair to Wittgenstein since Wittgenstein himself was aware of the limits of what can be said in philosophy, that philosophy itself provides no theses about ultimate reality or about what it means to live an enlightened life. But recognising this, it seems to me, should increase our doubts about Canfield's attempts to draw at times quite close comparisons between Wittgenstein's attacks on mentalism, the priority of thought, and his notion of a practice on the one hand, and the Zen teaching concerning actions without thought on the other. As I have suggested, one should not say *much* more than that clearing up these philosophical confusions may remove an initial intellectual prejudice against taking seriously any teaching which speaks of emptying oneself of all thoughts and concepts. Certainly, one can see how what Wittgenstein shows, unlike mentalism, would be consistent with Zen teaching. It might be interesting to compare the relation of what he has shown to this teaching with the relation of the Mādhyamika dialectic to Zen.[5]

How Wittgenstein's recognition of the limits of philosophy is to be taken itself raises important philosophical questions about the relation of philosophical enquiry to character. To what extent can distinctions be drawn between the character in a man's work and the character of the man? Is that itself a misleading way of posing the question? Clearly, one cannot say in general that the connection between work and a man's character is contingent. And yet, it is also good to remind ourselves that, as Sinyavsky says, 'One can live like a fool and have interesting thoughts from time to time'.[6]

Notes

1. John V. Canfield, 'Wittgenstein and Zen', *Philosophy* 50, no. 194 (October 1975).
2. Philip Kapleau (Boston, 1965), pp. 231–2. Quoted by Canfield on p. 392.
3. O. K. Bouwsma, 'Anselm's Argument', in *The Nature of Philosophical Enquiry*, J. Bobik (ed.) (University of Notre Dame Press, 1970).
4. Trans. Burton Watson, *The Complete Works of Chuang Tzu* (New York, 1968).
5. I owe this suggestion to a valuable conversation on this topic with Glyn Richards. No doubt the spiritual orientation of the dialectic would pose similar difficulties to those raised in this paper.
6. Andrey Sinyavsky, *Unguarded Thoughts*, trans. M. Harari (Collins, 1972). These issues are taken further in Essay 13.

13
Authorship and Authenticity: Kierkegaard and Wittgenstein

'In this age, and indeed for many ages past, people have quite lost sight of the fact that authorship ought to be a serious calling implying an appropriate mode of personal existence.'[1] So wrote Kierkegaard in his *The Point of View for my Work as an Author*. He accused metaphysicians of losing sight of this serious calling. There is a comic pretentiousness in the disparity between their speculative systems, and the actualities of human existence. Kierkegaard said that they built castles in the air, dwellings no one lives in, and created a fantastic language for fantastic beings. Wittgenstein recognised that the problems which lead to metaphysical systems are deep problems. Nevertheless, he said that language in such systems is idle language which has gone on holiday. His aim was to bring words back from their metaphysical to their ordinary use; to bring us back from castles in the air to rough ground. Wittgenstein insisted that what is ragged should be left ragged.

Kierkegaard and Wittgenstein oppose philosophy's foundationalist pretensions, its claim to possess a rational measure by which all our practices must be assessed. No such rationale exists, and no theses concerning it can be 'said'. What philosophy provides is an elucidatory 'showing' of what our practices come to, in face of our tendencies to be confused about them. Foundationalism's direct method of demonstration is replaced by an indirect method of perspicuous representation.

But how can there be a serious philosophical authorship after the demise of foundationalism? What style can philosophy have? In their struggles with this issue, both writers adopted striking literary devices. Kierkegaard wrote a number of pseudonymous works, claiming that the perspectives elucidated in them were not his, but those of the pseudonymous authors. Wittgenstein presented his work in

200

numbered paragraphs, in which we meet different voices he argues with, and voices expressing different perspectives. His early readers found this difficult to grasp and many critics concluded that Wittgenstein provides us with no more than, what he himself called, disparagingly, an album of unconnected remarks.[2] Both authors endeavour to teach us conceptual differences, without claiming that these differences form a systematic unity. But, it has been asked, how can such endeavours constitute a serious philosophical authorship? If Kierkegaard, in his pseudonymous works, shows us a variety of perspectives, what is his *own* relation to them? If Wittgenstein introduces us to a variety of voices, how can he have *a voice of his own*? No matter how confused he might be, the foundationalist has a noble aim: he wants to be our guide in helping us to distinguish between the rational and the irrational. Since Kierkegaard and Wittgenstein forsake this task, how can there be a philosophical voice which is no voice in particular?

Once the tasks of foundationalism are forsaken, does not philosophical enquiry become no more than a form of aestheticism, a parody of, or an ironic play with, real voices? In fact, this possibility worried Kierkegaard in his student dissertation, *The Concept of Irony*, in which he suggests that there is a necessary tension between Socrates' elucidations of different possibilities, and the actual life Socrates has to live, a tension which involves Socrates in irony:

> The ironist stands proudly withdrawn into himself; he lets mankind pass before him, as did Adam the animals, and finds no companionship for himself. By this he constantly comes into conflict with the actuality to which he belongs . . . For him life is a drama, and what engrosses him is the ingenious unfolding of that drama. He is himself a spectator even when observing some act . . . He is inspired by the virtues of self-sacrifice as a spectator is inspired by them in a theatre; he is a severe critic who well knows when such virtues become insipid and false.[3]

In rejecting every definition of piety and justice put to him, by suggesting further possibilities and never coming to rest in a definition of his own, there is a danger of Socrates' life becoming one of 'infinite negativity'. Kierkegaard thought that because, in his view, Socrates 'lives hypothetically and subjunctively, his life finally loses all continuity. With this he sinks completely into mood. His life becomes *sheer mood*.'[4]

Josiah Thompson has argued that Kierkegaard succumbs to this danger in his own work. In depicting aesthetic, ethical and religious perspectives in his pseudonymous works, he suggests, Kierkegaard is simply playing with possibilities. This form of play developed early in him. One day, Kierkegaard's father returned home too late to take his young son for a promised walk. They imagined going on the walk instead: acting out the scenes they might have witnessed and the people they might have met. Kierkegaard noted, later, that too much of his childhood was lived in the imagination. Yet, Thompson argues, the child was developing an appetite for the imaginary which would lead him to philosophy: 'Slowly, inevitably, a singular thought has taken root in the young boy's mind. It is not necessary to live in the world. On the contrary, the world – its resistance, its burdens, its conflicting demands – can be transformed. One need only dream. Narcissus has found his solitary pool, and Kierkegaard his future: he will be a dreamer.'[5]

Thompson reminds us that Kierkegaard succumbed to this aestheticism in his life. His nephew related an incident in which Kierkegaard, hearing a poorhouse inmate say she would be happy if someone gave her some money, approached her, gave her, with a flourishing gesture, the exact amount she had asked for, and disappeared without saying a word. Later, in philosophical tranquillity, he enjoyed thinking of possible ways in which the old woman might have thought of the incident. The old woman simply occasions a mood. According to Thompson, so do the pseudonymous works. They are 'Nonparticipants in life, they are its critics and spectators.'[6] The fact that Kierkegaard is their single author does not imply any singlemindedness in him. On the contrary, the pseudonyms testify to the activity of a playful aesthete, withdrawn from the actualities of life, which is all philosophy can be once its metaphysical pretensions have been put aside. Thompson concludes that in the pseudonymous works, 'there is an underlying black humour. For finally the joke is on the reader, and the smarter he is, the sooner he realises it. But to see through all the pseudonyms, to recognise that the vision of any one of them is not to be preferred to that of any other, is finally to join Kierkegaard in his cloister. It is to share with him that peculiarly modern laceration – 'I must believe, but I can't believe' – which since his time has become even more painful.'[7] Looking at the range of Kierkegaard's pseudonymous works, Thompson says: 'It is as if his life had been refracted by a powerful prism into a multitude of images, each of which retained some mark of the original.'[8]

Kierkegaard shares the fate he ascribed to Socrates in his doctoral dissertation. Is this Wittgenstein's fate too? In his philosophisings about religion, R. F. Holland finds that modern laceration in him – 'I must believe, but I can't believe' – which creates tensions for his authorship. On the one hand, Wittgenstein says, 'I cannot kneel to pray, for it is as though my knees were stiff. I am afraid of dissolution (of my own dissolution), if I were to become soft.'[9] But, on another occasion, he says, 'I am not a religious person, but I cannot help seeing every problem from a religious point of view.'[10] In these remarks, Holland argues, we have a tension between Wittgenstein's philosophical investigations and the actuality to which he belongs; the same tension that worried Kierkegaard in his doctoral dissertation. Wittgenstein seems to give an independent sense to 'seeing the world (or seeing life, seeing one's work) from a religious point of view and being a religious person.'[11] Holland has difficulty in seeing how this is possible: 'We are presented with the suggestion that a person's point of view can be religious although he himself is not.[12] But how can a point of view be made religious except by a religion? And must not the religion enter the viewpoint through the mind of the person who is taking this view?'[13] The danger is that the philosophical point of view which is called 'religious' is no more than *pathetisch* religion. Expounding the notion of the *pathetisch*, Holland says he 'might speak controversially of Mahler's *pathetisch* pantheism, and . . . might also use the term or the English word 'sentimental', in describing the man who muttered words such as "Gott", "Himmel" and "Danke" when looking over the mountains from his chalet at Terchtesgarten in 1939.'[14] If this were our final verdict, Wittgenstein's investigations would make no more contact with religion than Kierkegaard's pseudonyms have contact, according to Thompson, with the subjects they purport to engage with.

Can it really be said, however, that Kierkegaard and Wittgenstein lack integrity as philosophical authors because they reduce philosophical enquiry to a form of aestheticism? Do they, like Kierkegaard and his father on their imaginary walk, doff their hats at the various possibilities in human life without engaging with any of them? Thompson's attempt to depict Kierkegaard as a playful aesthete, based on biographical evidence, is manifestly unreliable. For example, in his use of Kierkegaard's treatment of the woman from the poorhouse, he omits to say that Kierkegaard was severely critical of his own conduct. In the second volume of *Either/Or*, he attributes the incident to the aesthete and subjects it to moral censure: 'So what you wanted was to play the part of fate; what you really enjoyed were the multifarious reflections which could be spun from this.'[15] The dangers of aestheticism in the realm of the intellect are clearly recognised: 'One is struck by seeing a clown whose joints are so limber that all necessity for maintaining the human gait and posture are done away. Such are you in an intellectual sense, you can just as well stand on your head as on your feet, everything is possible for you, and by this possibility you can astonish others and yourself; but it is unwholesome, and for the sake of your own tranquillity I beg you to see to it that what is your advantage, does not end by being a curse. A man who has a conviction cannot turn topsy-turvy upon himself and all things. I warn you, therefore, not against the world but against yourself, and I warn the world against you.'[16] The problem for Thompson is obvious: how can the author of this blistering attack on aestheticism be called an aesthete?

R. F. Holland says that 'it *is* possible for a charge of sentimentality to be thoughtfully mounted against any philosopher who camps under the portico of historical religion instead of going inside',[17] but says also that Wittgenstein cannot be found guilty of it. The aesthete goes as he pleases where religion is concerned, but, Holland argues, this cannot be said of Wittgenstein: Wittgenstein 'takes up a position that is actually very austere, like an unfurnished room by comparison with what is available in the historical religions. I would also say that if someone is prone to sentimentality, then sentimental he is going to be, when he gets the chance. There is no sign of Wittgenstein's being that way inclined and plenty of evidence in the other direction.'[18]

Since it can be shown that Kierkegaard's and Wittgenstein's attacks on metaphysical systems do not involve reducing philosophy to a form of aestheticism, it may be thought that we can conclude, without more ado, that both were concerned with the struggle for clarity, the working through to grammatical distinctions we are tempted to confuse or ignore. The only difference between them it may be said, is that Kierkegaard was concerned with combating confusions about Christianity, whereas Wittgenstein combated confusions in a wide range of contexts. I shall now examine this view at some length.

Kierkegaard wanted to dispute what he called 'the monstrous illusion', namely, the widespread conviction, in the Denmark of his day, that one could be a Christian simply by being a citizen. People who embraced aesthetic or ethical perspectives in their lives thought

they were Christians. Kierkegaard did not think they could be disa-
bused of this fact by any direct method. He writes: 'there is a difference between writing on a blank sheet of paper and bringing to light
by the application of a caustic fluid a text which is hidden under
another text.'[19] The pseudonymous works were meant to act as such
a fluid by giving perspicuous representations of aesthetic and ethical
perspectives. Kierkegaard says:

> if real success is to attend the effort to bring a man to a definite
> position, one must first of all take pains to find HIM where he is
> and begin there . . . In order to help another effectively I must
> understand more than he – yet first of all surely I must understand
> what he understands. If I do now know that, my greater under-
> standing will be of no help to him.[20]

Contrary to Thompson's suggestion, Kierkegaard's pseudonymous
works are not exercises in aesthetic self-indulgence. Rather, they call
for a disinterested reflectiveness in the elucidation of different perspectives. E. D. Klemke comments:

> One of the most impressive features of Kierkegaard's writings is
> the remarkable philosophical detachment with which he wrote. A
> high degree of disinterestedness pervades his writings and dis-
> plays the objectivity with which he could practice even on matters
> which have a highly subjective and personal concern.[21]

Kierkegaard himself testifies: 'So in the pseudonymous works there
is not a single word which is mine. I have no opinion about them
except as a third person, no knowledge of their meaning except as a
reader, not the remotest private relation to them.'[22] He does not look
for a philosophical underpinning for his own Christian beliefs. On
the contrary, Kierkegaard says: 'One single word of mine uttered
personally in my own name would be an instance of presumptuous
self-forgetfulness, and dialectically viewed would ensure with one
word the guilt of annihilating the pseudonyms.'[23] Of course,
Kierkegaard's hope was that when aesthetic and ethical perspectives
are seen for what they are, those who confused them with Christianity would realise the error of their ways, and turn to Christianity. But
even if this does not happen, and they preferred to stay where they
were, at least the monstrous illusion would have been dispelled:
'Therefore it is possible for misunderstanding to be removed and

become agreement and understanding, but it is possible also for it to be removed and to become real disagreement.'[24] It follows that clarity is in 'every man's interest, whether he be a Christian or not, whether his intention is to accept Christianity or reject it.'[25]

This search for clarity is found in Wittgenstein too. In his work we find at least five different contexts in which he discusses the relation of philosophy to religion. Having discussed them elsewhere, I shall be no more than note them here.[26] First, Wittgenstein criticises philosophers who argue that all forms of religious belief are meaningless. Second, he criticises confused grammatical accounts of religious belief. Third, he discusses the distinction between religion and superstition. Fourth, he discusses reactions to different forms of religion, emphasising that which are called 'higher' or 'lower' must be a personal matter. Fifth, he notes that we have to be pragmatic in our reactions to religion. Sometimes, there may be little to say about a phenomenon claimed to be religiously significant. (He saw a blinding flash and that was that, except that he keeps talking about it!) When one of Wittgenstein's pupils wrote to tell him that he had become a Roman Catholic, Wittgenstein replied, 'When I hear someone has bought himself equipment for tight-rope walking, I'll be impressed when I see what he does with it.' In all five contexts, Wittgenstein is bringing out the grammar of our practices. In order to do so, what we need is not more information, but clarity concerning what lies before us. Holland, on the other hand, is in danger of succumbing to *pathetisch* philosophy when he endorses A. E. Taylor's view that, in religion, there is a 'never wholly removable misfit between the real and the categories in which we try to confine it.'[27] We are reminded of Locke's claim that our faculties are inherently inadequate to grasp reality, and Berkeley's apt reply, ' . . . that we have first raised a dust and then complain we cannot see.'

In this struggle for clarity, Wittgenstein urged his students, 'Go the bloody hard way', but Holland wonders whether it is hard enough. He poses this question because, when A. E. Taylor gives the same advice, it involves doing something Wittgenstein does not do: 'When Taylor gives the advice the sense of it is: Don't let the difficulties bring you to a halt. Commit yourself to a traditional form of worship, and do not be content with some wishy-washy kind of 'philosophical religion'.'[28] An historical religion, Holland reminds us, presents us 'with *this* founder, *these* scriptures, *these* beliefs' and he says, 'I am inclined to go along with the suggestion that to take all that away is to strip religion of its body and turn it into a pale sort of ghost.' Taylor speaks of 'the thin and sentimental devotions of eighteenth century English Deism'.[29] But what of Wittgenstein? Holland replies: 'Wittgenstein of course said that he was not religious. Taylor, however, in agreeing, would have added that looking at things . . . in the way Wittgenstein did was just one form among others of that dilute thing, philosophic religion, which is a surrogate for genuine religion.'[30]

It is true that Wittgenstein did not embrace any historical religion but, as Holland admits, the accounts he gives of religion are not reductive. There is certainly no question of Wittgenstein constructing a deistic philosophic religion. One of the main objects of his attack was the deistic assumptions which still pervade twentieth century philosophy of religion. Kierkegaard would have enjoyed the irony in the claim by contemporary purveyors of philosophic religion, still a recognisably English mode of philosophising, that they have gone the hard, systematic way in philosophy. Wittgenstein thinks that kind of philosophy is as wishy-washy as the devoutness Taylor saw Deism generate.

At times, Holland suggests that the obedience to authority which religion calls for 'is a scandalum to the philosophic mind.'[31] At the outset of his paper, he argues as though there is a *necessary* tension between philosophy and religion:

> Philosophy consists in the struggle for clarity. In religion there is no virtue in arriving at that. What is wanted is charity, not clarity. I would go as far as to suggest that clarity is a hindrance to the kind of spirituality expressed in religious devotion. In any case it is not available there: you can only see through a glass darkly, and even then your account of what you see is subject to unexplained alteration at the hand of authority. The meek acceptance of this is *docility* – one of the loveliest words in religious language; but in the vocabulary of philosophy it is suitable only for animals.[32]

The difficulty is in knowing how seriously these remarks are intended, since later in his paper, he endorses the following very different comments by Taylor:

> In a critical age, like our own, the 'option' for Christianity or any other historical religion, must bring a perpetual tension into one's intellectual life from which acquiescence in a 'religion within the limits of reason' would leave us free . . . We could get rid of the

tension equally readily by blind acquiescence in tradition and authority, or by a cheap and easy rejection of both.[33]

As we have seen, Wittgenstein does not construct a philosophic religion, but neither do we find in him, as Holland would agree, blind acquiescence to, or cheap and easy rejection of religion. In fact, the intellectual effort involved in paying attention to particular cases, captures the spirit of Wittgenstein's attitude to religion exemplified in the five different contexts in which he discusses the relation of philosophy to religion.

We have been emphasising what philosophical enquiry became for Kierkegaard and Wittgenstein. They taught us conceptual differences, elucidated a heterogeneity of perspectives, which cannot be reduced to the unity of any metaphysical system. But misleading conclusions have been drawn from their philosophical endeavours, even by those sympathetic to them. It has been said that according to Kierkegaard and Wittgenstein, all perspectives other than one's own must be regarded as alternatives; moral criticism of others is impossible; all perspectives can be given equal plausibility. Anyone who advances such conclusions, it is said, surrenders any claim to serious philosophical authorship. But do these three conclusions follow from Kierkegaard's and Wittgenstein's methods?

First, E. D. Klemke claims that the purpose of Kierkegaard's literary style of presentation in the pseudonymous works 'is to show that to a disinterested and cognizing subject there are always genuine ethical *alternatives*. Reflection does not reduce the multiplicity to a unity . . . A scientific or philosophical ethics – in the sense of a discipline which can remove ultimate differences concerning the good, etc. – is hence a chimera.'[34] Klemke's conclusion is correct, but it does not entail regarding all perspective as alternatives. People differ morally, not simply in the choices they make given the same alternatives, but in what they are prepared to count as alternatives. To say that all moral perspectives other than one's own *must* be seen as alternatives, is already to impose a definite attitude towards them which is but one possible attitude among others.[35] Nothing in Kierkegaard's or Wittgenstein's methods need lead to such an imposition.

Second, Klemke thinks that, according to Kierkegaard, 'There is no immediate ethical relationship between one individual and another. Therefore, any individual can question only himself ethically. None can question another . . . Therefore, the attempt to find intersubjectively valid ethical judgements ("One ought to do . . .") is futile. There are, and can be, no such judgements.'[36] Wittgenstein's insistence that in ethical matters he has to speak for himself, has been thought to lead to the same conclusions. But the absence of a science of ethics does not imply that people do not reflect on moral matters.[37] There is a difference between reflective and unreflective criticism, the former often being one of the marks of moral responsibility.[38] Moral differences do not rule out the possibility of criticism of others. Kierkegaard and Wittgenstein are simply calling attention to the moral form such criticism takes.

Third, Klemke thinks that Kierkegaard is saying: '*All* of the various modes of existence, that is, all of the alternative answers to the questions "What is the good?", "What ought I to do?", etc. can be given equal plausibility to the genuinely reflective man.'[39] This suggestion is contradictory, since the judgement of 'equal plausibility' implies the very notion of a common rationality Kierkegaard and Wittgenstein are attacking. So far from being the only judgement open to the genuinely reflective man, such a man would recognise its vacuity.

Neither Kierkegaard nor Wittgenstein, then, hold the three views attributed to them. But neither need they embrace the only mode of judgement many think is open to them once a science of ethics is rejected. It is the mode of judgement Klemke ascribes to Kierkegaard. Speaking of moral judgement, he says: 'the condition for such certitude (as distinct from rational and objective certainty) is passionate inwardness, not reflection. The problem is, therefore, "resolved" by an existential choice, a leap.'[40] To argue in this way, however, suggests that the possibility of reflection and objectivity *does* depend on a science of ethics. Further, by placing 'the choosing self' outside all possible relations, movements and institutions, the notion of such a self and its choice or leap become as metaphysically suspect as the science of ethics they were meant to replace.

The essential burden of Kierkegaard's and Wittgenstein's remarks need not involve these difficulties. Think of the ways in which various things may absorb us.[41] This does not involve a choice externally related to what is embraced, any more than we have an external relation between willing and acting. In criticising the notion of a science of ethics, Kierkegaard and Wittgenstein clear a conceptual space in which our allegiances to various values can be themselves. They show that these allegiances cannot be reduced to a unity and combat confusions concerning them. Wittgenstein says in *Culture and Value*, 'My ideal is a certain coolness. A temple providing a setting for the passions without meddling with them'.[42]

Having noted the various misunderstandings concerning Kierkegaard's and Wittgenstein's philosophical methods, are we now able to endorse the previous suggestion that nothing separates them? O. K. Bouwsma is correct in noting an analogy between what he calls 'the logical aspects' of their investigations: 'There is illusion in both cases. The task in both cases is conceived as that of dispelling illusions. The illusion is in both cases one of misunderstanding certain languages . . . But those who seek to understand ordinary language and those who seek to understand the Scriptures run into confusion due to mistaken expectations concerning what the language must mean.'[43] Bouwsma says that the indirect method by which such confusions are unravelled is what Socrates, Kierkegaard and Wittgenstein have in common:

> the way to dispel an illusion is not by presenting the subject in a direct way – one must change the person who is under the illusion. No one is going to understand what it means to become a Christian until he has first understood what such a man is before he becomes a Christian. Those young friends of Socrates also had to come to understand something about themselves before they could join Socrates in asking his questions. All of us who learn from Wittgenstein had to come to understand something about ourselves, about our confusions, before we could return to where we were when as children we understood. Philosophy is generally an ailment which children don't have. There is no commonsense answer to a philosophical problem – hence the long way round.[44]

The only difference between Kierkegaard and Wittgenstein, it may be thought, is that 'Wittgenstein's interest is more general because he is interested in all philosophical confusion, and not simply in confusions that arise in connection with Christianity.'[45]

Yet, as Bouwsma recognises, it would be misleading to be content with this conclusion. This is because it gives insufficient weight to the fact that 'Kierkegaard introduces the distinctions he needs for his special purposes' whereas 'Wittgenstein introduces those that anyone may need in clearing up confusion.'[46] As we have seen, Kierkegaard's special purposes concerned his hope of freeing people from 'the monstrous illusion'; from confusions concerning what it means to become a Christian. This aim was his main priority. To be sure, philosophical clarifications are provided in the course of pursuing it, but these, for Kierkegaard, are a secondary consideration. From the outset he saw himself as a religious writer in Christendom, and he speaks of his *tactics* in his pseudonymous works. He insists that anyone who does not appreciate these tactics, misunderstands the whole corpus of his work:

> Supposing that . . . a reader understands perfectly and appraises critically the individual aesthetic productions, he will nevertheless totally misunderstand me, inasmuch as he does not understand the religious totality in my whole work as an author. Suppose, then, that another understands my works in the totality of their religious reference, but does not understand a single one of the aesthetic productions contained in them – I would say that this lack of understanding is not an essential lack.[47]

Bouwsma brings out well how Kierkegaard's religious priorities affect the task he took himself to be confronted with; a task importantly different from Wittgenstein's:

> In the work of Wittgenstein there is ordinary language we understand. That ordinary language is related to words or expressions that give us trouble. In ordinary language we discover the corrective of the language which expresses the confusion. In the work of Kierkegaard there corresponds to ordinary language in Wittgenstein the language of Scriptures, which Kierkegaard understands. Without this latter assumption Kierkegaard cannot be effective. And this is not how it is in Wittgenstein. There, ordinary language is taken to be language which we all understand. Here, there is agreement.[48] But Kierkegaard's task is in that way more formidable. He has first to teach us how to understand the language of Scripture.[49]

But what form does the teaching take? As Bouwsma says, 'The question is as to how much of what Kierkegaard describes as the illusion is to be described as grammatical.'[50] What needs to be emphasised is that Kierkegaard is not simply clearing up grammatical confusions but, in depicting aesthetic, ethical and religious perspectives, challenging people about the meaning of their own lives. Bouwsma is right in saying that Kierkegaard 'was not . . . merely presenting possibilities. There is more. He was more interested in filling our hearts with something like terror. You are at stake. What is to become of you?'[51] Kierkegaard did this in relation to clearing up 'the monstrous illusion'. I think it would be problematic to argue that Kierkegaard thought, in a wider context, that philosophical reflection, if carried out with integrity, should lead one to see Christianity as the only adequate positive answer to the question of the meaning of life.[52]

Holland seems to find tensions in Wittgenstein's authorship because he thinks that he, too, aspires to a religious point of view. When Wittgenstein says that he cannot help seeing every problem from a religious point of view, Holland assumes that he must be expressing some form of religious belief. Naturally, he then wonders which form of religion it is. He agrees with Taylor that 'A man who is religious without having any religion in particular is hard to come by for the same reason that it would be hard to find a man who is a good citizen, but a citizen of no city in particular.'[53] But did not Wittgenstein say, 'The philosopher is not a citizen of any community of ideas, that is what makes him a philosopher'[54]? On Holland's view, what could this mean?

Among dictionary definitions of 'religious' we have: 'strict', 'rigid', 'scrupulous' and 'conscientious'. Rush Rhees suggested to me that it is dangerous to say more of Wittgenstein's remark: he applied himself to philosophy religiously, that is all. It would be absurd to ask in which historical religion this application takes place! Holland seems to appreciate this sense of 'religious application' when he says of Wittgenstein: 'The fact that the problems were there had the same sort of significance for him as the fact that good and evil are there. This is how it was that the sphere of his work and the sphere of the ethical were both seen by Wittgenstein from a religious point of view. And one of the consequences of the two being connected in this way was, I think, that his work demanded of him what a religious vocation would have demanded.'[55] But, then, Holland turns the philosophical vocation into a religion: 'His work, I suggested, was like a religious vocation in what it demanded of him. If that was right, we have in effect arrived at the following result already – Wittgenstein cannot pray lest he become soft. And he cannot become soft because his religiously given, or as we might also venture to say, his divinely appointed vocation, will not allow it. In short, God does not want him to worship.'[56] But no such result follows from saying that Wittgenstein applied himself to philosophy religiously. The problems he wrestled with were conceptual, not personal. Thus, it is a mistake to suggest, as Bouwsma does, that a philosophical clarification of the language of Scripture is deficient if one does not respond to it religiously as Kierkegaard did: 'We get, accordingly, a grammatical elaboration of the language when what is required is obedience and surrender. The elaboration is cheap in that one can indulge in that and enjoy at the same time one's intellectual respectability.'[57] But the grammatical elucidation may take the form of clarifying that the language of Scripture makes demands of its readers. This is not itself a form of religious surrender, but why should it be? Philosophy is concerned with clarity, not religious confessions. No doubt, if clarity does not lead to confession that is an offence in the eyes of Christianity. But it does not follow that Christianity is an offence to philosophy,[58] or that grammatical clarifications are cheap.

Wittgenstein's problems have their roots, not in his personal life, but in tendencies of thought to which anyone can be susceptible, since they arise from the language we share. This remains so, even if we agree with Holland's further claim that religion influenced the way in which Wittgenstein saw philosophical problems: 'the ethical and . . . the Supernatural, entered into the conditions of their existence. In other words, the wonder was that these great problems – concerning the foundations of knowledge, and the relation between thinking and reality, and what it is to say something – should be there at all.'[59] If this wonder is the result of religious influence, we may ask whether someone could see philosophical problems as Wittgenstein did, without having in him the possibility, at least, of religious belief.[60] On the other hand, we must remember that this religious influence is consistent with Wittgenstein's saying, 'I am not a religious man'.

Given that Kierkegaard's aims differ from Wittgenstein's, why not bring our deliberations to a close by saying that while Kierkegaard fully appreciated the clarificatory role of philosophy, he turned from it quite consciously to pursue his religious purposes?[61] After all, does he not say, 'All honour to learning and scholarship, all praise to the man who can control the material detail, organising it with the authority of genuine insight, with the reliability that comes from acquaintance with the original sources'?[62] But this conclusion is too simple. Kierkegaard's comments refer to scholarship in general. We need to pay attention to what he says about philosophy in particular. When we do so, we find that Kierkegaard ignores aspects of authenticity in philosophical authorship which one finds in Wittgenstein.

Kierkegaard says: 'I can very well call Socrates my teacher – whereas I have only believed, and only believe in One, the Lord Jesus Christ.'[63] Why did Kierkegaard turn from Socrates to Christ? Partly, because he saw that philosophy as such cannot determine the meaning of life. Socrates's achievement was to recognise this. He reveals the comic aspect of trying to attach one's eternal happiness to philosophy: 'The comical appears only when the subject with an infinite passionate interest tries to attach his eternal happiness to philosophical speculation. But the speculative philosopher does not pose the problem of which we speak; for precisely as a speculative philosopher he becomes too objective to concern himself about an eternal happiness.'[64] Thus Kierkegaard revises his early criticisms of Socrates. He no longer accuses him of infinite negativity. On the contrary, he regards the famous Socratic ignorance concerning the nature of the good life as the highest attainment of paganism: 'Humanly speaking, that was surely a magnanimous undertaking.'[65] But, where the meaning of one's life is concerned, one cannot remain with these negative conclusions. Hence, Kierkegaard continues: 'But Christianity is a power far too great to be willing as a matter of course to make use of a man's magnanimous resolution . . . wherefore Christianity or Governance took the liberty of so arranging my subsequent life that there could be no misunderstanding (as indeed there was not from the beginning) as to whether it was I that stood in need of Christianity or Christianity that stood in need of me.'[66]

Kierkegaard, as I noted at the outset, wants authorship to be a serious calling. He protests against the assumption 'that one need not enquire about the communicator, but only about the communication,'[67] and insists that we should see whether an 'author's personal existence comports with his communication'.[68] Kierkegaard writes in his Journals: 'I surely do not deny that I still recognise an *imperative of understanding* and that through it one can work upon man, *but it must be taken up into my life*, and that is what I now recognise as the most important thing.'[69] But because the imperative of understanding cannot determine the meaning of life in some theoretical way, Kierkegaard assumes that it can only be taken up into one's personal life if it serves some other purpose. In his case, that purpose was the aim of bringing people to Christianity. Kierkegaard does not give sufficient attention to ways in which philosophical imperatives *as such* can be taken up into a person's life and, as a result, neglects important aspects of authentic authorship in philosophy.

The same neglect, it seems to me, is found in Holland's treatment of Wittgenstein. As we have seen, he sees Wittgenstein's struggle for clarity as an expression of his wonder at the world; a wonder which is shown in his endeavours to show us language as a city with no main road. This involved Wittgenstein in elucidations of perspectives he did not embrace personally. Holland says: 'As a matter of fact, there is a kind of insight that enables a few gifted people who have it, not only to feel the full force of spiritual possibilities which they do not occupy, but even to be better perceivers of what is involved than the occupants themselves; and Wittgenstein probably had that insight.'[70] But Holland has difficulty in seeing how the struggle for such insight could be connected with one's personal problems. He says: 'the idea of somebody's arriving at a view of *his own problems* by that route is preposterous'.[71] Similarly, Kierkegaard says, 'The person of an abstract thinker is irrelevant to his thought.'[72] But what of non-abstract, non-metaphysical thinkers, such as Socrates and Wittgenstein? Kierkegaard's view is that in relation to the philosophical work of such thinkers, questions concerning their personal lives simply do not arise. According to him, that is what such thinkers have come to realise. Bouwsma concurs with this judgement: 'whereas Kierkegaard's interest lies in saving Christianity for the world or to make sure that Christianity is understood, Wittgenstein is interested in saving intelligence – which means us – from the corruption that comes as natural to us. Purity of heart would be incidental to this'.[73] Wittgenstein would not agree. To accept Kierkegaard's, Bouwsma's and Holland's conclusions would be to miss an important aspect of what is involved in philosophical authorship for Wittgenstein. No doubt Holland and Bouwsma want to remind us that the source of Wittgenstein's philosophical problems is not personal. They arise from a wonder at the world. Quite so, but *the struggle with these problems is personal.* In fact, the struggle for clarity has analogies with a moral struggle. It is in this context, it seems to me, that Wittgenstein's concern with style is deeper than Kierkegaard's.

In 1937, Wittgenstein wrote: 'What one writes about oneself cannot be more truthful than one is.'[74] According to Rush Rhees,[75] Wittgenstein said, later, that self-deception must have a harmful effect on one's style, and that a person's state of soul could hide these deficiencies from him. He thought something akin to this had happened in Mahler's music. Holland spoke of Mahler's *pathetisch* pantheism. Wittgenstein wrote in 1948:

If it is true that Mahler's music is worthless, as I believe to be the case, then the question is what I think he ought to have done with his talent. For quite obviously it took a *set of very rare talents* to produce this bad music. Should he, say, have written his symphonies and burnt them? Or should he have done violence to himself and not written them? Should he have written them and realised that they were worthless?[76]

But how could Mahler recognise this? Wittgenstein writes: 'I can see it, because I can compare his music with what the great composers wrote. But *he* could not'.[77] Self-deception is likely to get in the way: 'If nobody you admire is like you, then presumably you believe in your own value only because you are *you*. Even someone who is struggling against vanity will, if his struggle is not entirely successful, still deceive himself about the value of his own work.'[78] Rhees said that Wittgenstein's own struggle to overcome the tendency to lie to himself about his own self-deception, drove him, at times, near to madness. Here, there is little distinction between Wittgenstein's philosophical struggle with the issue and his personal struggle with it in his work, hence the remark: ' . . . how can I be a logician if I'm not a human being?'[79]

Rush Rhees was with Wittgenstein on one occasion when he was thinking of sending to the publishers, as soon as possible, a draft of *Philosophical Investigations* which he had almost finished. He was very gloomy about it all. Rush Rhees said to him, 'You must know that it's head and shoulders above most of what is produced.' Wittgenstein replied, 'There's talent enough in it', but kept walking around the room, scowling. Contrast this with Kierkegaard's confident assertion that, from the outset, he knew he was a religious writer, and that, through the disinterested elucidations of his pseudonymous works, he was hoping to awaken others to an understanding which he possessed, but which they lacked. I shall not comment further on Kierkegaard's tactics as a religious writer in Christendom. What I do want to say is that, in Wittgenstein's case, we have a man greatly concerned with the style of his writing; absorbed, one might say, with how one can be an authentic philosophical author.

Notes

1. *The Point of View for my Work as an Author,* trans. Walter Lowrie (Oxford: University Press, 1939) p. 44.
2. See his Preface to *Philosophical Investigations.* Wittgenstein could not have been more wrong about his achievement.
3. *The Concept of Irony,* trans. with an introduction by Lee M. Capel (London: Collins, 1966) pp. 300–302.
4. Ibid.
5. Josiah Thómpson, *Kierkegaard* (London: Gollancz, 1974) p. 40.
6. Ibid.
7. Ibid., p. 147.
8. Ibid., p. 139.
9. *Culture and Value,* ed. G. H. von Wright, trans. by Peter Winch (Oxford: Basil Blackwell, 1977) p. 56.
10. *Ludwig Wittgenstein: Personal Recollections,* ed. Rush Rhees (Oxford: Basil Blackwell, 1981) p. 94.
11. R. F. Holland, 'Not Bending the Knee', *Philosophical Investigations,* Jan. 1990, p. 20.
12. I am not concerned with whether Wittgenstein was, in fact, a religious person. It would not affect the conclusions of my paper if it could be shown that he was.
13. Ibid.
14. Ibid., p. 21.
15. *Either/Or,* vol. ii, trans. Walter Lowrie (Oxford: Oxford University Press, 1946) p. 11.
16. Ibid., p. 14.
17. Holland, 'Not Bending the Knee', pp. 27–8.
18. Ibid.
19. *The Point of View,* p. 40.
20. Ibid., p. 27.
21. E. D. Klemke, *Studies in the Philosophy of Kierkegaard* (The Hague: Martinus Nijhoff, 1976) pp. 10–11.
22. *Concluding Unscientific Postscript,* trans. David F. Swenson (Princeton University Press, 1944) (p. 551, but unpaginated in text).
23. Ibid.
24. *That Individual* in *The Point of View,* p. 123.
25. *My Position as a Religious Writer in Christendom and My Tactics,* ibid., p. 159.
26. See Essay 15.
27. Holland, 'Not Bending the Knee', p. 27.
28. Ibid., p. 25.
29. Ibid., p. 27.
30. Ibid., pp. 25–6.
31. Ibid., p. 27.
32. Ibid., pp. 18–19.
33. Ibid., p. 25.
34. 'Some Misinterpretation of Kierkegaard', op. cit., p. 28.
35. Cf. 'What Can We Expect From Ethics?', *Proc. Aristotelian Soc.,* Supp.

Vol., 1989, where I argue against Bernard Williams's claim that critical reflection on ethical diversity entails viewing different moral perspectives as options or alternatives. This essay is in my collection, *Interventions in Ethics*, (Macmillan, 1992).

36. Klemke, *Studies in the Philosophy of Kierkegaard*, p. 34.
37. This is not denied by my claim in 'What Can We Expect from Ethics?' that intellectual reflection does not determine *the form* of the good life.
38. See Rush Rhees's 'Papers on Ethics' in *Without Answers* (Routledge & Kegan Paul, 1969).
39. Op cit, pp. 28–9.
40. Ibid.
41. I owe this suggestion to Peter Winch's 'Moral Integrity', in *Ethics and Action* (London: 1972).
42. *Culture and Value*, p. 2.
43. O. K. Bouwsma, 'Notes on Kierkegaard's "The Monstrous Illusion"', in *Without Proof or Evidence, Essays of O. K. Bouwsma*, ed. J. L. Craft and Ronald E. Hustwit (Lincoln and London: University of Nebraska Press, 1984) p. 85. Cf. Essay 6.
44. Ibid., p. 79.
45. O. K. Bouwsma, 'A New Sensibility', in *Toward A New Sensibility: Essays of O. K. Bouwsma*, edited and introduced by J. L. Croft and Ronald E. Hustwit (Lincoln and London: University of Nebraska Press) p. 4.
46. Ibid.
47. *The Point of View*, p. 6.
48. This is too sweeping a claim. For example, it ignores Wittgenstein's discussions of conceptual indeterminacy, and of how some people may be complete enigmas to others. See Essay 9.
49. 'Notes on Kierkegaard's "The Monstrous Illusion"', p. 85. I have discussed the implications of this difference, for Wittgenstein's methods, in *Belief, Change and Forms of Life* (London: Macmillan, 1986).
50. Ibid., p. 83.
51. 'Notes on Kierkegaard's "The Monstrous Illusion"', p. 74.
52. Michael Weston seemed to urge a consideration of this wider view in a discussion of the second version of my paper at a seminar at the University of Essex.
53. Holland, 'Not Bending the Knee', p. 25.
54. Ludwig Wittgenstein, *Zettel*, trans. G. E. M. Anscombe (Oxford: Basil Blackwell, 1967) para. 455.
55. Holland, 'Not Bending the Knee', p. 23.
56. Ibid., p. 24.
57. 'Notes on Kierkegaard's "The Monstrous Illusion"', p. 77.
58. For a further discussion of the distinction see my Critical Notice of C. Stephen Evans, *Kierkegaard's Fragments and Postscript* and H. A. Nielsen, *Where the Passion Is: A Reading of Kierkegaard's Philosophical Fragments*, *Philosophical Investigations*, vol. 9, no. 1, Jan. 1986.
59. Holland, 'Not Bending the Knee', p. 22.
60. I owe this consideration to my colleague, R. W. Beardsmore.
61. This suggestion was put to me by my colleague H. O. Mounce in a

discussion of the first version of this paper at the Philosophical Society at the University College of Swansea.

62. *Concluding Unscientific Postscript*, p. 15.
63. *The Point of View*, p. 41.
64. *Concluding Unscientific Postscript*, p. 54.
65. Ibid., p. 97.
66. Ibid.
67. *The Point of View*, p. 45.
68. Ibid.
69. *Journals*, ed. and trans. Alexander Dru (OUP, 1951) p. 15.
70. Holland, 'Not Bending the Knee', p. 20.
71. Ibid.
72. *Concluding Unscientific Postscript*, p. 319.
73. 'A New Sensibility', p. 4.
74. *Culture and Value* (Rush Rhees's translation). Peter Winch's published translation reads: 'You cannot write anything about yourself that is more truthful than you yourself are.'
75. The comments on Wittgenstein which follow I owe to seminars on *Culture and Value* by Rush Rhees at the University College of Swansea in 1979.
76. *Culture and Value*, p. 67.
77. Ibid.
78. Ibid.
79. See Ludwig Wittgenstein, *Letters to Russell, Keynes and Moore*, ed. G. H. von Wright, assisted by B. F. McGuinness (Oxford: Blackwell, 1974) pp. 57–8.

14
Advice to Philosophers who are Christians

CARDINAL MERCIER LECTURE, 1988[1]

According to Alvin Plantinga, 'we who are Christians and propose to be philosophers must not rest content with being philosophers who happen, incidentally, to be Christians; we must strive to be Christian philosophers.'[2] He gives advice on the character such striving should have. I think his advice is bad advice, bad for philosophy and bad for Christianity. Here I shall concentrate, in the main, on the philosophical aspects of this bad advice. The aspects I have in mind are of two kinds: first, Plantinga's appeal to considerations external to philosophy which distort the spirit of philosophical enquiry; second, Plantinga's conception of philosophical enquiry itself.

The Appeal to External Considerations

Plantinga claims, 'Christianity, these days, and in our part of the world, is on the move . . . There is also powerful evidence for this contention in philosophy' (p. 253). How is this supposed to be established? By comparison, it seems, with the state of philosophy in the fifties *vis-à-vis* Christianity: 'the public temper of main-line establishment philosophy in the English speaking world was deeply non-Christian. Few establishment philosophers were Christian: even fewer were willing to admit in public that they were, and still fewer thought of their being Christian as making a real difference to their practice as philosophers' (p. 253). These three characterisations of the fifties are very different from each other.

The first sign that Christianity in philosophy was not on the move in the fifties is supposed to be the fact that few Christians were in the philosophical establishment. Is that supposed to have been a bad thing? Plantinga assumes that it was. In that case, the remedy is obvious: Christians must become part of the philosophical establishment, or set up an establishment of their own. Plantinga is obviously pleased to announce that this is exactly what has happened: 'But things have changed. There are now many more Christians and many more unabashed Christians in the professional mainstream of American philosophical life. For example, the foundation of the Society for Christian Philosophers is both an evidence and a consequence of that fact. Founded some six years ago, it is now a thriving organisation with regional meetings in every part of the country; its members are deeply involved in American professional philosophical life. So Christianity is on the move, and on the move in philosophy, as well as in other areas of intellectual life' (p. 253).

That conclusion has not been earned; not, at least, if 'on the move' is supposed to be a commendatory description. If the phrase is merely descriptive, indicating that Christians can now be found where they could not be found in the fifties, very little follows from the fact in terms of Christian or philosophical commendation. To say that Christianity is on the move would not be to indicate the direction in which it is moving. To think otherwise would be to use what Flannery O'Connor called 'the language of the herd'. Writing to the novelist John Hawkes, she said: 'You say one becomes "evil" when one leaves the herd. I say that depends on what the herd is doing. The herd has been known to be right, in which case the one who leaves it is doing evil. When the herd is wrong, the one who leaves it is not doing evil but the right thing. If I remember rightly, you put that word, evil, in quotation marks, which means the standards you judge it by there are relative; in fact you would be looking at it there with the eyes of the herd.'[3]

In the same way, one might say that if someone argues: 'Christians used not to be part of the philosophical establishment, now they are, so Christianity is on the move' or 'Christians used not to be part of the philosophical establishment, but now they have a philosophical establishment of their own, so Christianity is on the move', one should again reply: 'That depends on what the establishment is doing'. This reply is as relevant to philosophy as it is to Christianity. Does the fact that there is a philosophical establishment show that philosophy is on the move? Surely, it can at least be argued that the reverse is true: and 'establishments' tend to be restrictive, self-congratulatory and stultifying. If this is so, the philosophical health of one's soul depends on keeping clear of them. Of course, in one sense, this is Plantinga's complaint against the philosophical establishment of the fifties with respect to Christian concerns. The answer, however, is not to commit the same mistake, compound such circumstances, erect similar obstacles, in the name of Christianity. It is not how something stands with respect to an establishment which determines whether that 'something' deserves to be called Christianity or philosophy 'on the move'. This would be to judge Christianity and philosophy by an appeal to external considerations. Rather, judgements which are themselves Christian or philosophical should be brought to bear on the respective establishments. Establishments may be healthy, but their health is not simply a matter of their being establishments.

The second consideration Plantinga appeals to is the fact that now, in America, unlike in the fifties, Christians who are members of the philosophical establishment are not ashamed to say that they are Christians. It is, of course, true that it is a condemnation of a Christian to say that he is ashamed to say he is a Christian in the professional circles in which he moves. On the other hand, that philosophers who are Christians are now not ashamed to say so does not, in itself, show that something called 'Christian philosophy' is on the move. In fact, it shows nothing at all about the philosophical quality of the work of the Christians concerned. Philosophers who are not ashamed to say they are Christians may still make up a pretty poor bunch of philosophers. Incidentally, readiness to testify cannot, in abstraction, be commended. Much depends on the circumstances, the spirit and the tone. In certain contexts, the ever-ready testifier may exemplify a lack of those very truths to which he takes himself to be a witness.

The third consideration Plantinga appeals to, in attempting to show that Christian philosophy is on the move, is the fact that now, unlike in the fifties, Christians think that being a Christian makes a real difference to the way in which they practise philosophy. Now, Christians have a Christian philosophy. How does Plantinga think of this? Does he allow that if philosophers in the fifties thought otherwise, they could have arrived at this conviction philosophically? If not, if he is suggesting that philosophers in the fifties did not espouse a Christian philosophy simply because the external pressure against doing so was so strong, or because it was not fashionable to do so, it will be no answer to cite the fact that nowadays Christians do espouse a Christian philosophy. The answer why is obvious: the new practice may be just as much a matter of fashion as the old practice; just as much the result of pressure, pressure, for example, from the Society for Christian Philosophers.

If some Christians today say that there is such a thing as Christian philosophy, I take it that they think that such a claim can be defended philosophically. In the same way, the philosophers of the fifties would have been saying that there is no such thing as Christian philosophy, and they advanced philosophical reasons for saying so. The nature of philosophy is itself a philosophical question, and the answer cannot be taken for granted. The question, 'Can there be a Christian philosophy?' is itself a philosophical question. It cannot be answered by saying, 'Of course there can, and we have regional meetings to prove it'. Once again, that would be an attempt to answer, by an appeal to external considerations, what ought to be discussed philosophically. It is at this point that we need to turn to considerations which are internal to philosophy.

Before doing so, however, I want to show how external considerations are also at work in the advice Plantinga gives to a student who is a Christian proposing to study philosophy; advice which I think any student wanting to study philosophy should ignore. Plantinga laments that 'most of the major philosophy departments in America have next to nothing to offer the student intent on coming to see how to be a Christian in philosophy' (p. 254). He outlines the likely fate of a Christian college student who becomes a graduate at Princeton, Berkeley, Pittsburgh or Arizona: 'There she learns how philosophy is presently practised. The burning questions of the day are such topics as the new theory of reference; the realism/anti-realism controversy; the problems with probability; Quine's claims about the radical indeterminacy of translation; Rawls on justice; the causal theory of knowledge; Gettier problems; the artificial intelligence model for the understanding of what it is to be a person; the question of the ontological status of unobservable entities in science or anywhere else; whether mathematics can be reduced to set theory and whether abstract entities generally – numbers, propositions, properties – can be, as we quaintly say, "dispensed with"; whether possible worlds are abstract or concrete; whether our assertions are best seen as mere moves in a language game or as attempts to state the sober truth about the world; whether the rational egoist can be shown to be irrational, and all the rest' (pp. 254–5). We may or may not be depressed at the fact that these are, allegedly, the burning questions of philosophy today. We may or may not be depressed at some of Plantinga's descriptions of what he takes these issues to be. But if this depression is itself intellectual, Plantinga can give no account of it. Why not?

He tells us: 'Philosophy is a social enterprise; and our standards and assumptions – the parameters within which we practise our craft – are set by our mentors and by the great contemporary centres of philosophy' (p. 255). Saying this is unobjectionable in so far as it is taken as an indication that philosophy and its problems, like any other subject, has a history and diverse traditions. The subject is not the creation of an individual. Nevertheless, the critical character of philosophical enquiry is an essential feature of it. Think of the critical character of the great works of philosophy. Of course, a student may agree with his teachers, but whether he has made that agreement his own will be shown in his independence in criticising other views. Failure to display that independence leads to charges of unthinking conformity and slavish adherence. Such is the picture we get from Plantinga's description of his graduate student. He says, 'It is then natural for her, after she gets her Ph.D., to continue to think about and work on these topics. And it is natural, furthermore, for her to work on them in the way she was taught to, thinking about them in the light of the assumptions made by her mentors and in terms of currently accepted ideas as to what a philosopher should start from or take for granted, what requires argument or defence, and what a satisfying philosophical explanation or a proper resolution to a philosophical question is like' (p. 255). But the crucial question concerns how the student is related to these activities Plantinga describes. Has she made them her own? In a give-away remark, Plantinga reveals that she has not: 'She will be uneasy about departing widely from these topics and assumptions, feeling instinctively that any such departures are at best marginally respectable' (p. 255). But if it is simply a question of respectability, no serious concern with philosophy is involved, no matter how clever the publications may be. Plantinga says of the graduate student's story, 'From one point of view this is natural and proper' (p. 255). I would deny that it is proper from any point of view. We all know the play of fashions in philosophy, the way one book supplants another on the student's shelves as one influentially-placed philosopher succeeds another. But these tendencies, however widespread, are not ones of which we, as philosophers, should be proud.

Plantinga says that from another point of view the fate of the graduate student is 'profoundly unsatisfactory' (p. 255). But what this amounts to is a fear that Christians will 'devote their best efforts to the topics fashionable in the non-Christian philosophical world' (p. 255). But is the remedy that Christians should devote their philosophical attention to what is fashionable in the Christian world? 'Christian philosophers', Plantinga tells us, 'are philosophers of the Christian community and it is part of their task as *Christian* philosophers to serve the Christian community. But the Christian community has its own questions, its own concerns, its own topics for investigation, its own agenda and its own research programme' (p. 255). There are wider issues involved in these remarks, but, for the moment, let us simply note that, once again, there is no discussion of whether the philosophy student in question has made these philosophical concerns his own. As far as anything we have been told so far goes, one fashion has been exchanged for another. In neither case has any serious commitment to philosophy been described. Plantinga wants the Christian philosopher to display autonomy, integrity and boldness. Heeding Plantinga's advice thus far would not lead to any of these virtues. On the contrary, one follower of fashion in Princeton or Berkeley has simply been replaced by another follower of fashion in Grand Rapids or Arkadelphia, Arkansas. The spirit of philosophical enquiry has yet to emerge. Given Plantinga's advice so far, it never will.

Religious Belief and Philosophical Enquiry

Plantinga clearly believes that there is such a thing as Christian philosophy. He also believes that there is such a thing as non-theistic philosophy. He says that the Christian philosopher may well think of 'topics of current concern in the broader philosophical world . . .' in 'a different way' (p. 256). Why does he think this? Much of the answer can be found by noting the conception of philosophy Plantinga wants to reject. Having rejected it, I suspect Plantinga thinks that his conception of philosophy is the only alternative. I want to show that this assumption is mistaken.

Plantinga is opposed to a conception of philosophy as the arbiter of either the truth or the rationality of religious belief: 'What I want to urge is that the Christian philosophical community ought not to think of itself as engaged in this common effort to determine the probability or philosophical plausibility of belief in God' (pp. 260–1). If the Christian thinks that he must justify his religious beliefs, as though they were probable or improbable hypotheses awaiting a verdict based on evidence common to believer and unbeliever alike, he will thereby not only fail to do justice to the character of religious belief, but also, notoriously, base his faith on the fiction of common evidence. In pointing this out, Plantinga is quite correct. It has indeed been a scandal in the philosophy of religion that it has been assumed, for so long, that foundationalism and evidentialism are the appropriate philosophical modes for discussing religious beliefs. But these conclusions are arrived at by reflecting on the character of religious belief. They do not lead to Plantinga's conception of a Christian philosophy. These conclusions are not confined to philosophers who are Christians or to something called a Christian mode of philosophising. Any philosopher reflecting on the logic or grammar of religious belief may reach these conclusions.

Plantinga also objects to the claim that philosophy can arrive at a set of criteria which determine the rationality or meaningfulness of any belief, religious belief included. These claims, as we know, led logical positivists to conclude that religious beliefs are meaningless. Plantinga quotes J. J. C. Smart saying in 1955: 'The main danger to theism today comes from people who want to say that "God exists" and "God does not exist" are equally absurd.' Why did philosophers come to such a radical conclusion? They did so because they adopted the 'verifiability criterion of meaning' 'which said, roughly, that a sentence is meaningful only if either it is analytic, or its truth or falsehood can be determined by empirical or scientific investigation – by the methods of the empirical sciences' (p. 257). As Plantinga says, no good arguments were given to show why these restrictive philosophical definitions should be adopted. He says of Christian philosophers: 'What they should have said to the positivists is: "Your criterion is mistaken: for such statements as *God loves us* and *God created the heavens and the earth* are clearly meaningful: so if they aren't verifiable in your sense, then it is false that all and only statements verifiable in that sense are meaningful"' (p. 258).

But how does Plantinga know that the meaning of these religious beliefs cannot be captured by the positivists' criteria? Surely, by reflecting on the place these beliefs have in people's lives and the roles they play there. Plantinga, of course, would also oppose a less restrictive, but, nevertheless, *common* set of criteria for what constitutes knowledge by which religious claims are to be assessed. He quotes remarks by David Tracy to indicate the viewpoint to which he is opposed. Tracy says:

In principle the fundamental loyalty of the theologian qua theologian is to that morality of scientific knowledge which he shares with his colleagues, the philosophers, historians and social scientists. No more than they can he allow his own – or his tradition's – beliefs to serve as warrants for his arguments. In fact, in all properly theological inquiry, the analysis should be characterised by those same ethical stances of autonomous judgement, critical judgment and properly sceptical hard-mindedness that characterises analysis in other fields.[4]

Plantinga wants the Christian philosopher to turn from these other fields to the preoccupations of his own. Speaking of his graduate student who becomes attracted to Quine's philosophy, he says, 'It should be natural for her to become totally involved in these projects and programmes, to come to think of fruitful and worthwhile philosophy as substantially circumscribed by them' (p. 256). Plantinga responds: 'This is understandable; but is also profoundly misdirected. Quine is a marvellously gifted philosopher: a subtle, original and powerful philosophical force. But his fundamental commitments, his fundamental projects and concerns, are wholly different from those of the Christian community – wholly different and, indeed, antithetical to them . . . So the Christian philosopher has his own topics and projects to think about' (p. 256). This response, in itself, however, would be insufficient, since philosophers might have no objection to concentrating on topics taken from the Christian community, taking them as a starting point, as long as they are then made subject to some common method of assessment. Such a position has been well expressed by John Wippel:

> Thus for the Christian it may be that in certain circumstances some revealed datum serves as a leading question or working hypothesis for his philosophical inquiry. While as a believing Christian he will continue to assent to this datum or believe in it, he may now decide to investigate it as a possible object of rational or philosophical demonstration. If he succeeds in finding rational evidence which supports it, then and to that extent his procedure will be strictly philosophical in the moment of proof. In other words, in the moment of proof his procedure cannot be described as Christian philosophy. But since in the moment of discovery it was his religious belief that first suggested this particular issue to him as a possible subject for philosophical investigation, one might refer to such a procedure as Christian philosophy in the order of discovery.[5]

Plantinga rejects such a conception of proof and wants to insist that when the Christian philosopher 'thinks about the topics of current concern in the broader philosophical world, he will think about them in his own way, which may be a *different* way' (p. 256). Yet, how can Plantinga draw this conclusion? Is it not by philosophical reflection that one can come to see that Tracy's and Wippel's conception of common standards is a confused one? And is not that reflection open to Christian and non-Christian alike? It does not lead us to a conception of Christian philosophy. On the contrary, it leads us away from such a thought.

Why does Plantinga think otherwise? Part of the answer is that he *assumes* that if Christian and non-Christian ways of thinking are said to be subject to philosophical enquiry, that *must* mean that these modes of thought are to be assessed by common criteria. Since Plantinga does not believe these common criteria exist, he seems to reach the over-hasty conclusion that Christian and non-Christian modes of thought cannot be subject to common methods of philosophical enquiry. Plantinga says, 'Of course, if the verificationists had given cogent *arguments* for their criterion, from premises that had some legitimate claim on Christian or theistic thinkers, then perhaps there would have been a problem here for the Christian philosopher, then we would have been obliged either to agree that Christian theism is cognitively meaningless, or else revise or reject those premises' (p. 258).

Even here, in what may look like a concession to the broader philosophical community, what premises should have a legitimate claim on Christians is not specified. Further, the force of the apparent concession is blunted by remarks such as the following: 'Even if there were a set of methodological procedures held in common by most philosophers, historians and social scientists, or most secular philosophers, historians and social scientists, why should a Christian theologian give ultimate allegiance to them rather than, say, to God, or to the fundamental truths of Christianity?' (pp. 263–4). In any case, Plantinga's main position is that these counter-arguments against what is fundamental in Christianity simply do not exist. He says, 'Of course if there *were* powerful arguments on the other side, then there might be a problem here. But there aren't: so there isn't' (p. 266). He therefore concludes: 'Christian philosophers must be wary about assimilating or accepting presently popular philosophical ideas and procedures; for many of these have roots that are deeply anti-Christian. And finally the Christian philosophical community has a right to its perspective; it is under no obligation first to show that this perspective is plausible with respect to what is taken for granted by all philosophers, or most philosophers, or the leading philosophers of our day' (p. 271).

It would be unfair to Plantinga to suggest that he does not have philosophical arguments for these conclusions, but they are arguments which constitute a form of negative apologetics. When Plantinga says that 'the modern Christian *philosopher* has a perfect right, as a philosopher, to start from his belief in God. He has a right to assume it, take it for granted, in his philosophical work' (p. 264), what he means is that nobody can produce a general criterion of basicality – means of gauging whether a truth-claim is basic – to show that there is any impropriety involved in the Christian taking belief in God as basic in his perspective. Of course, he has to admit that he too possesses no such general criterion by which the unbeliever could be shown why belief in God should be basic. Believer and non-believer cannot stop each other from committing themselves to the fundamental beliefs of their perspectives. That is how far Plantinga's philosophising seems to take us. It does not follow at all from these conclusions, however, that Christian and non-Christian modes of thought cannot be the subject of a common mode of philosophical enquiry. In seeing what the characteristic concerns of such an enquiry are, we shall see how philosophy can go far beyond the somewhat arid limits of Plantinga's philosophical enterprise. We will be able to give substance to some of Plantinga's assurances; assurances which seem rather hollow in the light of his philosophical practices. Plantinga says:

> Of course I don't mean for a moment to suggest that Christian philosophers have nothing to learn from their non-Christian and non-theist colleagues: that would be a piece of foolish arrogance, utterly belied by the facts of the matter. Nor do I mean to suggest that Christian philosophers should retreat into their own isolated enclave, having as little as possible to do with non-theistic philosophers. Of course not! Christians have much to learn and much of enormous importance to learn by way of dialogue and discussion with their non-theistic colleagues. Christian philosophers must be intimately involved in the professional life of the philosophical community at large, both because of what they can learn and because of what they can contribute. Furthermore, while Christian philosophers need not and ought not to see themselves as involved, for example, in a common effort to determine whether

there is such a person as God, we are all, theist and non-theist alike, engaged in the common human project of understanding ourselves and the world in which we find ourselves. If the Christian philosophical community is doing its job properly, it will be engaged in a complicated, many-sided dialectical discussion, making its own contribution to that common human project. It must pay careful attention to other contributions; it must gain a deep understanding of them; it must learn what it can from them and it must take unbelief with profound seriousness. (pp. 279–81)

Despite these remarks and the reference to dialogue and a many-sided dialectical discussion, it must be remembered that the dialogue and discussion is supposed to be between some people doing something called Christian philosophy, and other people doing something called non-Christian philosophy. What I am insisting on is that the dialectical discussion, the common attempt at understanding, can refer to a mode of philosophical enquiry in which Christians and non-Christians can share. In the course of this enquiry issues, fundamental issues, arise on which the philosophical procedures advocated by Plantinga throw little light. Let us examine some of these.

First, it is possible for a Christian or a non-Christian to be philosophically puzzled about the grammar of belief in God. What kind of belief is it? Is 'God' a proper name? Does it make sense to ask what it stands for? It is clear that possessing a Christian belief does not, in itself, clarify these questions for us. Plantinga's negative apologetics will not prevent these puzzles from arising. For example, Plantinga says of the graduate student who is attracted by Quine's philosophy: 'Of course she will note certain tensions between her Christian belief and her way of practising philosophy' (p. 256). But can Plantinga take that for granted? After all, he admits to having a philosophical acquaintance who 'suggested that Christians should think of God as a *set* . . . the set of all true propositions, perhaps, or the set of right actions, or the union of those sets, or perhaps their Cartesian product' (p. 256). Plantinga depicts these suggestions as an attempt to harmonise perceived tensions between Quine's views and Christianity. But what if the suggestions were simply advanced as an account of the grammar of belief in God? How would Plantinga try to show the inadequacy of this account? Plantinga and his philosophical acquaintance are, presumably, disagreeing about the conceptual character of the same or similar religious beliefs. The religious beliefs are the same, but the philosophical accounts are different.[6] At least one distinguished philosopher of religion, whose religious background was not dissimilar to Plantinga's, nevertheless thought that Plantinga's philosophical projects concerning religious belief were fundamentally misconceived. Speaking for myself, while I might see how a philosopher of mathematics may say that thinking about sets gives glory to God, I think it confused to say, as Plantinga does, that the infinity of sets leads naturally to the belief in an infinite mind which can think them all, that it shows 'that sets owe their existence to *God's* thinking things together . . . that sets are indeed collections – collections collected by God' (p. 270). Such a conclusion, it seems to me, does not do justice to either the notion of infinity or the notion of divine activity. Religious concepts are being torn from their natural setting and brought into contexts where the proposed language concerning them is merely idling. I am not arguing for this conclusion now. My point is that my reaction is a possible one in face of Plantinga's suggestion about how a Christian philosopher should argue about sets.

Faced with these different philosophical accounts, one has no option but to continue the discussion, hoping that clarity will be achieved. In the course of the discussion, one may get someone to see that he is confused, or he may get one to recognise one's own confusion. There is no by-passing such discussion and the hazards it involves if we want to pass from philosophical puzzlement to clarity. In such a discussion, it may become impossible to draw a sharp line between philosophical and religious difficulties. The course of the argument may cloud or clarify a person's religion or atheism, and he may lose or gain either as a result. We cannot legislate in an a priori fashion about such matters. If I am confused about the sense in which belief in God is basic, I can only be freed from my confusion if I can be brought to see what led me into it in the first place. Simply being told that no general criterion of basicality has been found which prevents the Christian saying that belief in God is basic, will not be of much help here. What I am puzzled about is the kind of basicality that belief in God has, or what believing in God amounts to. Here, a non-confused non-Christian may be of infinitely greater help than a philosophically confused Christian. Coming to see what belief in God means is a matter of bringing out its grammar and clearing away the tendencies of thought which stand in the way of the clarity I desire.

Plantinga is right in thinking that belief and unbelief cannot be assessed by common evidence or common criteria of rationality. But this should not lead to notions of Christian and non-Christian philosophies. Plantinga wants to insist that perspectives, for example, Christian perspectives, should not be assessed by criteria of meaning which are alien to them. But this insistence on the differences between perspectives, on differences between beliefs and concepts which feature in our lives, was one of the main features of Wittgenstein's *Philosophical Investigations*, published posthumously in 1953, a work about which and its influence on philosophy, Plantinga, and reformed epistemologists generally, are interestingly, if not surprisingly, silent. This may be because Wittgenstein's work shows the possibility of a common method, a common engagement in disinterested enquiry which Christians and non-Christians alike can participate in. As we have seen, Plantinga is deeply suspicious of the notion of a common method. He assumes that the practice of a common method entails believing in the availability of common criteria of truth or rationality by which any belief can be assessed. But what if disinterested enquiry reveals a variety of meanings and conceptions of truth which cannot be reduced to any single paradigm? But this variety *can* only be revealed by clarifying the grammar of the various concepts involved in the language-games we play.

Plantinga is wrong, therefore, in suggesting that it is only with the benefit of hindsight that we can appreciate the inadequacy of the logical and epistemological parameters set by the collection *New Essays in Philosophical Theology*, published in 1955; 'a volume of essays that was to set the tone and topics for philosophy of religion for the next decade or more' (p. 257). The inadequacy of those parameters had *already* been exposed in Wittgenstein's work. What is true is that those insights, for the most part, were not appropriated in the philosophy of religion.

A comparison of Wittgenstein and Plantinga on 'what we take for granted' reveals how rich and substantial Wittgenstein's method is in contrast to Plantinga's negative apologetics. Plantinga says, as we have seen, that the modern Christian philosopher has a perfect right to start with his belief in God, to take it for granted. This right is established by the failure of any philosopher to produce a criterion of basicality which shows that the Christian philosopher cannot do this. By contrast, in *On Certainty*, Wittgenstein discusses a variety of propositions which we take for granted. It can be said that these propositions underlie others. The central question concerns what we mean by 'underlying' in these contexts. The propositions are basic, not because of any epistemic or phenomenological properties they may be said to possess, but by virtue of the place they occupy in human life. The propositions, such as 'There are physical objects', 'There are human beings', 'The earth has existed for a long time', are held fast by all that surrounds them. Instead of the aridity of negative apologetics, Wittgenstein endeavours to give perspicuous representations of what those surroundings are. The surroundings will not be the same in each case. Appropriating these insights for the philosophy of religion involves bringing out the basicality of belief in God, showing the kind of surroundings which hold it fast. So one does not *begin*, philosophically, by asserting the basicality of the beliefs. On the contrary, their basicality is something which has to be shown by giving perspicuous representations of their status. This is a difficult undertaking, as difficult in the case of 'Thou art God' as it is in the case of 'That's a human being'. Plantinga, it is true, does say that belief in God is connected with experiences such as 'hearing God speak', 'feeling punished by God', 'desiring to praise him', etc. The trouble is that they too are called properly basic, and the whole game of negative apologetics begins again. What is missing is a living presentation of the grammar of these beliefs and expressions. Without this, it is no good saying to someone philosophically puzzled by what these expressions and beliefs come to, that they are clearly meaningful to other people and then challenge him to show why they shouldn't be.

In elucidating the surroundings in which belief in God is held fast, the philosopher is not doing something called Christian philosophy, any more than he is doing non-Christian philosophy in elucidating the surroundings which hold certain forms of atheism fast. He is simply doing philosophy. Certainly, he is not embracing a religious or atheistic perspective by elucidating its grammar. His concern is with their conceptual character, not with their truth. Indeed, clarity about their conceptual character will bring one to see why philosophy cannot determine truth in such matters. Of course, the philosopher will be interested in what it means to speak of truth in such contexts, but that interest is not itself a desire to embrace those truths.

Wittgenstein talked of language as a city with no main road. Again and again in the history of philosophy, philosophers have wanted to postulate something, metaphysically, as the main road, seeing all other roads as subsidiaries or minor in relation to it. Wittgenstein wants to release us from this presumption. He wants to reveal the constant temptations which beset us, temptations to obscure the variety of the world. He wants, as far as possible, to give us clarity concerning that variety; to give us a disinterested view of it. Is not this a philosophical passion which characterises his work? If this is our understanding, too, of what a philosophical interest is, then we can see, at the same time, why there cannot be a Christian philosophy, a Marxist philosophy or any other philosophy of that kind.

Of course, we do not *start* with a conception of philosophy as disinterested enquiry. We start with our puzzles and difficulties. By working through them, some may come to conclusions they wish to describe as Christian or Marxist philosophy. But, then, they will have reached these conclusions by listening to argument and counter-argument. The method of procedure will not itself be Christian or Marxist. The person who thinks the variety philosophy should recognise is being distorted by these conclusions will try to get someone who reaches these conclusions to look at them again. This, too, can only be achieved by discussion, the philosophical discussion which cannot be bypassed.

In any event, whatever conclusions are reached, this openness to discussion is very different from an attitude which says that the parameters for discussion must be determined *ab initio* by Christian or Marxist values. Suppose someone says that they intend calling these latter procedures 'philosophy'. True, no one can stop him doing so. All we can do, then, is to show the differences involved between these procedures and disinterested enquiry. What cannot be allowed is that Christian or Marxist philosophies, so conceived, can pretend to carry on in the spirit of disinterested enquiry.

It may be thought that we cannot give ourselves to disinterested enquiry without sacrificing some traditional religious claims. For example, it may be asked, how can we say, philosophically, that the city has no main road, while at the same time believe, religiously, that God is the creator of the city. The answer is that, in thinking a tension exists here, a religious belief is being misconstrued as a theoretical explanation. To say that all things are created by God, is not to give a theoretical explanation of all things. Such a displacement of religious belief occurs when Plantinga says: 'Belief in the existence of God is in the same boat as belief in the truths of logic, other minds, the past and perceptual objects; in each case God has so constructed us that in the right circumstances we acquire the belief in question' (p. 262). Belief in God does have something to do with all the factors Plantinga mentions. We pray, 'God be in my mind, and in my understanding'. We are asked to look on others as our neighbours. Past, present and future are said to be in God's hands and we see him in his creation. But are these religious beliefs captured by Plantinga's reference to the way in which we are allegedly constructed? The shift from 'creation' to 'construction' marks the shift from religious belief to a confused epistemological theory. The same reference to 'construction' has led some Reformed epistemologists to displace the belief that all men are created in the image of God, with a confused philosophical or psychological thesis which says that all human beings have been so constructed that they know that there is a God.[7]

Plantinga holds that fundamental Christian beliefs are not answerable to philosophical justification. I agree, but I come to this conclusion as a result of philosophical reflection.[8] It is not a presumption with which I begin. This does not mean that religious beliefs are ultimately based on philosophical justifications after all, since the philosophical procedures referred to are those which seek to clarify the grammar of religious concepts themselves, and not ones which impose alien criteria and tests on these concepts. But there is risk involved in philosophical enquiry. The conclusions I have come to cannot be guaranteed in advance, and one may not arrive at them. But the man who is genuinely philosophically puzzled has no choice. He has to go where the argument takes him. With Plantinga, it seems, things are different. As we have seen, he believes that although the 'Christian philosopher does indeed have a responsibility to the philosophical world at large; . . . his fundamental responsibility is to the Christian community, and finally to God' (p. 262). Contrast this with Wittgenstein's remark: 'The philosopher is not a citizen of any community of ideas; that's what makes him a philosopher.'[9]

In concluding, I must not be taken to have suggested that there is a necessary tension between a Christian and the disinterested enquiry I have talked of. Of course, many Christians have viewed such enquiry with distrust and dislike, and that is always likely to be the case. But for others, it need not be so. While genuinely giving himself up to disinterested enquiry, a Christian may also feel that through it those beliefs which mean so much to him will be shown to possess a distinctive grammar and to play an equally distinctive role in human life. Simone Weil made a remark once by which she probably meant more than this. But at least the Christian conviction I have indicated, as a Christian who gives himself to disinterested enquiry, might find a place in her words when she said that, if she pursued truth without fear, she would find herself, in the end, falling into the arms of Christ.

Notes

1. This paper was one of the Cardinal Mercier Lectures delivered at the University of Leuven 1988. A wider consideration of Plantinga's epistemology of religion was given in the 1987 Aquinas Lecture 'Shaking the Foundationalists', delivered at Blackfriars, Oxford. Material used in that lecture appears in *Faith After Foundationalism* (Routledge 1988).
2. Alvin Plantinga, 'Advice to Christian Philosophers', *Faith and Philosophy*, vol. 1, no. 3 (July 1984) p. 271. All quotations from Plantinga are from this paper.
3. Flannery O'Connor, *Letters of Flannery O'Connor: The Habit of Being*, selected and edited by Sally Fitzgerald (New York: Vintage Books, 1980) p. 456.
4. David Tracy, *Blessed Rage for Order* (New York: Seabury Press, 1975) p. 7.
5. John F. Wippel, 'The Possibility of a Christian Philosophy: A Thomistic Perspective', *Faith and Philosophy*, vol. 1, no. 3 (July 1984) p. 280.
6. I am not denying the possibility that in some instances the philosophical differences may themselves reflect religious differences between the philosophers concerned. Religious belief itself is, after all, a ragged phenomenon.
7. See Nicholas Wolterstorff, 'Can Belief in God be Rational?', in *Faith and Rationality*, edited by Alvin Plantinga and Nicholas Wolterstorff, University of Notre Dame Press 1983. I do not claim to have argued fully for my counter-conclusions here. I am only indicating the direction such argument might take. For a fuller account see D. Z. Phillips, *Faith After Foundationalism*.
8. This does not commit me to the view that no religious belief can be confused. See Essays 6 & 7.
9. Ludwig Wittgenstein, *Zettel*, trans. G. E. M. Anscombe (Oxford: Basil Blackwell, 1967) para. 455.

15

Religion in
Wittgenstein's Mirror

There is a well-known remark in Wittgenstein's *Philosophical Invest-igations* which even some philosophers sympathetic to his work have found very hard to accept. It reads:

> Philosophy may in no way interfere with the actual use of lan-guage; it can in the end only describe it.
> For it cannot give it any foundation either.
> It leaves everything as it is. (*PI*, I, para. 24)

Surely, it is said, that is carrying matters too far. Wittgenstein's hyperbole should be excused as a harmless stylistic flourish.

That reaction does a great disservice to Wittgenstein's work, whether one is sympathetic to that work or not. It obscures, or even ignores, what a philosophical problem was for him. When we are puzzled philosophically, Wittgenstein argued, what we stand in need of is not additional information, but a clearer view of what lies before us. We need to appreciate how we have become confused concerning the diverse areas of discourse in which we are engaged. This is why Wittgenstein says that he is not trying to get us to believe something we do not believe, but to do something we will not do.[1] In striving for clarity, it is difficult for us to leave everything as it is. Wittgenstein expressed his philosophical ideal as follows in 1931: 'I ought to be no more than a mirror in which my reader can see his own thinking with all its deformities so that helped in this way, he can put it right' (*CV*, p. 18).

This ideal remained Wittgenstein's to the end of his life. He strove after it in every area of philosophical inquiry he engaged in. In 1950, the year before his death, he wrote of religious belief:

> Actually I should like to say that in this case too the *words* you utter or what you think as you utter them are not what matters, as

much as the difference they make at various points of your life. How do I know that two people mean the same when each says he believes in God? And just the same goes for belief in the Trinity. A theology which insists on the use of *certain particular* words and phrases, and outlaws others, does not make anything clearer (Karl Barth). It gesticulates with words, as one might say, because it wants to say something and does not know how to express it. *Practice* gives the words their sense. (*CV*, p. 85)

Wittgenstein's appeal to practice has been badly misunderstood in contemporary philosophy of religion. No single account can be given of it, since different things need to be said in different contexts. What does it mean to give practice its due, by being no more, as a philosopher, than a critical mirror? In this essay I shall consider five contexts in which this question needs to be answered.

I

The first context to consider is that in which we may be tempted to think that all forms of religious belief are confused. We fail to give religious practice its due because we bring to it preconceptions concerning what words *must* mean. For example, we may assume that all words operate as names and refer to objects. Thus, when we come across the word 'God', we start looking for the object it stands for. We may even think that we can come across pictures, such as Michelangelo's painting of God creating Adam, or the Last Judgement, in which we actually have depictions of the reference of the names 'man' and 'God'. But, of course, it will be said, this old man in Michelangelo's *Creation of Adam* no more exists than the man in the moon.

Wittgenstein is too optimistic when he says of Michelangelo's painting, 'we certainly wouldn't think this the Deity. The picture has to be used in an entirely different way if we are to call the man in that queer blanket "God" and so on' (*LC*, p. 63). The philosopher J. L. Mackie used the picture precisely in the way Wittgenstein thought to be obviously mistaken. He thought that while a believer need not commit himself to every detail in the painting of the Last Judgement, *some* details of this kind must be an approximation to a description of an empirical event, if the notion of a Last Judgement is to mean anything. Mackie says: 'I am saying only that talk about a last judgement *can* be understood literally' (Mackie, 1982, p. 3). But if by 'literal' use we mean 'standard' use, why should we assume that the literal is always the empirical or the factual? When we speak of Creation or the Last Judgement, we are not talking metaphorically, or in some non-literal sense. For Mackie, Michelangelo's painting is taken to be an attempted approximation to empirical accuracy; a case of Michelangelo 'doing his best', as Wittgenstein comically remarks (*LC*, p. 63). We might then say, 'Of course, I can't show you the real thing, only the picture'. Wittgenstein retorts: 'The absurdity is, I've never taught him the technique of using this picture' (*LC*), a technique which applies to pictures of aunts and plants. Wittgenstein says, 'I could show Moore the picture of a tropical plant. There is a technique of comparison between picture and plant' (*LC*). But this use cannot be invoked where our use of the word 'God' is concerned: 'The word "God" is amongst the earliest learnt – pictures and catechisms, etc. But not the same consequences as with pictures of aunts. I wasn't shown [that which the picture pictured]' (*LC*, p. 59).

Even if we are sympathetic to religion, we may interpret Wittgenstein's remarks in a disastrous way. We may take him to be pointing out a shortcoming in religious pictures, as though they *try* to refer to God, but fail to do so because God is transcendent.[2] This interpretation ignores the fact that Wittgenstein is endeavouring to clarify *the kind* of picture concerning God this picture is. This is shown in the use made of it; a use which will fix the meaning of 'divine transcendence'. The meaning of 'transcendent', like the meaning of any other word, does not transcend its use. If it made sense to claim otherwise, which it does not, the meaning of religious concepts would be said to be beyond our practices; that is, beyond what we do with them. In thinking this, we would be turning away from the practices that we need to be clear about. Wittgenstein emphasises the point as follows:

> Religion teaches that the soul can exist when the body has disintegrated. Now do I understand this teaching? – Of course I understand it – I can imagine plenty of things in connection with it. And haven't pictures of these things been painted? And why should such a picture be only an imperfect rendering of the spoken doctrine? Why should it not do the *same* service as the words? And it is the service which is the point. (*PI*, II, p. 178)

If we wanted to understand what Michelangelo's painting shows about creation, we should have to pay attention to the nakedness of the figures in it: 'Naked came I from my mother's womb, and naked shall I return thither'. In Socrates' account of divine judgement in the *Gorgias*, both the judged and the judges are naked. Naked at birth, what comes our way comes from God. Naked at death, it is the state of one's soul which reveals purity or shame. Clothing, worldly status, is what is said to obscure these spiritual realities.

If we look at religious pictures as Mackie looked at them, it is not surprising to find description giving way to explanation. This is exactly what happened in post-Enlightenment thought. How *could* people possibly believe such things? Anthropologists, sociologists and psychoanalysts suggested that the belief was the superstitious product of a primitive mentality, unavoidable at that stage of human development. Wittgenstein showed that such thinkers are themselves in the grip of primitive superstition: 'In other words it's just false to say: Of course, these primitive peoples couldn't help wondering at everything. Though perhaps it is true that these people *did* wonder at all the things around them – To suppose they couldn't help wondering at them is a primitive superstition' (*CV*, p. 5). The appeal to necessity, which seeks to be explanatory, is idle. We need to concentrate on what the wonder amounted to in people's lives; to concentrate on practice.

In the same way, it is idle to claim that people in a scientific culture *cannot* entertain religious hopes and fears. Wittgenstein insists: 'we cannot exclude the possibility that *highly* civilised peoples will become liable to this very same fear once again; neither their civilisation nor scientific knowledge can protect them against this' (*CV*, p. 5). This does not mean that science cannot threaten religion. Wittgenstein acknowledges in 1930: 'All the same it's true enough that the spirit in which science is carried on nowadays is not compatible with fear of this kind' (*CV*, p. 5). But this incompatibility cannot be said, in general, to be between a sophisticated mode of understanding and primitive superstition. Rather, it is an incompatibility between the values, interests and spirit of two very different modes of thought.

If we say that religious belief is *necessarily* confused, we have failed, philosophically, to mirror its practices. In emphasising this, Wittgenstein calls into question the intellectualist assumption that religion is an outmoded way of thinking. He combats the prejudice which asserts that 'the science of culture is essentially a reformer's science' (Tylor, 1920, p. 453).

II

Even if we do not think religious belief is necessarily confused, we may still fail to mirror its practice in our philosophical accounts. We may be participants in religious practices and still give conceptually confused accounts of them. This is the second context we need to take into account. In 1950 Wittgenstein wrote:

> If someone who believes in God looks round and asks: 'Where does everything I see come from?', he is *not* craving for a (causal) explanation, and his question gets its sense from being the expression of a certain craving. He is, namely, expressing an attitude to all explanations – But how is this manifested in his life?

That is the crucial question for Wittgenstein. He continues:

> The attitude that's in question is that of taking a certain matter seriously and then, beyond a certain point, no longer regarding it as serious, but maintaining that something else is even more important. Someone may for instance say it's a very grave matter that such and such a man should have died before he could complete a certain piece of work; and yet, in another sense, this is not what matters. At this point one uses the words 'in a deeper sense'. (*CV*, p. 85)

Someone whose intellectual powers are failing in old age may regret, as a grave matter, some work he has not completed. But he may come to look at old age and its infirmities as something that comes from God. This acceptance influences how he regards his earlier powers. He comes to see them as gifts of grace which the Lord gives, but also takes away.

The question, 'Where did everything come from?' may lead to this religious reflection. Yet, when someone philosophises about this reflection, he may do so in terms of a super-explanation. He may feel that he cannot do justice to his religious belief unless he does this. Dominant philosophical trends may influence him. That is why

Wittgenstein wrote in 1947: 'God grant the philosopher insight into what lies in front of everyone's eyes' (*CV*, p. 63). In making this insight explicit, the philosopher neither adds nor takes anything away from what is there to be appreciated. He does not replace practice with his own theories. Wittgenstein warns: 'Don't concern yourself with what, presumably, no one but you grasps' (*CV*, p. 63). Instead, he insists: 'Anything your reader can do for himself leave to him' (*CV*, p. 77). Wittgenstein's appeal to practice has been greeted with a chorus of impatience. In philosophy, disputes will arise about whether certain philosophical accounts of religion distort or do justice to religious practices. Agreement may not be forthcoming. As a result, many come to feel that these philosophical discussions are pointless. For example, Stewart Sutherland writes:

> Much stimulus to the philosophical discussion of religious belief is to be found in the writings of D. Z. Phillips, but equally much sterile debate has resulted because both Phillips and his opponents have at times argued as if one appropriate criterion of the acceptability of his account of, say, petitionary prayer or the belief in eternal life, is whether or not this is what Christians *really* believe. Phillips has given weight to this by his interpretation and application of Wittgenstein's dictum that 'philosophy leaves everything as it is'. This is not the place for a full discussion of Phillips' views. It suffices to define my own enterprise over against his (and his opponents') by pointing out that I welcome his accounts of petitionary prayer and belief in eternal life; *but* I welcome them as interesting constructions upon or revisions of the Christian tradition rather than as they are apparently offered, descriptions of the most essential or continuing elements of that tradition. It is not clear that Phillips would accept my emphasis on the terms 'construction' or 'revision'. (Sutherland, 1984, p. 7)

It should be clear that I would not accept this emphasis, but not because I want to show that my account of these beliefs is right and that the account offered by my opponents is wrong. I reject Sutherland's emphasis because it misses what Wittgenstein meant by a philosophical problem.

Sutherland describes himself as a theological reformer. He wants myself, and others, to admit that we, too, are prescribers rather than describers. I have nothing against theological reform, but it is different from the philosophical reflection I am concerned with. The language we use in religious practices may confuse us. We have seen already how we may be tempted to look for the object which the word 'God' stands for. To rid ourselves of these confusions we must unearth the tendencies which lead to them. This is no easy matter. Part of the work involves trying to give perspicuous representations of the practice we are tempted to distort. Wittgenstein explicitly contrasts this kind of discussion with desires to reform practice. He writes as early as 1931: 'I might say: if the place I want to get to could only be reached by way of a ladder, I would give up trying to get there. For the place I really have to get to is a place I must already be at now. Anything that I might reach by climbing a ladder does not interest me' (*CV*, p. 7). What we need in order to dissolve our philosophical puzzlement is not more facts or reforms which tell us how we *ought* to think, but, rather, clarity about the ways in which we *do* think. Wittgenstein writes: 'One movement links thoughts with one another in a series, the other keeps aiming at the same spot. One is constructive and picks up one stone after another, the other keeps taking hold of the same thing' (*CV*, p. 7). Sutherland may want to reform practices. Wittgenstein wants to mirror their grammar.[3]

Sutherland's theological impatience is matched by a philosophical impatience in others. Whereas he wants to reform religious practice, they want some method by which its character can be settled once and for all. In response to my work, they have said that if believers reject the accounts of their belief I offer, their rejection is the last word on the matter. The believers' account is final. Wittgenstein certainly does not agree. He writes:

> Christianity is not a doctrine, not, I mean, a theory about what has happened and will happen to the human soul, but a description of something that actually takes place in human life. For 'consciousness of sin' is a real event, and so are despair and salvation through faith. Those who speak of such things (Bunyan for instance) are simply describing what has happened to them, *whatever gloss anyone may want to put on it.* (*CV*, p. 28, my italics)

According to the impatient philosophers, we must accept the believers' gloss. The suggestion is baffling. These philosophers would not dream of advocating this procedure elsewhere in philosophy. I can be told any day of the week in my local pub that thinking is a state of consciousness. Does that settle the matter? I can also be told that thinking is a brain-state. Does that settle it too? No philosopher is going to accept these procedures. Why advocate them, then, in the philosophy of religion? On this view, no philosopher could capture deformities of thought in his philosophical mirror since, if every gloss is to be accepted, there are no deformities to mirror.

As an example of a misleading theological gloss, Wittgenstein referred to the historical status of the Gospel narratives. He writes:

> God has *four* people recount the life of his incarnate Son, in each case differently and with inconsistencies – but might we not say: It is important that this narrative should be no more than quite averagely historically plausible *just so that* this should not be taken as the essential, decisive thing? So that the *letter* should not be believed more strongly than is proper and the *spirit* may receive its due. (*CV*, p. 31)

Some theologians see the variations and inconsistencies as indications of what is essential in the Gospels, whereas Wittgenstein sees them as indications of what is inessential: 'historical proof (the historical proof-game) is irrelevant to belief. This message (the Gospels) is seized on by men believingly (i.e. lovingly). *That* is the certainty characterising this particular-acceptance-as-true, not something *else*' (*CV*, p. 32). We do not believe on the basis of a second-best account. What is essential for belief is not hidden: 'The Spirit puts what is essential, essential for your life, into these words. The point is precisely that you are only SUPPOSED to see clearly what appears clearly even in *this* representation' (*CV*, p. 32).

In disputing the gloss on religious beliefs which theologians, believers or philosophers may give, Wittgenstein does not take himself to have tampered with these beliefs in any way. His touchstone is what is shown in practice. He says of the believer: 'If I say he used a picture, I don't want to say anything he himself wouldn't say. I want to say that he draws these conclusions' (*LC*, p. 71). These conclusions are found in a believer's practice, not in his philo-sophisings about them. Wittgenstein acknowledges that a philosopher would have to revise his account if he found a believer drawing conclusions he did not expect him to draw: 'I want to draw attention to a particular technique of usage. We should disagree, if he was using a technique I didn't expect' (*LC*, p. 71). Once the unexpected technique comes to light, its practice has the last say: 'All I wished to characterise was the conventions he wished to draw. If I wished to say anything more I was merely being philosophically arrogant' (*LC*, p. 72). Philosophy mirrors practice; it does not change it.

III

As a result of our conclusions so far, it may be thought that we cannot be critical of any religious practice.[4] An absurd conservatism has been attributed to Wittgenstein.[5] In the third context I want to consider, however, philosophical reflection reveals confusions *in* religious practices. It may be asked how this is possible if Wittgenstein's final appeal is to practice. Difficulties arise only if we think of practice in too formal or restricted a way. If we think 'practice' must refer to something as formal as a ritual, and say that appeal to practice is final, we come to the unhappy conclusion that no ritual can be confused. But Wittgenstein's use of 'practice' is not confined to these formal senses. He means no more by 'practice' than 'what we do'. If some things we do are confused, how is this to be pointed out except by reference to other things we do? What does not make sense is the suggestion that all our practices might be confused. Wittgenstein says: 'It is true that we can compare a picture that is firmly rooted in us to a superstition; but it is equally true that we *always* eventually have to reach some firm ground, either a picture or something else, so that a picture which is at the root of all our thinking is to be respected and not treated as a superstition' (*CV*, p. 83). These remarks were written in 1949, but as early as 1930 Wittgenstein recognised the possibility of confused rituals and practices: 'Of course a kiss is a ritual too and it isn't rotten, but the ritual is permissible only to the extent that it is as genuine as a kiss' (*CV*, p. 8). Whether a ritual is superstitious is shown in its practice. Philosophy, in making this explicit, is not prescriptive.

Wittgenstein certainly thought it important to distinguish between religion and superstition: 'Religious faith and superstition are quite different. One of them results from fear and is a sort of false science. The other is a trusting' (*CV*, p. 72). For example, it is superstitious to think that there is some kind of queer causal connection between sin and worldly punishment. Being distanced from God is not a causal consequence of sin. Sin, pride and envy, for example, create the distance in simply being what they are. Praying to avoid God's anger is thus not a praying to avoid consequences, but a praying to avoid becoming a certain kind of person. Wittgenstein writes: 'God may say to me: "I am judging you out of your own mouth. Your own actions have made you shudder with disgust when you have seen other people do them"' (*CV*, p. 87). If we are only afraid of sin's consequences, there is no disgust. A person may see a natural disaster which befalls him as punishment. There are two different ways he may think about it. 'If he is ill, he may think: "What have I done to deserve this?" This is one way of thinking about retribution. Another way is, he thinks in a general way whenever he is ashamed of himself, "This will be punished"' (*LC*, pp. 54–5). Wittgenstein thinks that the first way of thinking is superstitious. The belief that at some future event, final punishments of this kind will be meted out, he takes to be a confused version of belief in a Last Judgement. He comments: 'Queerly enough, even if there were such a thing, and even if it were more convincing than I have described, belief in this happening wouldn't be at all a religious belief' (*LC*, p. 56). He can make little of the way certain forms of predestination seek to explain the outcome of divine judgement so conceived. In them, man 'was created so that the interplay of forces would make him either conquer or succumb. And that is not a religious idea at all, but more like a scientific hypothesis' (*CV*, p. 86). The proposed explanation makes nonsense of ethical ideas: '"Out of his goodness he has chosen them and he will punish you" makes no sense. The two halves of the proposition belong to different ways of looking at things. The second half is ethical, the first not. And taken together with the first, the second is absurd' (*CV*, p. 81).

Sometimes, Wittgenstein equates the distinction between religion and superstition with a distinction between what he calls a higher and lower level of expression. In 1937 Wittgenstein wrote:

> In religion every level of devoutness must have its appropriate form of expression which has no sense at a lower level. The doctrine, which means something at a higher level, is null and void for someone who is still at the lower level; he *can* only understand it *wrongly* and so these words are not valid for such a person. (*CV*, p. 32)

Taking predestination as his example, Wittgenstein says:

> at my level the Pauline doctrine of predestination is ugly nonsense, irreligiousness. Hence it is not suitable for me, since the

only use I could make of the picture I am offered would be a wrong one. If it is a good and godly picture, then it is so for someone at a quite different level, who must use it in his life in a way completely different from anything that would be possible for me. (*CV*, p. 32)

How do we know the level to which particular religious pictures belong according to Wittgenstein? Peter Winch writes:

His attitude towards the acceptance of pictures involved in religious belief was not a settled one; and this is one reason for not regarding what he says as constituting a theory. He treats different cases differently and his reactions to particular cases are avowedly very personal sometimes. (I am reminded of the remark in his *Lecture on Ethics*, that on certain matters he has 'to speak for himself'.)[6]

In what sense could the distinction between religion and superstition be said to be a personal one? The answer is that the same religious picture, the same form of words, may be superstitious in one practical context, but not in another. So if we ask whether a given religious picture is confused then, as Winch says, 'it is a question the force of which will only be apparent within the life of the believer; it is not one to which the philosopher can give any general theoretical answer' (1987, p. 74). On the other hand, *whether* a religious belief *is* superstitious is not up to the individual concerned to decide. Someone else may recognise that his belief is superstitious when he does not. Later, the person who was superstitious may come to recognise this; it is 'possible for someone who once did apply the picture without qualm later to think this had been possible only because he had failed to think about certain matters rigorously enough' (1987, p. 73). For these reasons, I do not think it is to the distinction between religion and superstition that we must turn to appreciate those reactions to religious beliefs where every person *must* 'speak for himself'.

IV

We must turn to our fourth context if we want to appreciate the sense in which reactions to religious beliefs must be personal. Here, too, we may speak of higher and lower levels of expression, but in this fourth context, this distinction will *not* correspond to that between religion and superstition. For example, we have seen already that whereas the Pauline picture of predestination, for Wittgenstein, would be 'ugly nonsense', he acknowledges that it may have a higher expression in someone else's life, where it might be 'a good and godly picture'. The further question to be raised now is this: are there *lower* expressions of belief, for Wittgenstein, which he does not regard as nonsense or superstitious? Clearly, there are. He may regard such beliefs as banal, vulgar, shabby or uninteresting. In so regarding them he is, of necessity, speaking for himself. We need to look at examples to illustrate this point.

Consider Wittgenstein's reactions to miracles. Sometimes, he simply disbelieves the reports he has heard. 'It would be an instance if, when a saint has spoken, the trees around him bowed as if in reverence. – Now, do I believe that this happens? I don't' (*CV*, p. 45). On the other hand, he might respond to the movement of the trees in this way, after the saint had spoken, without believing there to be any queer causal connection between the saint's words and the movement of the trees: 'The only way for me to believe in a miracle in this sense would be to be *impressed* by an occurrence in this particular way' (*CV*, p. 45). But there is a third possibility: 'And I can imagine that the mere report of the *words* and life of a saint can make someone believe the reports that the trees bowed' (*CV*, p. 45). The belief is vague, not one which invokes any causal connection. It seems to be an extension of the impression the saint's words made on the person. Speaking for himself, however, Wittgenstein adds, 'But I am not so impressed' (*CV*, p. 45).

Consider a different kind of example. I recall an elderly widow asking me why God had called her two sons home before her. She proceeded to provide her own answer. She said that if she went into a garden to pick flowers, she would not choose weeds, but the best blooms. In taking her sons to himself, God had picked the best blooms. Does this picture imply that the longer one lives, the less one counts in the eyes of God? Obviously not. She does not push the picture in that direction. She is saluting her sons, that is all. Her practice is decisive. It need not be confused or superstitious. On the other hand, I do not find the picture very helpful. It sustained her, but it would not sustain me. Here, she and I have to speak for ourselves.

In other examples, it may be hard to determine whether the practice of belief is superstitious or not. Wittgenstein asks:

> What would it feel like not to have heard of Christ?
> Should we feel alone in the dark?
> Do we escape such a feeling simply in the way a child escapes it when he knows there is someone in the room with him. (*CV*, p. 45)

When I look at what the presence of Christ means to a certain person, I may be inclined to call the belief superstitious: 'No great harm can befall me. He's always there, unseen and unheard. But if the worst comes to the worst, he'll intervene to stay the blow.'[7] How little that has in common with, 'The Lord gave, the Lord hath taken away. Blessed be the name of the Lord.' On the other hand, religious belief may be far removed from the Book of Job without being superstitious. A person may go through life, not overtaxed, comforted by the thought of the cosy, Constant Companion. I am reminded of the lady who was comforted by the thought that she could always cuddle up to God. Even when tribulations occur, they are perceived in terms of a religious romanticism. Such words at funerals are often thought to be wonderful. We may find these reactions banal and shabby, but they are fixed, regulative paradigms in the lives of those they sustain. These pictures, the Mills and Boon products of religion, are 'laid up in heaven', occupying a grammatical position which others reserve for a God of a very different kind. It is pictures such as these that led the dramatist Dennis Potter to say: 'the human dream for *some* concept of "perfection", some Zion or Eden or Golden City, will surface and take hold of whatever circumstances are at hand – no matter how ludicrous. Even in a future land of Muzak, monosodium glutamate and melamined encounters, the old resilient dreams will insist on making metaphors and finding illumination in the midst of the surrounding dross. There is, then, no place where "God" cannot reach' (Potter, 1983, Introduction, p. 3). What god emerges and our reactions to him are another matter. Here, everyone has to speak for himself.

Underlying the treatment of all these examples is Wittgenstein's question, 'How should we compare beliefs with each other? What would it mean to compare them? . . . The strength of a belief is not comparable with the intensity of a pain' (*LC*, p. 54). The strength of a belief is measured, partly, by what a person is prepared to risk for it, by the way it governs his life. For Wittgenstein, these considerations affect what he wants to say about the character of the belief.

This is illustrated in Wittgenstein's hints about spiritualism: 'Cf Flowers at seance with label. People said: "Yes, flowers are materialised with label." What kind of circumstances must there be to make this kind of story not ridiculous?' (*LC*, p. 61). What if explanations carry no weight with the participants? What if they regard attempts at explanation as blasphemous? For Wittgenstein, that they do so affects the character of their practice. He does not insist that we *must* assume that these spiritualists are playing the game of offering explanations. Wittgenstein's attitude even extends to cases where duplicity is involved: 'I have a statue which bleeds on such and such a day in the year. I have red ink etc. You are a cheat, but nevertheless the Deity uses you. Red ink in a sense, but not red ink in a sense' (*LC*, p. 61). We may or may not be impressed by the fact that a phenomenon which depends on cheating leads to a devotion such cheating could never have anticipated. Some may speak of gullibility, while others say, 'Look, God even used the cheat.' I have been in churches where the statue 'bleeds'. For some, the availability of an explanation destroys its impressiveness, while for others it does not. At other times, reactions depend on the statue in question.

Wittgenstein does not call the beliefs in the examples we have considered superstitious or confused, but he does not call them impressive either. I suspect he would call most of them lower expressions of belief. Whether he or we find particular expressions of belief high or low, however, is a matter of personal reaction; reactions in which we all speak for ourselves. This is something the philosopher of religion ought to point out. It means that in considering reactions to religious beliefs, we cannot divide them neatly into reactions to beliefs we find spiritually impressive, and reactions to beliefs we find superstitious or confused. Philosophers must find room for the ugly, the banal and the vulgar for these, too, may be forms of religious belief.

V

In the fifth and final context I want to consider, philosophers' relations to practices are seen to be far more pragmatic than they often suppose. Mention of a pragmatic attitude will increase misgivings many philosophers will have felt already about the conclusions reached in this essay. They fear that talk of pragmatism is simply an excuse for intellectual sloppiness or even dishonesty. Its result, they would argue, is to let people get away, without criticism, with all sorts of confused, and possibly dangerous practices. I want to show that such misgivings are without foundation.

Of course, the misgivings I have mentioned are bound to be felt by those who think that *all* forms of religious belief are necessarily confused. But then, as indicated in the first context we considered, Wittgenstein finds this general thesis philosophically suspect.

Taking a pragmatic attitude to religious practice, as we saw in the second context we considered, does not mean that Wittgenstein lets anyone, participants included, whether they happen to be philosophers or not, get away with confused accounts of religious practice. Consider, for example, a religious belief Wittgenstein says he understands: 'Suppose someone before going to China, when he might never see me again, said to me, "We might see one another after death" – would I necessarily say that I don't understand him? I might say [want to say] simply, "Yes, I *understand* him entirely."' When Lewy suggests that Wittgenstein might mean only that he expressed a certain attitude, Wittgenstein replies, 'I would say "No, it isn't the same as saying I'm very fond of you" – and it may not be the same as saying anything else. It says what it says. Why should you be able to substitute anything else?' (*LC*). But he does not hesitate to criticise certain philosophical accounts of such meetings: 'Philosophers who say: "after death a timeless state will begin" or: "at death a timeless state begins", and do not notice that they have used the words "after" and "at" and "begins" in a temporal sense and that temporality is embedded in their grammar' (*CV*, p. 22).

In the third context we considered, it is clear that taking a pragmatic attitude to religious practice does not condone superstition. Whenever reflection shows superstition to be present in practices, Wittgenstein does not hesitate to point it out. Although Wittgenstein distinguishes between religion and superstition, one cannot save religion from criticism by calling anything open to such criticism 'superstition'. The reason why is obvious: superstition sometimes takes a religious form. Religion is capable of making a distinctive contribution to superstitious practices.

It is the fourth context which will probably cause most concern if we speak of a pragmatic attitude to what might be regarded as lower expressions of religious belief. It may seem that where such religious beliefs are concerned, their adherents can say what they like. But is this true?

What if a believer said that the meeting he longed for after death was like a meeting between human beings on earth. A myriad of objections would occur to one. How could one meet one's father or wife after death despite the cessation of the circumstances which give such relationships their sense? How can one meet a friend again when the friend was drowned when ten years old and one is dying aged ninety-one? And so on for a hundred other questions. Suppose someone responded: 'I know what I mean even if these practical contexts are absent', what then? A humorous incident related by Norman Malcolm, concerning Wittgenstein, illustrates what our reply should be. Malcolm writes: 'On one walk he "gave" to me each tree we passed, with the reservation that I was not to cut it down or do anything to it, or prevent the previous owners from doing anything to it: with those reservations it was henceforth *mine*' (Malcolm, 1958). Without the appropriate practice, such a 'gift' is no gift at all. Similarly, it may be said, without the appropriate practice, the 'hope of a meeting' is no hope of a meeting at all. As A. G. N. Flew once said, the 'hope' 'dies a death by a thousand qualifications' (Flew, 1955, p. 96). It is no good saying that it is an ordinary hope, but that one is unaware of the details, since it is the details which make the hope an ordinary one.

If a believer were making claims such as these, Wittgenstein would agree with the philosophical objections made against them. But why should we assume that believers are making such claims? Their practice may show that they are not. The hope of meeting a loved one after death may dominate a life without the person who entertains the hope bothering himself about the kind of details we have discussed. In that sense, the hope is a vague one. Someone says he will see his dead friend again. Wittgenstein comments: 'He always says it, but he doesn't make any search. He puts on a queer smile. "His story had that dreamlike quality." My answer would be in this case "Yes", and a particular explanation' (*LC*, p. 63). For Flew, the vagueness which surrounds this story *disqualifies* it. For Wittgenstein, the vagueness *qualifies* the story; it shows us the kind of story it is. It is a story 'laid up in heaven'; a fixed paradigm which governs a person's life.

In such a story images of 'sleep' and 'waking' may be used. *Must* we say they are confused? Must we say that death is being confused with a sleep of long duration? But when a person speaks of waking from the sleep of death 'it does not keep him from the terrible recognition that his brother is not asleep but dead: he does not try to wake the corpse, and he knows it would make no sense to speak of waking it. There is no need to ask him, "Don't you know what death is? Don't you know what it is when someone's dead?" He would not bury or cremate his brother when he was asleep. And yet he may go on using this imagery.'[8] As we have seen, this does not mean that the user of the imagery cannot become confused:

> We may speak of people who have died as 'the departed' because they are not here; they are no longer among us. When my brother had died it is obvious – too obvious – that he is not among us. But if I thought it must have sense to speak of 'where he is' or to say 'he must be somewhere', this would show a confusion of grammar. And this may be because the grammar of personal names and personal pronouns is not clear to me. (Ibid.)

Believers may talk of meeting loved ones again at the end of time, or of the meeting 'happening outside time'. Rhees comments:

> Here there are images which must be left as images. We might call some of them deep and others tawdry, that is all. But this does not mean that the distinction between what there is and what will be is unimportant; or that we can give an equivalent expression of the belief in which the difference of 'now' and 'then' has vanished. (Ibid.)

At one point in *Lectures and Conversations*, Wittgenstein is reported as saying that he himself does not speak of seeing friends after death (*LC*, p. 63). But he does not always take himself to be denying or contradicting what is said by those who do. He is taking a far more pragmatic attitude than many philosophers think appropriate. By all means point out confusion and superstition when practice reveals it. Yet, there will be times when, confronted by beliefs which are obviously important in people's lives we, as philosophers, may feel that there is little we can say about them or even make of them. In that case, is it not philosophically arrogant to want to say more? Religious allegories may cause confusion or they may not. Even when they do not, some will be able to appropriate them while others will fail to do so. Wittgenstein said as much of Bunyan's *The Pilgrim's Progress*: 'If anyone gets upset by this allegory, one might say to him: Apply it differently, or else leave it alone! (But there are *some* whom it will confuse far more than it can help)' (*CV*, p. 77).

Philosophers are reluctant to leave things alone. They are tempted to make matters tidier than they are. But as we have seen in the five contexts we have considered, the relation of philosophy to religious practice cannot be summed up in any once-and-for-all fashion. Neither can the practices themselves be summed up in this way. These are the things Wittgenstein shows in his philosophical mirror. If we appreciate how he does this, we see that while Wittgenstein describes actual uses of language, he does not interfere with them. He does not try to give them foundations either in terms of preconceived paradigms of rationality. In fact, he shows how searching for such foundations is confused. Wittgenstein's mirror shows that he is striving constantly after that end which is extremely difficult to achieve – to leave everything where it is. In *Culture and Value* the whole task is summed up thus: 'My ideal is a certain coolness. A temple providing a setting for the passions without meddling with them' (*CV*, p. 2).[9]

Notes

1. Quoted in Rush Rhees, 'The Philosophy of Wittgenstein' (Rhees, 1970, p. 43).
2. See Essay 4.
3. For a further discussion of this distinction see my paper, 'Grammarians and Guardians' (Phillips, 1988b). The paper is placed in a wider context in my *Faith After Foundationalism* (Phillips, 1988a).
4. See Essays 6 & 7.
5. This accusation, with others, equally unfounded, constitutes what has been called 'Wittgensteinian Fideism'. I challenged the accusation, with textual evidence, in *Belief, Change and Forms of Life* (Phillips, 1986). As far as I know, the challenge has not been answered by the critics who indulged in such accusations for twenty years. Some try to forget that the criticisms were ever made!
6. Peter Winch, 'Wittgenstein, Picture and Representation' (Winch, 1987, pp. 71–2).
7. I like the story of the mountain climber who, seeing his rope begin to fray on a steep climb, called out to the heavens in desperation, 'Is there anyone there?' A voice replied: 'I am here my son. I am always with you. Let go the rope. Underneath are the everlasting arms.' The climber paused, then shouted: 'Is there anyone else there?'

8. Quoted from a letter by Rush Rhees (4 August 1970) in response to my book, *Death and Immortality* (Phillips, 1970).
9. See Essay 13. An earlier version of the paper was read at a colloquium on Wittgenstein and the Philosophy of Culture at the Inter-University Centre, Dubrovnik, in May, 1989, and to the Philosophical Society of the University College of Swansea. I benefited from the discussions on those occasions.

References

Flew, A. G. N. (1955) 'Theology and Falsification' in *New Essays in Philosophical Theology*, ed. Flew, A. and A. MacIntyre (London: SCM Press).

Mackie, J. L. (1982) *The Miracle of Theism* (Oxford: Clarendon Press).

Malcolm,N. (1958) *Ludwig Wittgenstein: A Memoir* (London: Oxford University Press).

Phillips, D. Z. (1970) *Death and Immortality* (London: Macmillan).

Phillips, D. Z. (1986) *Belief, Change and Forms of Life* (London: Macmillan).

Phillips, D. Z. (1988a) *Faith After Foundationalism* (London: Routledge).

Phillips, D. Z. (1988b) 'Grammarians and Guardians' in *The Logic of the Heart*, ed. Bell, R. (London: Harper & Row).

Potter, Dennis (1983) *Brimstone and Treacle* (London: Methuen).

Rhees (1970) *Discussions of Wittgenstein* (London: Routledge).

Sutherland, S. (1984) *God, Jesus and Belief* (Oxford: Blackwell).

Tylor, E. B. (1920) *Primitive Culture* (London: Murray).

Winch, Peter (1987) *Trying to Make Sense* (Oxford: Blackwell).

Index of Names

Index of Subjects

259